GoD SaVe THe...

SeX PisTOls

A CoLLeCTOR's GUiDe...

To THe PRieSTs oF PuNK

seX P

GoD SaVe THe...

iSTOLS

A CoLLeCTOR's GUiDe...

To THe PRieSTs oF PuNK

GaViN WaLSh

Plexus, London

Acknowledgements

In Memory of My Grandparents

This book is also dedicated to the memory of Frisky, my dog, who used to go berserk howling along to 'I Wanna Be Me' (Nov 1974 - 15 Sep 1990).

In collecting the material reproduced or listed, I have enjoyed the assistance of the following people:
Ireland: Michael Candon; Stella Carroll; Marian Coyle; my family; Geoffrey Gorman; Tom Hayes; Paul Loftus; Colm 'Rolf'' O'Rourke; Robert Stewart, Brian Young.
UK: Agent Provocateur; Mike Ashman; Ben Chapman; Chris Charlesworth; Earl Delaney; Fred Dellar; Ken Dryden; Bill Forsyth; Tony Fouweather; Mick Gookey; Andy Halstead; P. Hand; Steve Hanney; Gary Harvey; Warren Jenkins; Simon P. Jones; Arthur Lancaster; Steve Llewellyn; Ed Lock; Dave Mac; Colin McCabe; Bob McKenzie; Neil McLean; Danny Marchant; Chris Moon; Lionel Moore; Alan G. Parker; Steve Pittif; Christopher Plummer; Bill Rudgard; Neil Russell; Nick Sands; Iain Scatterty; Dave Scott; Steve Severin; Marc Smith; Shaun Smith; Andy Taylor; Robert Tregilgas; John Welsh; Clive Whicelow; Steve Whitehouse; John and Kate Willicombe; Dave Wilson; Mark Woodley; Simon Wright; Marty Young.
USA: Rick Atwell (IL); Cinde Bear (OK); Roberta Bayley (NY); James Bradley Jr. (CA); Chuck Brogan (FL); Simon Callaghan (NY); Gary and Abbie Carelock (NY); Peter Carty (NY); Kevin Finkle (CA); Mike Galvin and family (CA); Jim Gibson (NY); Sean Joyce (IL); Karin Kaufman (CO); Paul and Mod Lang (CA); Liz (CA); Walter and Dena Pierrets (AZ); Richard A. Richards (CA); Joe Schafbuck (OR); John T. Shipley, Jr. (MD/PA); Peter Sisco (CN); Daniel G. Smith (MN); Jeff Tamarkin (WI); Bill Uhre (OK); Michael L. Warren (OR); Lori Weiner (IL); Barry Wickham (CA).
Australia: Lewis (Zoom); Bill Lovett; Mark Marnica; John Sobieray.
Argentina: Eduardo Gomez Kodela. **Austria:** Christoph Ulrich. **Belarus:** Sergei Pchelkin. **Belgium:** Daniel Biesemans. **Brazil:** Mariana Porto; Gerard Van Der Verm. **Canada:** Roger Brennan; Ken Hubert. **Croatia:** Damir Hadzic. **Finland:** Jukka W-M. Sateri. **Germany:** Ingo Eitelbach; Dirk Lohmanne; Benjamin Merhadi; Martin Tiedemann; Klaus Weber. **Greece:** Alexandros Paraskevopoulos; Makis Venieris; George Tsolakis. **Hong Kong:** Oliver Breit; Samvid Poon; John Ralston. **Hungary:** Matthias Csabai; Laszlo Kovacs. **Israel:** Omer Nuriel. **Italy:** Ricardo Bonelli. **Japan:** Trevor Grace; Mikio Moriwaki. **Malaysia:** Mohd. Abdusalam Abdurahman; **Mexico:** Eduardo Malvido. **Netherlands:** Paul Luxton. **New Zealand:** O. Berry; Gary Chapman; Roy Colbert; Jack and Mavis Dorothy Keechand; Stan (Scanz). **Philippines:** G-3 Misa; John A. Que. **Poland:** Wojciech Zajac. **Singapore:** L. Y. Heng; **Slovakia:** Joe Norocky. **South Africa:** Karen West. **Spain:** J.A. Gaspar. **Switzerland:** Urs Widmer. **Sweden:** Anders Johnsson; Mikael Kruus; Lars Sjogren. **Ukraine:** Victor Dubiler. **Zimbabawe:** Terry Van Der Werf.

I am especially indebted to the following people/organisations:
Joanne Bernstein (Royal Festival Hall); Susie Boone (Punch Publications); Sligo County Development Team; the *Connaught Telegraph*; Johnny Dean and Mark R. Paytress (*Record Collector*); Matt Gilsenan; Dave Goodman; John Koenig, Jeff Tamarkin and Deidre Rockmaker (*Goldmine*); Glen Matlock; Steven Maycock (Sotheby's); Leena Meinertas (Victoria & Albert Museum); Nicholas J. Orringe (Phillips); Pippa (Christie's); Glenn Terry (Australia); Lee Wood (*Spiral Scratch*); Jamie Reid, whose original Sex Pistols designs are replicated in this book, and, finally but most positively, to the **SEX PISTOLS**, the greatest rock'n'roll band to ever hit this universe!

Photos by permission of *Daily Mail*; Barry Plumber; Glitterbest; Pete of Shews; Screen on the Green; Warner/Reprise Records; *Evening News*; Jane A; *Evening Standard*; British Film Institute; Matrixbest; Virgin Records; all other photographs from Gavin Walsh's collection.

Thanks to everybody who helped out.

Contents

Introduction

Summer '02

Where do I begin? It's over two decades since I fell in love with the world's greatest rock'n'roll band, and fifteen years since I resolved to compile a collector's guide to the Pistols, irrespective of any hassles along the way. And boy – have there been hassles.

Well, here it finally is, after literally thousands of hours of collecting, continuous researching and compiling. This book does not claim to be the 'complete guide' to all the band's releases – nor can any other book. However, it does offer a visual record of the most fascinating band to exist in my lifetime so far. I hope readers will experience the same effect that I first felt, when the imagery and the artwork proved to be as breathtaking as the music.

Summer '77

So where did it all begin? Unlike other ex-punks who have published their memoirs, I can't claim to have 'been there': I wasn't at the Nashville, nor the 100 Club, not even the Roxy. Instead I grew up in Sligo, a town in the west of Ireland.

Like many teenagers of the day I felt apathetic and disaffected . . . until I was introduced to the notorious Sex Pistols. The first time I heard 'Anarchy', I was knocked for six to hear Johnny Rotten bellowing, 'I am an anarchist, I am an Antichrist!', it was nothing short of mind-blowing. With their confrontational attitude, the Pistols soon came to stand for everything I *loved*.

In no time at all, my fascination for the music widened to take on board all the imagery and paraphernalia. I spent my adolescence hopelessly infatuated by the Pistols and everything they stood for, hoarding anything and everything I could find relating to the band. As a young teenager, I longed for the summers when I could work six days a week as a kitchen porter/glass collector in a local hotel, accumulate as much money as possible and spend the seventh day travelling to Dublin (some 150 miles east of my hometown) in search of Pistols and punk rock records.

At first, I thought my hobby was a trifle weird, until one day, browsing in a bookstore, I spotted a magazine entitled *Record Collector* . . . What a relief – there were other wackos out there. From here, I would build up contacts with scores of fellow Pistols fanatics.

I always felt that, retrospectively, the band would be huge in terms of collectability. This belief was endorsed in 1980, when the Victoria and Albert Museum bought a collection of Pistols ephemera. Peter Doggett, editor of *Record Collector*, summed up the excitement caused by those early auctions in an editorial piece back in 1988: '. . . every year the Beatles dominate these memorabilia sales; but

other acts are leaving their mark. The Sex Pistols are the most collectable modern band when it comes to memorabilia . . .'

You didn't have to be an 'inside trader' to predict where it was all heading – but whilst the value of the band's memorabilia continued to rise rapidly throughout the 1980s, nobody could have predicted the way it would skyrocket in the Nineties. Posters that sold for around £1 in the band's heyday can now easily fetch a bid of hundreds at respectable auction houses like Bonham's, Christie's, Philip's and Sotheby's. And in the Pistols' eastern Mecca, Tokyo, figures quickly escalate beyond the budget of even the well-off western collector.

Amazingly, the band now frequently make the annual editions of both the esteemed Lyle's and Miller's Antiques Guides. In February 1998, the London Royal Festival Hall, one of Europe's leading art venues, staged an exhibition entitled *Destroy: Punk Graphics*. (The exhibition eventually made its way to the Canadian Arts Festival in Ottawa in early '99.) I was pleased to contribute to the event, but couldn't help noticing that, given how QEII was the Festival Hall's patron, it could be said that royalty was rubbing shoulders with anarchy. Punk was finally respectable.

On a recent round-the-world collecting binge, it was ironic to go from one store to the next only to hear the anticipated answer: 'Sorry man, that stuff just walks out the door, we don't even get a chance to put it on the wall anymore.' Quite hilarious, given what Johnny had said back in 1977: 'Collector's items? I'm afraid, if people treat us like an antique, then they can go to hell.' QED.

Where does it end? Maybe it doesn't. The fact that teenagers of today – kids who weren't even born when Rotten said goodbye at Winterland – are still willing to invest their money into Pistols product is testament to their place in the history of rock'n'roll. So many years on, we have documentary films and theses discussing the profound effects the band had, not only upon music, but on *society*. Perhaps we should all remember the wise words of the illiterate, twenty-year-old Steve Jones, right back at year zero: 'We're not a political band, we're a fun band . . .'

Gavin Walsh

Above: The boys promoting 'God Save The Queen'. Sid's dress code shows his general attitude of contempt.
Below: Promo shot of the band used extensively by Warner Bros to promote the release of Never Mind The Bollocks.

It was the era of détente; the Americans had just met up with the Reds in space, courtesy of Apollo 18 and Soyuz 19. This final Apollo flight signalled the end of the greatest adventure ever undertaken by mankind: the awesome American quest that had landed twelve men on the moon and returned each one of them safely to Earth had cost $40 billion, one failed mission (Apollo 13) and three dead men (Apollo 1).

In stark contrast, here on Mother Earth, this same superpower was extracting itself from an unwinnable war half a world away. This time the costs and losses were monumentally higher: some $400 billion, 4,865 helicopters and 58,132 body bags to come home. There were an additional 1.3 million north and south Vietnamese killed. At 7 a.m. on 30 April 1975, it was officially over as far as the USA was concerned.

In Britain, the daughter of a Lincolnshire grocer, Margaret 'Maggie' Thatcher, made political history when she succeeded Edward Heath as leader of the Conservative Party on 11 February. Although only in opposition at that time, she was the first woman to lead a major western political party, and, with her promise of a move back to right-wing roots, she was to set the wheels in motion for four consecutive wins over the Labour Party in what was to be a 'red out of vogue' era.

The British people also got their very first referendum on staying in the European Economic Community. The pros won with an outright majority of almost 70 per cent, but, if they thought Europe would be a bag of goodies, they were wrong: domestic unemployment stood at 1.3 million, coupled with a staggering annual inflation rate of 26 per cent and GNP at a sluggish £89 billion. The population passed the 56 million mark and the average industrial wage was £60 per week.

Also at this time, an ambitious 29-year-old began to manage a rock'n'roll group – but a rock'n'roll group unlike anything the recession-hit UK had seen up to that point.

Malcolm McLaren was, in many ways, the archetypal entrepreneur. A natural schemer, he dabbled in anything which involved fashion, culture, notoriety and, most importantly, money – albeit cash from chaos. Born on 22 January, 1946, into a middle-class Jewish family, his father took the high road when Malcolm was just two years old, and the young boy was farmed out to his maternal grandmother. He left school with few qualifications, scraping two O-Levels, and ended up working as a shop assistant. Eventually, he wound up in art college, where he teamed up with Vivienne Westwood. On leaving college in 1972, the pair opened a nostalgic 1950s rock'n'roll shop, Let It Rock, at 430 Kings Road, Chelsea. Changing its name to Too Fast To Live Too Young To Die the following year, the store specialised in fetish items such as rubber suits and bondage clothes.

The proprietor also solicited the part-time assistance of a young teenager, one Glen Matlock. Born on 27 August 1956, Glen was a quiet, affable ex-grammar school boy from Kensal Rise in west London. Also about this time, the premises were frequented by another pair of layabouts, Paul Cook and Steve Jones. Although they both hailed from Shepherd's Bush, on the same side of London as Glen, their backgrounds were very different from that of the shop assistant. Paul (born 20 July 1956) had been a similarly conscientious schoolboy before

hooking up with his friend Steve Jones; Steve (born 3 September 1955) was the streetwise product of a broken home; near-illiterate and a self-confessed kleptomaniac, he subsidised his interest in music by stealing instruments and equipment from rock stars' homes.

The three young McLaren acolytes wound up rehearsing as a band, with Warwick 'Wally' Nightingale making up a quartet: Steve on vocals, Paul on drums, Wally on guitar, and Glen on bass. They went through a spate of name changes in the summer of '74 before settling for the Swankers. Over the following year they practised and covered a variety of songs originally performed by 1960s artists. Although not formally managing the band, Malcolm was nonetheless enthusiastic over the idea of his proteges entering the rock'n'roll world.

The businessman showed his latent music-managerial skills when he flew out to New York City in the autumn of 1974, in an abortive attempt to manage David Johansen's US glam-rock band the New York Dolls. Malcolm dressed the Dolls in an outrageous, offensive mode: red patent leathers with communist insignia. Still signed to Mercury Records, however, they would never make it any further than the two albums they had already released.

It was in New York that Malcolm allegedly came upon the name 'Sex Pistols' – ostensibly that of an NYC street gang. He may not have succeeded with the Dolls, but he knew the potential of shock and brought the idea back to his King's Road emporium, which had since undergone another name change: this time it was provocatively renamed SEX.

Malcolm now took an avid interest in the fledgling ensemble, who had recently performed their first and only gig – a brief set at a party in a flat above Tom Salter's Cafe, 205 King's Road, in early 1975. The first thing was to offload Wally, whose main use had been that his father had access to a recording studio at the BBC, which the foursome used to sneak into in order to practice: he was duly fired in the spring of '75. The maestro manager, now firmly at the helm and determined to give his teenage desperadoes the name, impetus and direction they so badly needed, set about looking for

Malcolm McLaren and his partner Vivienne Westwood. Westwood, who defined the visual image of punk rock, would later move into haute couture.

Johnny Rotten with mandatory beer in hand, his usually spiky hair Brylcreemed into Teddy Boy style.

another guitarist. Malcolm ran the classic advertisement in *Melody Maker*'s 'musicians wanted' section (27 September 1975): 'WHIZZ KID GUITARIST, Not older than 20, Not worse looking than Johnny Thunders, Auditioning TIN PAN ALLEY.' Responding to the ad, Steve New joined up but only ever rehearsed.

Around this time, another adolescent started to visit the shop periodically. One particular Saturday afternoon in August, this uncouth youth stumbled into Malcy's (as the boys referred to him) SEX emporium. The hunchbacked, foul-mouthed yob, sporting a spiked green head coupled with a set of teeth to match and a T-shirt emblazoned with 'I hate Pink Floyd', was confronted by McLaren and persuaded to audition in front of his jukebox, singing along to Alice Cooper's 'Eighteen'.

John Lydon (born 31 January 1956) had been thrown out of their Finsbury Park, north London home by his first-generation Irish immigrant parents, for cropping and dying his formerly long hippie locks. Carrying a permanent stoop and manic stare from a childhood bout of meningitis, the intelligent, impoverished Lydon was one of life's natural outsiders.

John Lydon passed his audition and was immediately hired, although the band remained short of a guitarist. Malcolm, who was now their strategist, demoted Steve to lead guitarist, the position that had opened when Wally was given the bullet. Lydon, with absolutely no musical experience, was rechristened Johnny Rotten and given the position of vocalist and front man. The band were now the Sex Pistols, and they were on a one-way ticket to notoriety.

At this time, things were musically bleak. Teeny boppers the Bay City Rollers were at the top of the charts with 'Give A Little Love'. The rock'n'roll world was centred on the fag end of the glam-rock scene: flares and long hair were the norm. The mid-sixties revolution had undergone minor hiccups, thanks to the likes of Bowie and Bolan, but the majority of revolutionaries were now just laid-back hippies.

In London, the only alternative was the pub rock/rhythm 'n' blues revivalism scene pioneered by such notables as Brinsley Schwarz, Graham Parker and the Rumour and Dr Feelgood, who frequented such venues as the Red Cow, the Nashville, and the Hope & Anchor. Outfits like Joe Strummer's 101'ers were also playing the club circuit. Across the Atlantic, CBGB's and Max's Kansas City were hosts to another new movement, the first wave of the American New Wave: Blondie, Television, Talking Heads, the Heartbreakers, the Dead Boys, the Ramones, Patti Smith, and the Tuff Darts. Although all these bands were individualistic and talented, they lacked the vigour and fortitude necessary to break the mould.

Three months after their formation, the Pistols played their debut at St Martin's College of Art in a ten-minute set supporting Bazooka Joe (featuring none other than Stuart Goddard, who would go on to superstar status as Adam Ant) on 6 November 1975. Over the following weeks, the group gigged sporadically in venues across London. They were followed around by a group of fanatics from Bromley and Hartlepool, affectionately dubbed 'the Bromley Contingent': members included William Broad, Susan Dallion and eighteen-year-old John Ritchie, who quickly became fatally attracted to the band. These three went on to achieve prominence under their respective aliases: Billy Idol, Siouxsie Sioux and Sid Vicious – although the latter jokingly denied his involvement with the Bromleys.

Wall display at the 1950s rock'n'roll nostalgia shop, Let It Rock, at 430 Kings Road, Chelsea, London.

In February the band got their first real publicity, in a review for the trendy *NME* (21 February 1976). They had got the support spot on Eddie and the Hot Rods' Marquee Club gig and on their imminent tour. The Pistols threw a couple of chairs about and smashed up the Hot Rods' gear, whilst Johnny fondled a semi-nude acolyte, Jordan, on stage. The *NME* reviewer quoted one of them as saying, 'Actually, we're not into music, we're into chaos.' At this stage the band were playing Kinks, Who, Small Faces and Stooges cover versions, coupled with their own newly-penned nuggets 'Did You No Wrong', 'Seventeen', 'We're Pretty Vacant' and 'Submission'. Getting booted off the Rods' tour – and banned from the Marquee – didn't really matter, since the Pistols were stealing limelight from the headlining bands on account of the commotion they and their 'contingent' caused wherever they appeared. They rapidly earned themselves a horrid reputation, and were consistently told 'don't come back' at practically every venue they played.

On Valentine's night they played at a private party thrown by the artist and mentor of the 'Alternative Miss World', Andrew Logan, at Butler's Wharf in London's docklands. The late Derek Jarman was there and filmed them in Super 8 – the first ever footage of the band. A few days later, they played at another Valentine's celebration – Bucks College in High Wycombe on 20 February. Somewhere in the crowd that night was promoter and punk's patron saint, Ron Watts. Watts was immediately impressed with what he saw – music for the kids of the street, by the kids of the street, with little or no musical experience or financial assistance – and booked the Pistols into the 100 Club, at 100 Oxford Street in London's West End, for the end of the following month.

On 30 March the Pistols supported Plummet Airlines at the 100 Club, to a miserable audience of 50 people. Rotten had brought some friends along and got pissed before climbing on stage. Sadly, this manifested the first signs of internal rot – with Johnny taunting Glen on stage for a fight, detesting him for his 'lower-middle-class values' and what, compared with his own, seemed to be a cushy and educated upbringing. The seeds were planted for an eventual split – either Matlock or Rotten would have to go sooner or later. Cook and Jones, who were also from working class backgrounds, were starting to side with Rotten.

On 3 April, the Pistols played their first gig at the Nashville in West Kensington as support to Joe Strummer's pub rock/r'n'b outfit the 101'ers. Dave Goodman, who co-owned a P.A. hire company which covered the mushrooming pub rock scene, was contacted by the Albion Agency who were organising the gig: 'They just rang us up and said, "Look, do you wanna do a cheap gig tonight at the Nashville, it's a young band called the Sex Pistols" . . . and 'cos the van was still loaded up, I thought, "Oh well, why not?" Y' know, save us unloading it, take it back, do it. So we met up down there and the band that turned up were the 101'ers. So we went to try and ring the agency, "What's going on, y' know, we've been conned into doing two bands." And then – just enough time for them to do a soundcheck – the Pistols turned up and blew us away and blew Joe Strummer away. He went on, he got so wound up he kicked one of our monitors. The band remarked – like they'd done some gigs before that – "Oh, we could hear ourselves tonight." Y' know, it's like they'd never done a

soundcheck before. And we said, 'If you're doing any more gigs, we'd come and do them." "Great, here two weeks time." And we just carried on then and did most of the gigs. They left to us to organise it, take them up north, book bed and breakfast, we used to squeeze everyone in a little tiny van, and off we'd go.'

With his desire for publicity, McLaren was already paving the next step: he booked the quartet into a club in seedy Soho, the El Paradise Strip Club, for the following night, Sunday 4 April. The band subsequently reappeared at the Nashville supporting the 101'ers again, but the night degenerated into fiasco when the band joined in a fracas among the audience. Teenager Neil Tennent (later of the Pet Shop Boys) was there and wrote a piece for the *NME* of 8 May. The Pistols were banned from yet another venue.

Ron Watts got the group a residency at the 100 Club on Tuesday nights, commencing 11 May. They were at last *headlining*. By now the band were attracting live gig reviews in the music papers, with *Sounds* giving them their first major feature in the 24 April issue. In May they made their first recording, at the Majestic Studio with pro-

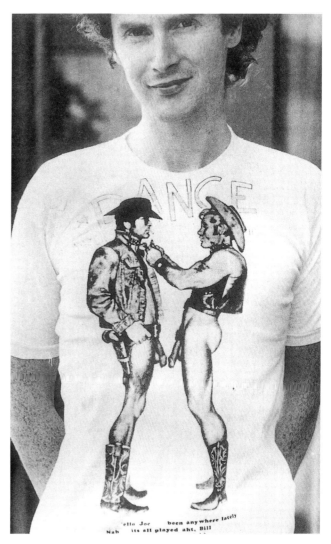

McLaren models the t-shirt that was obviously designed to offend. However, it was Sid Vicious who would make the design notorious.

ducer Chris Spedding, where they cut three tracks: 'Problems', 'No Feelings' and 'Pretty Vacant' (subsequently released on bootleg vinyl in West Germany – see 'Pistols Piracy' section).

The following month saw the tables turned: the 101'ers supported the Pistols on one of their regular Tuesday slots. However, this time Strummer had had enough. He was so awed and incensed by the Sex Pistols' attitude, dress and music that he immediately disbanded the 101'ers, cropped his hair, dumped his flares and set about forming the Clash. They made their own private debut in Chalk Farm, Camden, a mere three months later, with a completely different line-up from the 101'ers. The Damned were also spawned at the Tuesday spot, when they supported the Pistols at the 100 Club on 6 July, their first proper gig.

The end of July saw the band recording at their own studio in Denmark Street, London WC1, with original sound engineer Dave Goodman: 'It wasn't really a rehearsal, it was that Malcolm had played me the Chris Spedding tapes and I said, "I could do better on my four track." So it was easier to take my four-track gear to their rehearsal studio and set it up, we had the control room upstairs – in Steve's sorta bedroom – and the band were there. So we just spent a long time going over and over, getting the backing tracks and dubbing some guitars on. And we took backing tracks, transferred it to an eight-track and went to Riverside Studios in Hammersmith and put the vocals on, and a few more guitars. And it was mixed somewhere in north London – Decibel Studios – but that was basically it.' The Pistols now had seven decent quality tracks recorded: 'I Wanna Be Me', 'Seventeen', 'Satellite', 'Submission', 'Pretty Vacant', 'Anarchy In The UK' and 'No Feelings'. (These and the subsequent sessions at Gerrard Street, in December 1976, surfaced on the classic *Spunk Rock* bootleg.)

In August the band were scheduled to headline Europe's first punk rock festival, at Mont de Marsan, but, due to their reputation,

Original flyer for August 1976 all-night Screen on the Green gig. Note the strength of this early punk bill: one year on, not only would the Clash be too big to play support, but the banned Pistols would have to tour under an assumed name in order to perform in their homeland.

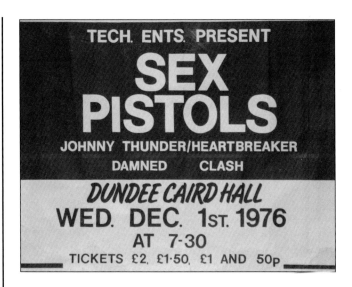

Very rare promo poster for a December 1976 Scottish gig. These early posters are extremely rare.

they were dropped by the organisers. They did, however, make their television debut at the beginning of the following month when Granada TV broadcast Tony Wilson's *So It Goes*, featuring the group playing 'Anarchy'.

The first weekend in September was another first, their debut outside of Britain. The band *et al* headed for France, where they played the Club de Chalet du Lac in Paris on 3 September. Another unique gig followed when they played to inmates of HM Prison Chelmsford on the 17th. (Dave Goodman has since released a recording of this gig in both wax and compact formats.)

Not to be outdone by the French, the 100 Club organised their very own punk rock festival – albeit with disastrous consequences. Planned as a two-day event, it kicked off on Monday 20 September. The Pistols headlined the first night, supported by the Clash, Subway Sect and Suzie and the Banshees – the latter two making their own debuts. Suzie's (subsequently 'Siouxsie') drummer was Johnny Rotten's best friend, the nineteen-year-old Sid Vicious in his first stage appearance. Sadly, on the closing night a girl lost the sight in one eye when a bottle was thrown – inevitably, Sid Vicious was blamed and subsequently indicted. As a result, all the punk bands were banned from the venue.

On 8 October 1976, the giant corporate label EMI snatched the band for £40,000. Determined not to miss the latest bandwagon, EMI outbid fierce competition from another big muscle in the music biz, Polydor. EMI's Terry Slater had seen the group at the 100 Club and was taken aback by their energetic vibrancy and unsophistication. This led to EMI's A&R manager Nick Mobbs signing the band up, and they were immediately put to work on their debut single, 'Anarchy In The UK'. Chris Thomas – noted for his work with Roxy Music, the Beatles and Pink Floyd – was brought in on production. Money was talking, which was supposedly everything the band stood against – or at least claimed to. But the fat cats at EMI would soon discover the price of being at the forefront of fashion and notoriety.

On 12 November the Pistols enjoyed their second television

appearance, on the BBC1 programme *Nationwide*, which once more featured the forthcoming 'Anarchy', coupled with an interview with Malcolm. Towards the end of the month, on the 28th, their third television appearance went out via *The London Weekend Show*. This featured four tracks from a recent gig at Notre Dame Halls, and a fine interview with Johnny conducted by Janet Street Porter.

On Friday 26 November, 'Anarchy In The UK' was released to an unsuspecting public, in some seven countries. It was an anthem of the times, with Johnny bellowing the opening lines, 'I am an antichrist, I am an anarchist . . .' The flipside was another Pistols classic, 'I Wanna Be Me' – pure unadulterated punk rock. (EMI cocked up the release by incorrectly crediting Thomas for producing both sides. Dave Goodman, who was responsible for 'I Wanna Be Me', immediately initiated a lawsuit.) The single entered the national charts at number 38, but never had a chance to climb – due to events that took place five days later.

On Wednesday 1 December, Queen cancelled a guest spot on Bill Grundy's popular evening TV programme *Today* – which went out at peak time on Thames TV. The Pistols were ushered in to fill the void, via connections at EMI. Grundy heard Johnny utter a barely audible 'shit', and, sensing potential drama, pushed for more. Steve Jones gladly obliged with a string of expletives, and the rest is history. In a subsequent interview, Paul Cook quipped, 'Steve drank the most and Steve said the most!' As a result of Steve's eloquence, the group's notoriety went ballistic. Outraged reaction was unprecedented across Britain.

The Pistols had been booked into a nineteen-date 'Anarchy Tour' of Britain, starting on 3 December at Norwich University and winding down on 26 December at Harlesden Roxy in north-west London. Prior to the TV exchange things were bad enough, with the band virtually banned from playing any major venues. After it, things became a whole lot worse – as a result of the Grundy interview, the tour was shredded by local councils. Only three gigs were left.

Immediately after the broadcast and the subsequent mass-media saturation, EMI started to panic. Their staid executives decided they should dump the band as quickly and quietly as they could. Unknown to many people at that time, the whole business was an internal embarrassment to the company's directors, since EMI had a substantial shareholding in Thames TV and did not want to be seen to act too rapidly. While EMI gave the band a cooling-off period over the following month, the Pistols' management, Glitterbest – McLaren's corporate name – claimed their record label was making 'Anarchy' unavailable, even though demand was huge. Consequently, the single fizzled out of the national chart over the next four weeks.

Johnny Rotten and Steve Jones during their 100 Club residency, spring 1976: John, in his
Seditionaries bondage jacket, was the epitome of punk anti-fashion, its point lost on a thousand slavish imitators.

The celebratory year for the 25th anniversary of the Queen's accession to the throne commenced with the opening of the Roxy Club at London's Covent Garden, on Saturday 1 January. Punk rock's formidable second band, the Clash, were the major event. Support was provided by the all-female group, the Slits, who were giving their first gig. Meanwhile, the Pistols were preparing for their first proper foreign tour. They had been booked to play three gigs in the Netherlands, opening in Amsterdam, followed by a night in Rotterdam, then terminating back at the opening venue, the Paradiso Club.

EMI was still waiting for the first opportunity to dump the band. The Pistols gave them what they wanted when they created a scene at Heathrow en route to Holland on Tuesday 4 January. A phone call two days later severed the entire contract – much to the disbelief of McLaren, on the receiving end of the wire.

EMI released a statement to the press stating: 'In accordance with previously stated wishes of both parties, referring to the phone conversation of 6th Jan., documents terminating the contract between EMI and the Sex Pistols have now been agreed. EMI Records wish the Sex Pistols every success with their next recording contract,' further stipulating the reason as the band's 'disgraceful aggressive behaviour', coupled with the recording giant's own responsibility to 'encourage restraint'.

This was the start of the band earning 'money for jam'. They had done virtually nothing for EMI, bar record and release one single. Yet the contract termination left them £50,000 better off! They had received £20,000 down upon signing the previous autumn. Now they were to get the outstanding balance of £20,000, plus an additional severance fee of £10,000.

The saga of adverse publicity continued; on the return from their brief visit to the continent, Johnny Rotten was charged with possession of amphetamines. Musically, they soldiered on, entering the studios with their original sound man Dave Goodman to record more tracks, in what became known as *The Goosebury Sessions*.

Much as the rock'n'roll business world was discontented with the Sex Pistols, the band were having their own internal problems. Glen Matlock was displaying ill-feeling about continuing with the group; the feeling was mutual, as the others had never shown much appreciation of his talents. Johnny insisted Glen had likened the band to the Beatles, but, in the end, it seemed his main crime was admitting to liking Paul McCartney. Even the amiable Paul Cook saw him as 'always having been different to the rest of us, he'd been to grammar school and art school.' Towards the end of the month, Matlock was 'given the bullet'; he insisted he had already left.

With the original bassist out, the band hired as a replacement the kid who Malcolm saw as the archetypal punk: Sid Vicious, Rotten's sidekick. John Simon Ritchie was born on 10 May 1957, one year younger than his psychotic-charismatic friend. As a child, he had accompanied his mother, Ann Beverley, on the back of a motorcycle around Europe's 'hippie trails'. Ritchie was known as an unpredictable character in the punk world, and already enjoyed a certain status because of his nihilism and violence. Some two years previously, as a seventeen-year-old, he had gone berserk at a party,

attacking two policemen and knocking out one of the lawmen's teeth. Now a Sex Pistol at nineteen years of age, his reputation had gone before him.

Vicious had met and befriended Rotten, then Lydon, when they both attended Hackney College in London's East End. He got the name Sid from an albino hamster John owned, and Vicious, 'because he wasn't vicious, he's just a big baby who eats sweets.' He detested the name, and hence it duly stuck. Prior to joining the Pistols, as well as drumming for 'Suzie' and the Banshees he was vocalist for the Flowers of Romance – who were also given their name by Rotten. Sid's main contribution to punk rock was his very own anti-dance, the 'pogo'. Arguably the band's most fervent fan, he had been promised a place in the group for some time. The image of chaos that McLaren had always desperately sought to purvey was now firmly established.

Although the new line-up had not yet gigged, Glitterbest was actively pursuing a new record deal on their behalf to ensure the release of 'No Future', aka 'God Save The Queen'. The need was urgent, since to maximise publicity – and sales – the record would have to be released to coincide with the Queen's Jubilee month, which was June. Early March saw them once again go to Kingsway

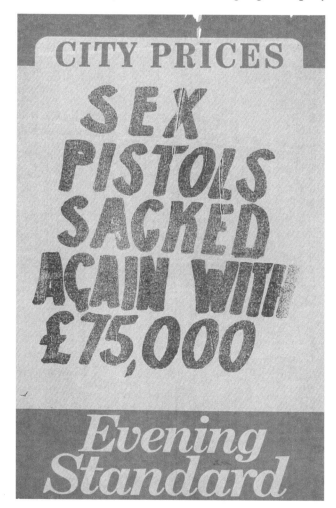

Original billboard for a March 1977 edition of the London Evening Standard. *It highlights the band's dismissal from A&M Records.*

Studios with respected producer Chris Thomas, where they laid down ten tracks. In what was to create major contention about the Pistols' musical abilities, Steve Jones stepped in and played bass in addition to fulfilling his normal role as guitarist.

Not having learned from EMI's mistake, another two giants were hunting McLaren for a deal with the band: CBS and A&M. CBS had just signed up the second most prominent act of the punk rock phenomenon, the Clash. Although they formed a year after the Pistols, they were now on the verge of releasing their debut single, 'White Riot', on 18 March, and were poised to release their brilliant, self-titled first album the following month.

With several record companies hot on the heels of Glitterbest, McLaren flew out to Los Angeles to meet A&M's founders, Herb Alpert and Gerry Moss. As a result of the meeting, on 9 March, the company's UK MD, Derek Green, signed a whopping £150,000 contract with the Pistols. The agreement provided an immediate cash injection of some £50,000 and was to last two years, in which time the band were committed to write 36 numbers. The following day saw the cosmetic solidifying of the deal, appropriately staged in front of Buckingham Palace for all the world's press to witness.

Whatever ideas A&M had in mind for a two-year working relationship didn't even last two weeks. Just seven days after signing, Malcolm was summoned to their offices for the contract to be terminated just like its predecessor. A repeat of their earlier contractual severance left the band with an impressive £75,000 – which comprised the original sum and a compensation fee of a further £25,000.

Although A&M never furnished a genuine reason for the cancellation, they told McLaren they were being subjected to 'industrial blackmail' and that other artists refused to share the label with the Pistols. A&M subsequently released a short statement stipulating, 'A&M will not be releasing anything by the group and has no further association with them.' Other factors included a fracas between the Pistols and the BBC's *Old Grey Whistle Test* host Bob Harris in the Speakeasy Club, in which Harris was allegedly assaulted only a few days after the signing of the contract.

Also, the press claimed that at the time the contract was signed the band had gone berserk in A&M's plush offices, throwing plants about and generally insulting their secretaries and executives. Whatever the reason, A&M were left with approximately 25,000

10 March 1977: the boys sign on the dotted line outside Buckingham Palace for a whopping £150,000. When A&M fired the band a mere two weeks later, they got to keep half of the dough.

Steve Jones (above) and Paul Cook (below) perform for the little-seen 'God Save The Queen' promo video.

copies of the Pistols' soon-to-be released single, 'God Save The Queen'. Consequently, all were burnt – all, that is, but approximately 100 which were sneaked onto the market. These singles are now among the most valuable records from the entire punk rock-new wave era, changing hands as of 1998 for c.£2,500.

Alas, the Pistols had no label to record or release their 'No Future' anthem. Malcolm wryly commented, 'I keep walking in and out of offices and being told take this cheque, go and don't come back! When I'm older and people ask me what I used to do for a living,' he joked further, 'I shall have to say, I went in and out of doors getting paid for it – it's crazy.' At this stage, the Sex Pistols were untouchable.

Meanwhile, American TV giant NBC filmed the band at a private gig in Notre Dame Church Halls, at London's Leicester Square, on 21 March. The concert was staged for the purpose of filming, but has unfortunately never been released. The gig itself marked a milestone for the group in that it was Sid Vicious's first time to join them on stage. Meanwhile Glen Matlock had formed a new band, aptly titled the Rich Kids, given the accusations he had endured from the Pistols.

Early the following month saw the band play their first public gig with the new bass player. It was staged at Islington's Screen on the Green cinema on 3 April. That night, the first ever Pistols film, titled *Sex Pistols Number One* – released on the continent as *When The Air Turned Blue* – was also screened. It was a cheap but impressive look at the band's short career to date, including most of their previous television appearances and some footage from the aborted Anarchy In The UK tour. The entire 22 minutes of live footage-cum-documentary was credited as a 'McLarenGlitterbest Production'.

The Pistols may have shown their first movie, but that same day saw CBS release the Clash's magnificent debut album. With the peak of the Jubilee year fast approaching, the Pistols desperately needed a record deal. Financial guru Richard Branson's Virgin label started to show interest, though the Pistols despised everything the millionaire stood for – a hippie-oriented label, with staff and artists alike wearing woolly jumpers. In any case Polydor, CBS USA and Chrysalis were still on offer – or, at the very least, willing to negotiate. On Friday 13 May, however, the Sex Pistols signed to Virgin.

On Friday 27 May, Virgin released 'God Save The Queen' just in time for the Jubilee celebrations. (Erstwhile member Wally Nightingale had penned the b-side, 'Did You No Wrong', although he was neither formally credited nor compensated.) It was widely anticipated the record would run into problems, but not to the extent that it did. The initial obstacle on its road to the top of the charts came from the workforce at CBS, to whom Virgin subcontracted out all its vinyl manufacturing, who refused to handle the record on account of its anti-monarchist statements.

The disc was widely banned from national radio and television stations. Practically all of the newspapers and the music press also ignored it, largely because their publishers would not accept advertising for it. Nonetheless, it was heading for number one in its first week of release – though, oddly, the official chart listing was left blank at whatever number the record had reached. Officially it peaked at number two, behind Rod Stewart's 'The First Cut Is The Deepest', but

Branson went on public record as stating that the chart was 'definitely fiddled' in order to keep the boys from the top. Virgin had never shipped as many singles in their first four years of existence.

Early June '77 saw the peak of the band's career. With the single hovering at the top of the charts during Jubilee week, they headed out on a private boat party on the River Thames, ostensibly to participate in the event themselves. (The hired boat was aptly named the Queen Elizabeth!) Accompanied by their usual frenzy of friends, fiends, hangers-on and scumbags, the band mimed to their freshly released anthem and also played a couple of live numbers. There to witness were Branson and co., various socialites, and, of course, the media.

The trip ended with the police boarding the boat and making numerous arrests for a litany of misdemeanours, from disturbing the peace to assault. Ironically, none of the actual band members were detained, although Malcolm and Vivienne were – for once, the boss took the rap. Among those arrested and subsequently convicted was a young Tracie O'Keefe, who received the harshest sentence – one month's incarceration. She would die the next summer of leukaemia.

Almost a week after the Thames incident, the band experienced yet another backlash – individual members were targeted this time, but not by the authorities. Their sleeve designer, Jamie Reid, had his nose and one leg broken in a frenzied attack by a gang in retaliation

Publicity material for 'God Save The Queen' appeared everywhere – even on the back of this London bus.

for the Pistols' mockery of the Royal Family. There was more to follow, when, five days later, on the night of Saturday 18 June, Johnny and producers Chris Thomas and Bill Price were ambushed and savagely beaten while leaving a pub. All three were razored in the attack, and required stitching.

Rotten was the prime target, his attackers hellbent on disfiguring him. They slashed his arm and face, but, fortunately, did not cause any lasting damage. The following night was Paul's turn: he was set upon at Shepherds Bush tube station by five men, stabbed, and coshed with an iron bar. This assault was more severe than any others, leaving the drummer lucky to be alive. Disturbingly for both the band and the authorities, the attacks were well-planned, and, most significantly, the assailants were men in their thirties, not rival teenage thugs from the rejuvenated Teddy Boy tribe.

Otherwise, the biz of making records and money proceeded. Virgin released one of the bands' earliest penned nuggets, 'Pretty Vacant', on Friday 1 July. Coupled with Iggy and the Stooges' 'No Fun', the 45 was released a mere five weeks after the controversial 'God Save The Queen', joining its predecessor in the Top Ten within one week of release. On 14 July, the Pistols made their debut on the popular weekly British music series *Top Of The Pops*, in what some fans, foes and critics alike saw as the ultimate sell-out. Commercialism was nigh.

It was subsequently revealed that footage was made for promotional purposes a week earlier, the band having mimed to the track. Knowing full well the importance of promotion, Branson had coerced the video from the band. Apparently, there was a tentative agreement between the Pistols' management and Virgin that the footage would not be turned over to the BBC. In the end it was, but the band were unable to do anything about it as, one day before the programme aired, they flew out to Denmark to kick-off a thirteen-date tour.

With just over half a dozen gigs behind them in the first half of their peak year – and half that again with the revamped line-up – Malcolm had arranged an extensive tour of Scandinavia. In what was to set an international precedent for the group, Finland set the pace by banning them outright from entering the country. Nonetheless, they kicked off at Daddy's Dancehall, Copenhagen, on the Wednesday night they arrived. (Some of those concerts have turned up in high quality audio and video formats, and represent the Sid-era line-up at its best in aural terms.)

Halfway through the dates, Sid had to fly back to face charges arising from the incident at the 100 Club the previous September, for which he was convicted and received a substantial fine. His solicitor successfully pleaded that a custodial sentence would impede his future with the group, thus avoiding any major hassles over completing the tour in Sweden. At the end of the month, when the tour had finished, they returned to the UK.

While the Pistols were busy fulfilling their touring commitments, Malcolm was in LA, planning a film on the band with cult movie director Russ Meyer. In August, the director flew into London to meet the group. The movie was provisionally titled *God Save The Queen*, but was changed to its more familiar appellation, *Who Killed Bambi?*. However, something about McLaren, the group, and, in particular, Rotten, did not gel with the Meyer script, and the agreement – if

there ever was one – was terminated. Malcolm and film student Julien Temple would eventually release a film on the band some three years later – well after their disbandment.

With the band's notoriety still massive, the average Briton could not expect to see the Sex Pistols play at home . . . until the oldest music paper in the land, *Melody Maker*, ran a cover story with details of an up-and-coming 'guerrilla' tour of the British mainland. Management, band and tour agents hotly denied any such plans. Nonetheless, on Friday 19 August the Pistols played at the Lafayette Club in Wolverhampton, billed as the SPOTS – either an acronym for Sex Pistols On This Stage or Sex Pistols On Tour Secretly, depending on who you believe. Advance fly posters simply stated 'Club Lafayette presents mystery group who will be known as the SPOTS – Friday 19th August – Admission £1.'

The ruse was repeated elsewhere without a hitch, since each venue was a private club and the only permission required came from the owners. Although it proved a successful method of circumventing the local authorities' blanket bans on the band, each venue was unannounced – unless the press got a leak – and limited in capacity. Other fictitious names used were 'Acne Rebble', 'the Hampsters', 'Special Guest', and 'the Tax Exiles'. The secret gigs tour gave the group the chance to play at least a half a dozen concerts in what was supposedly the Mother of Democracy – their home country.

Friday 14 October saw the release of the group's fourth – and final – single, 'Holidays In The Sun'. It quickly ran into trouble when a Belgian tour operator discovered the sleeve's graphics had been nicked from one of their brochures. Legal action led to the withdrawal and scrapping of all the remaining sleeves – however, within its first week of release, tens of thousands had been sold. (These pressings are very sought-after and constitute one of the more modest collectibles.) The b-side was another vintage track, 'Satellite', and once again the platter went Top Ten shortly after its release.

By now there were about half a dozen different bootleg albums in circulation, most of which were from live concerts in the summer of '76. For those who couldn't wait for the band's debut album there was an alternative: *Spunk Rock* – or simply *Spunk*, as the most famous Sex Pistols bootleg of all was also known – was made available in early October '77. It featured all of the group's best-known cuts, some twelve raw tracks recorded over two sessions: the rehearsal studios at Denmark Street, 13/30 July '76 and Goosebury Studios, Gerrard Street, 27 December '76.

For the masses, *Never Mind The Bollocks, Here's The Sex Pistols* was finally released on Friday 28 October 1977. The classic, seminal album made a piece of British history, entering the national album chart at number one on the very day of its release on the strength of advance orders alone. Critics were quick to point out that it was nothing more than a 'greatest hits' collection, considering all the previous four single a-sides were included alongside an additional eight cuts. Like previous releases, the album ran into legal problems due to its offensive title, but a court case brought by Nottingham police resulted in a victory for the group and Virgin Records – not to mention the sales generated by the adverse publicity.

With reaction to the band calming down somewhat, they kicked off a mini-tour of Britain and the Netherlands on 5 December that would take them right up to Christmas day. Malcolm was heavily involved in arranging passage to what he considered the ultimate market for his fledglings – the USA. They were lined up to appear on the popular NBC TV show *Saturday Night Live* on 17 December, following it up with an American tour. As usual, their track record and reputation went before them: the entire band were denied visas two days prior to their departure. The embassy in London gave several reasons, including their individual criminal records and what they termed 'moral turpitude'. But the liberal Democratic Party was in power, and Malcolm got the ban overturned.

By year's end, if anyone doubted the Sex Pistols' musical abilities they could not ignore their success in securing lucrative contracts. After the initial EMI and A&M debacles, Malcolm went on to sign international deals worth hundreds of thousands of pounds, coupled with the potential to turn that figure into millions over the coming years. In a short seven months after signing to Branson's Virgin label, the band were guaranteed a high-profile access to the home market, and, in addition, Virgin would handle pressings in Argentina, Brazil, Uruguay, Mexico, South Africa and New Zealand.

Virgin did not – in some places could not – gobble up the entire pie; instead, the global market was networked via a healthy spate of signings: Warner Bros (USA and Canada), Nippon Columbia (Japan), West Records (India), Wizard (Australia), Phonogram (Greece), Glitterbest/Barclay (a co-management deal with French entrepreneur Eddie Barclay's label which oversaw releases in France, Switzerland, Algeria and Zanzibar), and Virgin Europe/Ariola (Belgium, Italy, Netherlands, Portugal, Spain and West Germany). In the Far East, where demand was less, the records were released either by Express Songs (Thailand) or by Super Hits (also Thailand). The success of this strategy was registered in the annual analysis for 1977 by the prestigious *Investor's Review And Financial World*, in which the Sex Pistols were voted the leading businessmen of the year – for their manipulation of various record companies.

'I am an antichrist!': John poses for a 1977 publicity shot in the infamous 'Destroy' T-shirt. This blasphemous image – a naked Christ crucified upside down – may have spat in the eye of his repressive Catholic upbringing, but it was reputedly designed by manager and arch-rival Malcolm McLaren.

Not content with the traditional East Coast venues, Malcolm persuaded Warner Bros to let the band kick off their US tour in America's Deep Southern states, the ultra-conservative 'Bible Belt'. On 5 January, the band opened in Atlanta's Great South Eastern Music Hall and Emporium with Rotten bellowing, 'Well, my name's John and this is the Sex Pistols.' A half dozen more gigs followed, each one taking the group further on the westerly route to California.

Malcolm's famed business acumen proved sadly lacking in the choice of states and venues he had the group visit: the whole idea was to shock the American public, in particular the overtly religious right-wing, but all that happened was that controversy failed to translate into sales. After the initial 45-minute set in Georgia, the group played in Tennessee, Louisiana and Texas before winding up in California. Most of the concerts were recorded and at least three were filmed, eventually turning up in American director Lech Kowalski's *DOA – A Right Of Passage* movie and a spate of pirate videocassettes.

Unknown to Warner Bros, management and tour operators alike, the band were rapidly in decline over the nine-day period it took to perform the seven gigs, especially Sid. He had degenerated into a hapless heroin addict obsessed with outplaying Johnny Rotten as Mr Bad Guy, regularly mutilating and slashing himself on-stage. The late, esteemed Bill Graham promoted what was the band's largest ever gig, at Winterland, San Francisco on 14 January, supported by up-and-coming West Coast punk bands the Nuns and the Avengers. The Pistols gave a truly pathetic performance to 5,500 punters, after which John sneered at the heckling crowd, 'Ha, ha, ha, ever get the feeling you've been cheated? Goodnight.'

They were to be the last words that ever issued publicly from the Sex Pistols in two decades – backstage immediately after the gig, the band abruptly disintegrated, McLaren and Rotten pissed off with both the group and each other. Malcolm and the three remaining members announced that Rotten had been fired; Rotten, needless to say, insisted he'd walked out. Whichever is true, he immediately headed for New York and stayed with rock photographer and friend Joe Stevens.

On 16 January Sid also headed for the East Coast, but had a near-fatal OD on barbiturates and alcohol whilst in flight. Unconscious, he was rushed to hospital upon arrival at J. F. Kennedy Airport, thereby depriving McLaren of an intended quick departure to Rio de Janeiro.

Rio was another product of Malcolm's insatiable appetite for notoriety. With Sid hospitalised and Rotten fired, Cook and Jones headed off for Brazil on 17 January, to team up with the longstanding British fugitive, Scotland Yard's most wanted, Ronald Arthur Biggs – an excursion which was to last six weeks.

Ronnie Biggs, born in London in 1929, had helped relieve HM's Glasgow/London mail train of some 120 mailbags, valued at £2.6 million, in August 1963. Even though all the gang were quickly appre-

Paul Cook and John Lydon in Atlanta on the first night of their US tour, 5 January 1978.

Promo advertising the line-up for (what was to be) the band's final gig. The band put on a dismal show to 5,500 punters and hecklers.

hended, Biggs escaped from Wandsworth Prison two years later and went on the run, literally worldwide, before settling in Brazil. Thanks to his impregnation of a local girl, he could not be extradited.

McLaren soon joined the trio, in desperate need of another band member if only for cosmetic purposes. Hoping for yet more controversy, he attempted to arrange the trio into a foursome with Nazi war criminal Martin Bormann – in the shape of American actor Jim Jetter, in an SS uniform. The quartet recorded two tracks: 'No One Is Innocent', and an alternative version of 'Belsen Was A Gas'. The former was destined to become their first release since the departure of Johnny Rotten; much footage from this trip would later turn up in the Pistols' *Great Rock'N'Roll Swindle* flick. Biggs only received a modest one-off payment from McLaren for both his input to the hit single, having written and sung the lyrics, and his appearance in the film.

In March, with the three remaining band members back in London, Malcolm's continuing obsession with putting the Pistols' story in a motion picture led him to seek the services of novice director Julien Temple. Sid, his American girlfriend Nancy Spungen and the film crew were sent to Paris to shoot footage. Eddie Barclay – already responsible for the bands' releases in France – arranged to have Sid mime over a pre-recorded cover version of Sinatra's classic 'My Way'. With Sid's

drug problem worsening, it took almost an entire month to get him to produce three minutes of on-stage footage.

Virgin then released the first non-Rotten Sex Pistols single, and their first record in over eight months. It was issued as a double a-side: presumably Virgin couldn't decide which was the more inferior! Biggs' hilarious 'No One Is Innocent' was coupled with Sid's rendition of 'My Way' and released on 30 June. The single would peak at number six in the British charts.

After the seeming success of Sid's career as a 'cover artist', more rip-offs were in the pipeline. Next to be shammed were Eddie Cochran's 'C'mon Everybody' and 'Something Else'. Given the loss of Rotten and, some would argue, Matlock a year earlier, the band's musical abilities had reached a low ebb. Other two-bit artists were brought in to assist in the need for more releases, not to mention music for the forthcoming film. Even McLaren himself contributed a pair of tracks. Others who got involved included Ten Pole Tudor, the Black Arabs, Jerzimy, a couple of kids who just happened to be auditioning at the right time, and the aforementioned Biggs and Bormann. Although most of the summer was spent shooting the film, events were to take a dramatic twist in the months that followed.

Meanwhile, the bitter Johnny Rotten quickly showed his talents by reforming and cleaning up his public image, reverting to his birth-name John Lydon and presenting the rock'n'roll world with his post-Pistols outfit Public Image Ltd – or PiL. The band was formed in April with the original line-up of Lydon on vocals, ex-Clash guitarist Keith Levine, longstanding Lydon friend John Wardle (alias Jah Wobble) on bass and Jim Walker on drums. Although the line-up changed as often as an Italian Parliament, the group would go on to have a reasonably successful career in their fourteen-year life-span.

With Sid and Nancy both hopeless heroin addicts and in constant trouble with both cops and customs, Nancy never had any legal status to remain in the UK. On 15 August they played an impromptu gig to celebrate their departure for America the following day. They were emigrating to stave off the on-going publicity from their notoriously drug-ridden lifestyles.

The concert band were billed as the Vicious White Kids, while the gig was flogged as 'Sid Sods Off'. Set at Camden Town's Electric Ballroom, both line-up and gig were classic. Sid took vocals, Nancy was 'back-up vocals', while two ex-Sex Pistolians also joined: Glen Matlock played bass and Steve New took guitar. Another famed punkster pounded on tubs, the Damned's Rat Scabies (neé Chris Miller). As well as Sid's recent cover versions, they also used some early Pistols covers and Stooges classics.

In the meantime, Paul and Steve were gaining a reputation as session musicians, helping out with various artists on both sides of the Atlantic. Both played with Dave Goodman and Friends, and, more notably, teamed up with members of Thin Lizzy and the late Gary Holton to form what was mainly a live band, the Greedy Bastards. Their live debut, on 29 July, was a double since it was also former Lizzy road manager Frank Murray's Electric Ballroom opening night. Six months later, Cook and Jones, both sick of the controversy surrounding the Pistols, would ask for the offending expletive to be removed, abbreviating the name to the Greedies.

In the autumn, Steve produced some fine material for West

Coast punk band the Avengers, who had supported the Pistols at their last concert. Cook and Jones also guested along with Phil Lynott on the late ex-Doll Johnny Thunders' brilliant, aptly-titled debut album *So Alone*; they also joined him on stage with his band the Living Dead. And, of course, Malcolm McLaren was busy trying to find money to fill the bottomless pit that the Pistols film had become.

Meanwhile, Sid and Nancy had booked into Room 100 at New York City's famed Chelsea Hotel, which had been host to a litany of offbeat celebrities in years gone by. By now, both were completely hopeless smack addicts. The Sex Pistols' royalties were rapidly running dry. Nancy tried to emotionally blackmail her wealthy Jewish parents in Philadelphia for funds to sustain their habits. Both even travelled up to the middle-class suburb where Spungen's parents resided – to no avail. Arriving back in NYC, Nancy set about getting Sid started up as a solo performer.

Still obsessed with the fact that Sid was a Sex Pistol, Nancy – his self-proclaimed manager – persecuted promoters and venues alike until she secured a handful of gigs at NYC's long established showcase of the US new wave scene, Max's Kansas City. He played as the Sid Vicious Band, alongside various other well-known punk desperadoes: the Clash's Mick Jones on guitar, ex-New York Doll Arthur 'Killer' Kane on bass and Jerry Nolan on drums. The gigs were played back to back at the end of September, with support provided by Pure Hell and the Victims. In addition, Sid was messing around with another NYC band, the Idols, primarily comprised of ex-Dolls, some Heartbreakers and London Cowboys.

Most of these recordings made it onto a spate of bootleg albums; Virgin would take their share of the cake when John Varnom and ex-Pistols' roadie/tour manager John 'Boogie' Tiberi (whom Sid regarded as 'the fifth member of the band') put together a pathetic package entitled *Sid Sings* a year later.

The Sid Vicious concerts were nothing more than a re-enactment of how the Pistols had performed eight months earlier – except on a much smaller scale. Only a handful of punters turned up, and most of them to heckle at that. Sid was completely out of it, Nancy kicking him to perform as he lay on the floor on at least one occasion after he collapsed. Both were now doomed; the legend of having once been a Sex Pistol didn't cut it, and heroin had sapped all their finances.

In the early hours of Friday 12 October, the New York Police Department received a 911 call notifying them that somebody was dead in Room 100 at the Chelsea Hotel. Twenty-year-old Nancy Laura 'Nauseating' Spungen lay knifed to death on the floor. Lover Sid, who was in a comatose state from the effects of smack, barbiturates and alcohol, was immediately arrested and arraigned on murder charges under his real name, John Simon Ritchie.

A very rare shot – Sid, as always, goofs around for the camera, in a hotel bathroom that doesn't appear to have been trashed yet.

As was often the case, Sid attempts to steal the spotlight. The stalwart Cook 'n' Jones are happy just to be in the frame.

He was sent to New York's notorious Ryker's Island penitentiary and housed in the detoxification unit for smack withdrawal. Bail was set at US$50,000 – the equivalent of $1/2 million in normal circumstances, as the $50,000 had to be paid in cash. Vicious had to wait out the weekend till Monday morning, when Virgin wired the money from London. Both McLaren and Sid's mother, Ann 'Ma Vicious' Beverley, flew out to be with him. Given the sensationalism of the forthcoming trial, Malcolm hired the renowned attorney F. Lee Bailey to represent the punk junkie.

On 23 October – eleven days after Nancy's demise – Sid attempted suicide in Madison Avenue's Hotel Seville, severely slashing his wrists and claiming he 'had to keep a suicide pact with Nancy'. He survived and was detained in the psychiatric ward of Bellevue Hospital where he was placed under observation for a few weeks. Upon his release from Bellevue in November, he appeared at a preliminary court hearing and was indicted on a second-degree murder charge. He pleaded not guilty.

The ignominy that was part of the Pistols' hallmark was set to continue: although Vicious had restrictions placed on conditions of his bail, namely not to leave the US, and to undergo treatment for heroin addiction, he continued to hang around the club scene with other members of mostly defunct punk bands. One such club, Hurrah's, which had dropped a gay clientele in order to join the lucra-

tive new wave scene *à la* CBGB's and Max' Kansas City, was now hosting punk rock acts seven nights a week.

There, on 6 December, Sid became involved in a fracas with Todd Smith, brother of new-wave rock star Patti Smith. As usual, things got out of hand and the ex-Pistol smashed a glass into Smith's face, causing him severe eye damage. Bail was immediately revoked and Vicious was yet again remanded to Ryker's Island. This time bail was not so readily available: McLaren and Virgin both agreed to let Sid sit it out in prison for the Christmas period while they prepared for his forthcoming trial.

On a cold Tuesday morning, 2 January, John Simon Ritchie formally appeared before a NYC courtroom crammed with media personnel and assorted punks, to be charged with the murder of his lover, Nancy Spungen. Bail was refused and held over to the next hearing, scheduled for 1 February. The defendant entered a plea of 'not guilty'.

Throughout January, Sid remained in the tough Ryker's Island penitentiary while Malcolm and what remained of the Pistols – Paul Cook and Steve Jones – planned an album to sustain the massive costs that would be incurred in the trial. McLaren was not short of material, due to what the remaining three members had put down in the studio that previous spring and summer, and he was also plotting forthcoming releases with Virgin.

On 1 February, Sid applied for bail, and, much to the disbelief of the press and public, it was granted, albeit on much more stringent conditions than the previous sitting. He was to report daily for methadone treatment to help with heroin withdrawal. Furthermore, he was obliged to visit the police on a daily basis and was banned from attending nightclubs. Sid's mother and his latest girlfriend, Michelle Robinson, a part-time actress, were there to greet him on his release.

That night the trio threw a party in Robinson's Greenwich Village apartment at 63 Bank Street. Again the addict returned to his old vices, a combination of alcohol, barbiturates and smack – the latter reputedly supplied by 'Ma Vicious'. Unfortunately for the punk junkie, abstention from heroin for the previous two months, coupled with his detox treatment, had made his resistance extremely low. At 2 a.m. on Friday – less than 24 hours after obtaining bail – he slumped into a coma and died from a heroin overdose. The rise and fall of Sid Vicious was both as meteoric and nihilistic as the band he had so fervently idolised.

Although both Vicious and Spungen had publicly indicated that they would die before they were twenty, and Sid lost no time in stating how quickly he would join his 'baby', his death was subsequently ruled accidental. His mother was to later claim that she had, in fact, assisted in his suicide, since he was facing ruination on multiple fronts: the band he had lived for no longer existed, his lover/manager was dead, and he was facing a sentence of 25 years in jail for her murder.

Although the deceased junkie may have only been co-responsible for a mere trio of the Pistols' more controversial melodies – 'Holidays In The Sun', 'Bodies' and 'Belsen Was A Gas' (he was also wrongly credited with 'EMI' on most European pressings of *Bollocks*) – he was to have a successful, albeit posthumous, career in the months that followed. The Glitterbest/Matrixbest/Virgin money machine was put in full swing. Their first offering was Sid's rendition of the Eddie Cochran classic 'Something Else', coupled with the hilarious traditional 'Friggin' In The Riggin'', voxed by Steve Jones. The platter, released on 23 February, would go all the way to number three.

Very different events, which also took place in February, cast a

Sid ready for trouble, during the 1978 American tour.
When he wasn't being provoked himself, he was provoking
the hecklers at the front.

different light on the workings of the great rock'n'roll swindle. John Lydon initiated High Court proceedings against Malcolm McLaren, Matrixbest and Glitterbest, to wind up the Sex Pistols partnership. The court heard that the various monies paid to the band from terrified record companies and royalties from the previous records totalled to £880,000, of which the business account now held a meagre £30,000. McLaren was spending heavily on the projected movie. *The Great Rock'N'Roll Swindle* had truly become, according to Lydon, the Great Sex Pistols Swindle. Lydon succeeded in freezing all future royalties earned by the defunct band, but the full case would take almost seven years to settle.

A second album was finally issued, comprising some 24 tracks. (Collectors should watch for a copy from the initial batch of 10,000 featuring an extra track, 'Watcha Gonna Do About It?'.) Released on 2 March, *The Great Rock'N'Roll Swindle* was a double set in a gatefold sleeve featuring the hallmark of Malcolm's film: a dwarf called Helen and the *Swindle* logo on the front, accompanied on the rear by a shot of a dead Bambi – a reference to the Russ Meyer sham of two years previously – and a ridiculous handbill McLaren had designed urging kids to go crazy, from the Pistols Christmas Day '77 concert.

Inside the gatefold sleeve was a collage of shots from the very early days, right through to the Biggs send-up in Rio. Musically, the set was basically a bastardisation of Pistols and non-Pistols recordings. There were some early Pistols demo cover versions that had never before seen the light of day, plus new material from Cook, Jones and the late Vicious, and a host of artists who had recorded for McLaren the previous summer. The album would reach number seven.

With 'Something Else' high in the charts, Virgin next issued 'Silly Thing' on 30 March. The b-side featured Ten Pole Tudor screaming a pathetic 'Who Killed Bambi?'. Although Sid is not on either side, the publicity surrounding his recent death had its perks, as the single went Top Ten. Some two months later, on 22 June, Eddie Cochran's 'C'mon Everybody' was released, with two tracks on the b-side including a senseless, symphonic version of 'God Save The Queen' sung by McLaren. Like the previous Vicious vocal cut, the single went to number three. The *defunct* Sex Pistols had now notched up as many Top Ten hits in five months as in the entire two years of their active career.

Meanwhile, the remaining Pistols had effectively escaped the clutches of McLaren's management; there would be no more posthumous Pistols recordings. In the spring both Paul, Steve and Blondie members Frank Infante and Clem Burke contributed two tracks to one-time Runaway Joan Jett's (aka Joan Krome) debut album, *Bad Reputation*. Ironically or coincidentally, in this same year the Runaways themselves recorded a cover version of the last ever recorded Pistols track, 'Black Leather', on the b-side of 'Right Now'. Lydon's PiL continued to enjoy success and Matlock, having disbanded his Rich Kids at the turn of '78, found himself playing guitar with ex-Mott the Hoople main man Ian Hunter.

Summer '79 saw the spurious supergroup that never was. With Jimmy Pursey's Sham 69 also running out of steam, time and fashion, they received stage assistance from Cook and Jones. This resulted in the abysmal conglomerate that was the Sex Pistols Mark III – dubbed 'the Sham Pistols' by a sneering music press. The net

result was nothing more than a brief alliance in July, although collectors should note: a live four-track twelve-inch EP including 'Pretty Vacant', the Clash's 'White Riot' and two Sham tracks was released almost a decade later.

Back to the plethora of posthumous Pistols records: 27 July saw the release of a third album. By now Virgin had completely run dry of musical material, so an album comprised solely of interviews would have to suffice. In fairness to Virgin, they did include some music: an extract from Mike Oldfield's *Tubular Bells* as background accompaniment! *Some Product – Carri On Sex Pistols* was nonetheless an hilarious set of radio interviews, including the classic West Coast K-SAN interview with Paul, Steve and plenty of Joe and Josephine Soaps from the American public. The entire ragbag was put together by John Varnom – true to Pistols' form, it was riddled with expletives and, needless to say, went Top Ten.

Autumn saw the fourth single of the year, 'The Great Rock'N'Roll Swindle', accompanied by a shrieking cover of 'Rock Around The Clock' by Ten Pole Tudor. Issued on 5 October, the single would fail even to go Top Twenty, the horse having been flogged beyond death. However, the single was to create a controversy similar to 'Holidays In The Sun': the front cover was a piss-take of American Express's AMEX Credit Card. AMEX subsequently sued and the picture sleeve was withdrawn.

That same month saw the release of a 'greatest hits' compilation, aptly titled *Flogging A Dead Horse*. It featured all the previously released singles and their b-sides, although it managed to omit the essential early 'Satellite' and the disposable 'Rock Around The Clock'. This was positively the apogee of the 'scraping the barrel' syndrome.

All that now remained was a posthumous solo album from the late Sid Vicious, the deplorable *Sid Sings*, conceived, orchestrated and executed by John Varnom and John 'Boogie' Tiberi. The latter had recorded several tapes from Sid's shows at Max's Kansas City, NYC, where he played on 7, 28, 29 and 30 September that previous year. A combo of tracks was lifted from these different gigs, pressed onto wax and rush-released for the upcoming Christmas market on 7 December. (Collectors should be aware that there were three versions issued on the home market, each bearing purple Fender Stratocaster guitar-cum-swastika labels, and each containing a different poster.)

By and large, the entire Sex Pistols fiasco was over by the year's end. Malcolm was still obsessed with the film and was working frantically to realise it. Lydon was still suing McLaren, Glitterbest and Matrixbest. Cook and Jones had yet to make their mind up over which side to take, if any at all. The royalties were pouring in like never before, but were all frozen due to the outstanding Lydon vs McLaren *et al* court case. And so the close of the decade brought the Sex Pistols as a band to a definitive end.

The new decade would finally see two major developments in the Sex Pistols' grand finale: the film would be released *and* the ex-band members would successfully beat the McLaren management parties in the High Court. In all other respects, the group was truly dead.

The first minor controversy of the year would be on the first anniversary of the death of Sid Vicious. Up to 1500 fans held a parade in London from Sloane Square to Hyde Park to mark his memory. His mother, who was to have led the march, was unable to attend. She had OD'd the previous night and was in hospital when the punks had their day of remembrance. (Seventeen years later, she would succumb to a fatal OD, bringing the total number of deaths of people within or associated with the band up to ten.)

The film that started out as *Who Killed Bambi?* finally premiered in British cinemas as *The Great Rock'N'Roll Swindle* in May. Julien Temple's first movie proved to be a hilarious piece of nonsense that centred on McLaren's 'Ten Commandments' – basically his boasts of how he ripped off record companies for almost a million pounds. The film went to number three at the box office and *Variety* magazine affectionately dubbed it 'the *Citizen Kane* of rock'n'roll pictures'. Although the film carried an 18 certificate, the censor still busied himself by cutting seven minutes out, bringing the released version down to 104 minutes.

The Swindle was accompanied by *yet another* soundtrack, this time issued on a single platter. The last single release to cash in was the band's early cover version of 'Stepping Stone', coupled with BBC announcer John Snagge's narration of 'Pistols Propaganda' on the b-side. Yet again the single would fail to go Top Twenty. Virgin's last milking occurred at Christmas that year, when they released *The Sex Pack*: half a dozen 7" singles, all but one previously released, in a plastic wallet.

On the ex-Pistolian front, the turn of the decade saw Paul and Steve play with the Lightning Raiders. Additionally, Steve turned up as a session guitarist for Siouxsie and the Banshees and Gen X. The pair also found themselves playing leading roles augmented by the Clash's Paul Simonon and the Tubes in yet another film, this one shot in Vancouver, Canada. Lou Adler presided in the high chair, and it was eventually released to American TV titled *Ladies And Gentlemen, The Fabulous Stains* – aka *All Washed Up.*

Cook and Jones finally formed a true post-Pistols band, the punk/hard rock group the Professionals, along with ex-Lightning Raider Andy Allen and Ray McVeigh, in July 1980. The band would enjoy a limited success, but, as with everything else connected to the Pistols, fate was to intervene: while successfully touring the USA for the first time, on their way to a party after a gig in Duffy's, Minneapolis on 5 November 1981, Paul Cook, Paul Myers (ex-Subway Sect bassist who had since replaced Andy Allen), Ray McVeigh and their sound engineer, Kevin Harvey, were involved in a horrendous head-on car smash on Freeway 12, in which Paul was catapulted through the windscreen. The other three also sustained serious injuries, while the driver of the oncoming car was killed. The tour was terminated, and things would never be the same for the band, which dissolved in early summer '82.

Cook and Jones continued guesting on other artists' records.

Paul produced Bananarama's first album and single, and regularly played drums for them. In the mid-eighties he formed the Chiefs Of Relief from the ashes of Bow Wow Wow, and, in the nineties, played drums on ex-Subway Sect lead singer Vic Godard's stunning album *The End Of The Surrey People.* Since then, he's been back on *Top Of The Pops*, drumming for Edwyn Collins – ex-Orange Juice – during his surprisingly successful comeback.

Steve busied himself by teaming up with hardcore Queens, NY band Kraut. In the mid-eighties he joined Michael Des Barres in the ill-fated Chequered Past, a short-lived American hard rock band, also guesting on Des Barres' solo album in 1986. 1986/7 saw him kiss goodbye to a longstanding bad drug/booze habit and kick-off a solo career which resulted in two albums: one a series of ballads, the next a hard rock album proving he hadn't lost his touch as a rock guitarist.

In the late eighties/early nineties, Steve recorded for Axl Rose, Megadeth, ex-Duran Duran guitarist Andy Taylor, and a spate of Iggy Pop albums on which his superb axework best shone through. Also in the early 1990s, he formed Hollywood gloss rockers Fantasy 7 with vocalist Mark McCoy, whom Steve met at an AA meeting. In a magazine interview of the time, Jones was quoted as saying, 'I love palm trees, servants, gardeners and swimming pools . . . still, I guess it's a long way from hemp plants, birds and boozing.' The article went on to say he was spending two hours a day in the gym and using a 'non-chemical additive dietary system'. It was all a very far cry from the days of speed and anarchy.

In June '95, he formed LA supergroup the Neurotic Boy Outsiders (shortened to the Neurotic Outsiders) with Matt Scrum, Duff McKagan (both Guns N' Roses) and John Taylor (ex-Duran Duran), immediately securing a Monday residency at the Viper Club, Hollywood for the next twelve months. Also at this time, Steve played for P, the project/partnership between actor Johnny Depp, Gibby Haynes of the Butthole Surfers and blues-rock veteran Bill Carter, guesting on their eponymous album *P* in January 1996, and played lead guitar on John Taylor's solo album, *Feelings Are Good And Other Lies.* The Neurotic Outsiders' signing to Madonna's Maverick label produced a slightly above-average hard rock album, released in August '96. After a lukewarm reception and modest sales, the band disbanded. (The toxin- and additive-free Steve Jones was by now, in any case, a member of the reformed Sex Pistols.)

McLaren kept himself busy by firing Adam Ant from Adam and the Ants and renaming the remaining members Bow Wow Wow, headed by controversial fourteen-year-old, media-hyped schoolgirl Annabella Lwin as vocalist. After the controversy surrounding the singer, it was intended that Lieutenant Lush, aka George O'Dowd, alias Boy George, would take over the position. Alas, this never came to pass and after a decent commercial career with Malcolm credited as both producer and manager, the group disbanded in '83 following an abysmal American tour. Needless to say, both Adam Ant and Boy George picked up the pieces and went on to have phenomenally successful careers. Ironically, most of Bow Wow Wow teamed up with Paul Cook in the mid-eighties to form the aforementioned Chiefs Of Relief.

As seen in The Great Rock'N'Roll Swindle, *the line-up that supposedly plays the band's fifth hit single, 'No One Is Innocent': the great train robber Ronnie Biggs, two-bit actor Jim Jetter, and guitarist Steve Jones. Paul Cook is missing – as are John and Sid, neither of whom contributed a note.*

Malcolm enjoyed equal personal fame when he began his solo career in '82, and signed to the Charisma label – subsequently bought out by Virgin. Ironically, practically everyone connected to the band still ended up making dough for Branson, in one form or another. It was to become a lucrative career, spanning Afro-American rapper team shows, hip hop, and opera. (McLaren even managed to record a version of *Madam Butterfly*.) Later forays saw him record with Jeff Beck, Dave Stewart and Bootsy Collins, amongst others. At the start of the nineties, he was responsible for the classic track *Opera House*, used in British Airways ads. Subsequently, he joined up with French icon Catherine Deneuve for a record entitled *Paris*.

Lydon enjoyed chart success with his PiL throughout the eighties, but, following EMI's buy-out of Virgin in '92, the band were dropped and more or less folded. In the early part of the eighties, he had been a producer for many fellow rotters: the Bollock Bros, Rabbie Burns and his Ticket Touts, the Lydons and the O'Donnells, and his brother Jimmy's 4 Be 2s. An escapade with the latter in October '80, on the

Emerald Isle, resulted in John being incarcerated in Dublin's infamous 'Joy' jail. He and Keith Levine also produced a single for ex-*Sounds* features editor Vivien 'Militant' Goldman.

November '83 saw Lydon make his film debut in Roberto Faenza's *Order Of Death* – released as *Corrupt* in the USA, and rereleased on both sides of the Atlantic in the 1990s as *Death Sentence*. Lydon played a young psychotic-schizophrenic named Leo Smith, who, regarding himself as an 'angel of death', proceeded to kill corrupt cops from the New York Bureau of Narcotics. Co-starring alongside Lydon was Harvey Keitel as Fred O'Connor, the Chief of NYBN. The film was released to modest acclaim, and Lydon reputedly received a paltry £10,000 for his services.

In the mid-eighties he used his unique wailing vocals for Afrika Bambaataa's *Time Zone*, which was dubbed as a combo session of 'punk meets funk'. In 1986 he joined a host of talented artists, including REM's Michael Stipe and Fairport Convention founder Richard Thompson, in contributing to the Golden Palominos' brilliant *Visions Of Excess* album. The entire assembly and finished product were aptly described as a bunch of 'jazz/rock/funksters'. More recent offerings have included a best-selling autobiography and a collaboration with duo Leftfield on the popular hit 'Open Up'. After the Pistols reunion, his first post-PiL solo album was issued in 1997: the unexceptional *Psycho's Path*. Somewhere throughout all this, Lydon managed to tie the knot with ex-Slit Ari Up's mother.

Glen Matlock practically disappeared from the public eye after the Rich Kids called it a day. After the Kids went, he briefly formed the Spectres. Of the plethora of bands he played with since leaving the Pistols, none of them achieved much commercial success.

The intervening years have seen him guest with Iggy Pop on the soft-pop *Soldier* album, Bette Bright and the Illuminations, the Swingers, Jimmy Kurata, Jimmy Norton's Explosion, the Subterraneans (Mark III), the Hot Club, the London Cowboys, Gene October (ex-Chelsea), Rhode Twinn, Concrete Bulletproof Invisible (CBI), the Gang Show – which evolved into Glen Matlock's Big Living – the Mavericks, the late Johnny Thunders, the Role Models and Metal PLC, to name a few. He also joined the Pretty Things on-stage

It took almost a whole month to shoot the classic three-minute 'My Way' sequence with the hapless drug-addicted bassist. Everyone around Sid in Paris, during the Spring of 1978, knew this was the beginning of the end for him.

for a one-off gig, but, contrary to rumour, never appeared on any studio recordings.

He released his first ever solo album on 29 May 1996, entitled *Who's He Think He Is When He's At Home?*, on superfan Alan McGee's Creation label. By this time, the question posed by the record's title could be answered 'a Sex Pistol', given that the band's reformation had been officially announced two months earlier.

But the main story of the post-Pistols decades – or, indeed, of the Pistols' financial career – was to come in January of 1986. Cook and Jones finally sided with Lydon. It was solely Malcolm Robert Andrew McLaren against the entire group *and* the estate of the late Sid Vicious. Some years previous, the then supposedly down-and-out John Lydon had started the ball rolling when he brought a court action which resulted in McLaren losing the management companies Matrixbest and Glitterbest to the Official Receiver. Now the remaining Sex Pistols and Ann Beverley would receive well in excess of £1,000,000 in back royalties. Justice was finally seen to be done.

Many issues were out of the band's hands when film director Alex Cox decided to portray the lives and crimes of Sid Vicious and Nancy Spungen, in his eponymously-titled *Sid And Nancy (Love Kills)*. Lydon would have none of it, especially given that all the band scenes would have to be recreated and the close friendship between him and Sid re-enacted. Although original Pistols music was out of the question for copyright reasons, Glen Matlock took part in re-recording it. Steve Jones also contributed a track to the soundtrack, as did Joe Strummer. Gary Oldman effectively kicked off his career by playing the gaunt, drug-ridden Sid, while Chloe Webb played Nancy. The film premiered to considerable press interest at the Lumiere Theatre near Leicester Square, London, in July 1986.

More publicity for a defunct band came in a poll in the immortal American music/political magazine *Rolling Stone*, in the summer of '87. They voted the Pistols' seminal – and only – album *Never Mind The Bollocks, Here's The Sex Pistols* as rock's second greatest in their all-time Top 100. Predictably, it was pipped by the Beatles' *Sergeant Pepper*. However, its popularity among American critics in the USA did not quite match its sales with the general public, and it took an entire decade to go gold. At this time, *Bollocks* had only just sold 575,677 units and its highest position in the *Billboard* charts had been a meagre number 106. Over the next five years, the album would steadily sell as many units as it did in its initial ten – whether it was the ever-increasing popularity of the CD or the *RS* poll position can only be a matter of speculation. Either way, it was certified platinum, with sales of one million units, in May '92.

In October '92 there was much speculation that the Sex Pistols were to reform. Virgin issued their first Pistols single in nine years and first album in twelve. Both 'Anarchy' and 'Vacant' were reissued – to little avail. However, some twenty original tracks were digitally re-mastered and put out as *Kiss This*. The album made a decent chart appearance, albeit brief. The band themselves were involved in these reissues. However, when the day of the so-called 'reunion' arrived, in what was to be a rerun of the infamous Thames riverboat trip, Lydon had the last laugh when he appeared on video and wryly remarked to the scores of waiting journalists: 'We have heard the rumours – your rumours – and we have seen you coming. This is a boat trip of your own making.' By this time, the Scottish Sex Pistols tribute band had gone into their renditions of early Pistols nuggets.

Ironically, some three and a half years later the band would make a U-turn on the possibility of a reformation. During Christmas '95, the tabloids were buzzing with rumour. Not wanting to be caught red-faced again, the media tended not to take them seriously. But, in truth, all the ingredients were finally coming to fruition: Steve Jones had sorted out some on-going difficulties with the US Immigration authorities. Paul Cook, never without work, found him-

self back drumming with old chum Edwyn Collins. As the ex-Orange Juice man hit the big time with the smash-hit 'A Girl Like You', Cook found himself touring the world as part of a rock band once again.

Glen Matlock, having been through almost a dozen 'farting-around-London' bands, woke up to the fact that he was never going to make it solo. But the strongest ingredient was the main Rotter himself. John Lydon had said the Pistols would never play again, had proclaimed that rock'n'roll was dead, had said he would never tolerate Matlock again . . . Meanwhile, John Lydon and PiL had been drop-kicked by EMI for dismal sales, when they bought Virgin Records from the Branson empire. Money was talking again, and this time the Pistols were wagging their tails.

On Monday 18 March 1996, all four members appeared at their old haunt the 100 Club to confirm that it was official: the horror of twenty years earlier was rearing its ugly head again. MTV headlined the event, as did all the press. The Pistols attempted to be more obnoxious then ever, only this time, as 40-year-old punks, it all seemed ridiculous. The band would spend the next three months rehearsing in LA and giving scores of interviews to international magazines, seeming genuine in their claim that they wanted to kill

Fat and forty something . . . and back for the lure of the lucre. But Lydon (right) had lost none of his arrogant, egotistical menace.

off the conventional wisdom that 'the Sex Pistols couldn't play live'.

The reunion gigs included a major concert at Lydon's native Finsbury Park, north London, where the band headlined in front of 30,000 people. Not a small feat, given that the original Pistols' largest audience was 5,000, and even that was their final gig at Winterland.

But first there was some unfinished business from the heyday: the group had formerly been banned outright by the government of Finland. Now the 40-year-old veterans would kick-off their Filthy Lucre Tour on a ski-hill in a forest at the Messila Festival in Helsinki, Finland on Friday 21 June, playing to 15,000 punters.

The new fans may have been in nappies the last time the Pistols did the rounds, but old habits die very hard – the group had to leave the stage for ten minutes after a hail of bottles and projectiles was hurled by their adoring fans. Rotten reappeared, roaring, 'Get some fucking Finn up here to tell them I'm not a fucking target!'

Not one single new song, not one single change would be added to the set throughout the entire tour. Some critics claimed the Finnish gig, and one on the following day in Munich, were simply 'live dress rehearsals' in front of euphoric fans who knew no better.

Sunday 23 June, Finsbury Park, was the big one. That great British bastion the BBC, quick to ban the Pistols throughout their short career, gave it their full support: the show was broadcast live in FM stereo, doubtless causing discomfort to the bootleggers. The concert itself was superb, and even the anti-Pistols camp in the music press agreed that the band *could* and *did* play. The Pistols were finally in control. They even handpicked their support acts: Iggy Pop, the Wildhearts and Skunk Anansie. Lydon cheekily quipped to journalists about the bill, 'There were a hell of a lot of people who wanted to become involved, like Billy Idol, but we don't want it to look like an old survivors' day out; Iggy can get away with it . . .'

For the next month, the Pistols would play in almost a dozen countries across Europe. Times had changed a lot from the grey heyday of the late seventies. The Berlin Wall, as immortalised in 'Holidays In The Sun', had long since gone, as had the Eastern European regimes which fell with the demise of Soviet communism.

Although the Euro leg of the tour proved extremely successful, it was fraught with difficulties. The initial plan seemed to be mass saturation, but some gigs were unavoidably cancelled, generally due to low advance ticket sales. One gig, scheduled for Madrid on 2 July, was also cancelled, ostensibly because the venue manager 'feared a riot'. He had his reasons. One of the more notable gigs had taken place four days earlier at Copenhagen's Roskilde Festival: it had stopped abruptly after a mere fifteen minutes and a single warning from Johnny – 'You continue to throw broken bottles at us, and we'll go home' – after the band were targeted by a section of the 50,000-strong audience. One Danish headline read: 'Sex Pistols can't take it anymore, abandon stage in hail of bottles.' A fan on Denmark's TV2 channel blithely claimed, 'In the old days, they would have returned the bottles, they are getting old.'

All Greek and Irish dates – both Dublin and Belfast – were completely cancelled. Belfast City Council refused to grant the necessary permits for the 17 July Maysfield Centre Show because of 'blasphemous content'. Financial logic dictated the cancellation of the Dublin gig: it would not be worth travelling to the small island for a single

show. Instead, the band shoved in an extra London date at Shepherds Bush. The Euro leg was finally wound-down with another English gig, at the Phoenix Festival in Stratford-upon-Avon, 21 July.

After ten days' rest – on top of the previous eighteen years – the Pistols finally returned to America. Kick-off was Red Rock in Denver, Colorado on 31 July. Over the next 32 days they played in all the major US cities and criss-crossed into both Canada and Mexico. Gone was the ludicrous McLaren ideology of playing cities where you weren't wanted (the Bible Belt). This time they appealed to a younger and much different American youth culture. The big cities, New York and LA, even hosted two consecutive gigs, such was the demand.

Autumn saw the band head for destinations unheard of during their previous incarnation, such as Asia and Australasia. The massive Nipponese fan base finally got to see their idols when the band played gigs across Japan, culminating in Tokyo on 22 November. In Japan, Pistols material and recordings have always been treated like gold dust, so many collectibles disappearing forever into a hungry black hole of fandom.

By the time the tour had ended, Virgin Records America had issued both a single, 'Pretty Vacant'/'Buddies' ('Bodies'), and an album, *Filthy Lucre Live*. Both were direct from the Finsbury Park gig and were on the streets in record time, by 29 July. Virgin America also flooded the market with a host of press releases, posters, and all the usual memorabilia.

And, this time, marketing was what it was all about. When the Pistols toyed with the idea of reforming, it was realistically believed that each member would earn £1,000,000. If anything, given the sheer number of gigs and the fact that the band now drew crowds tens of thousands strong, whereas they only ever played to hundreds in their heyday, they were probably far in excess of that million-pound marker. It wasn't anarchy, it was only rock'n'roll. But what awesome rock'n'roll it was – as if the Pistols were re-claiming their own history.

Six years later, the Pistols honed their original repertoire further. As Queen Elizabeth II's Golden Jubilee was being celebrated with a mainstream rock concert at Buckingham Palace, the band couldn't resist reliving the controversy of 1977. They reformed for a second time, for the 27 July 2002 Pistols at the Palace gig – referring to Crystal Palace, the less prestigious public park in south-east London.

Many sneered at the 40-something Pistols for trying to recreate the filth and the fury of yore. Others relished the chance to wallow in spiky nostalgia, with couples taking their kids along for a day of sunshine and punk rock. Few were prepared for the revelation that was the reformed Pistols, assaulting their back catalogue with ferocity and skill. Their garage rock roots were paid tribute by every cover version they ever played, from the Who's 'Substitute' to the Creation's 'Through My Eyes' (the latter never officially committed to vinyl). Their original numbers were spat out with a new lease of life, the archives raided for everything the band ever played as a unit – their sole nod to the post-break-up era being 'My Way', with Rotten/Lydon laying on the histrionics in tribute to his late best mate Sid.

But still . . . There was not one single new note to be heard. While his personal legend has long credited their original manager, Malcolm McLaren, with the great rock'n'roll swindle, at the end of the day it was the Sex Pistols themselves who made cash from chaos!

PISTOLS

PLATTERS 45s

Anarchy In The UK/ I Wanna Be Me

* UK EMI, EMI 2566, 26 Nov 76, first pressing of approx. 5,000 copies. Incorrectly credits Chris Thomas for production on the b-side. Black bag. Fairly Common.
* UK EMI, EMI 2566, second pressing. Some in black bag, the remainder came in a standard EMI die-cut custom sleeve. Dave Goodman correctly credited for production on b-side. Fairly Common.
* UK EMI, EMI 2566, mispressed labels: 'Anarchy In The UK' is stated on both sides, though the record actually plays the correct tracks. Very Rare.
* UK EMI, EMI 2566, demo. Incorrectly credits Thomas for production on both sides, though a note on the sleeve states producer's credit for b-side should go to Goodman. Mostly issued in a white sleeve, some in black bags and others in EMI custom bag. Fairly Rare.

British demo copy of the Pistols' debut 45.

* UK EMI, EMI 2566. Disc states 'factory sample'. Some in black bag, some in die-cut sleeves. Goodman credited for b-side. Fairly Rare.
* UK EMI, EMI 2566, one-sided white label test pressing. Very Rare.
* Bg EMI, 4C-006-06294, withdrawn. Production credits for Thomas on both sides. NOC. Logo (first different) ps. Very Rare.
* NI EMI, 5C-006-06294, withdrawn. Production credits for Thomas on both sides. NOC. Black/white (second different) ps. Very Rare.
* WG EMI, 1C-006-06294, withdrawn. Production credits for Thomas on both sides. NOC. Black/white (third different) ps. A handful of pressings had the 'Anarchy In The UK' logo in orange. Very Rare.
* WG EMI, 1C-006-06294, withdrawn. Production credits for Thomas on both sides. NOC. Black/white (third different) ps with logo in standard red. Very Rare.
* WG EMI, 1C-006-06294, demo stamp on back ps. Black/white (German) pic. Very Rare.
* Au EMI, 11334. The first batch of the Australian pressing, limited number of copies (300 to 500) issued in this format. Red/buff standard EMI labels. In a one sided die-cut custom bag. Very Rare.
* Au EMI, 11334. 'A'-side demo copy with red/buff EMI labels. Very Rare.
* Au EMI, 11334, withdrawn. Black/white labels. Production credits for Thomas on both sides. In red EMI die-cut custom bag. Some of these were issued with a inner slip of paper stating that Dave Goodman was producer for b-side. Rare.
* Au EMI, 11334, withdrawn. Black/white

labels. Mispressed labels claim 'I Wanna Be Me' on both sides although it features the correct tracks. In EMI custom sleeve. Rare.
* Au EMI, 11334. 'A'-side demo copy with black/white labels. Very Rare.
* NZ EMI, EMI 2566, no ps issued. Ultra-rare, since it's the only foreign version that correctly credits Goodman on the b-side.
* Fr EMI. Withdrawn three or four days after release. Very Rare.
* Fr Glitterbest/Barclays, 640.112, July 77. Initial pressing of 1,000 which credits the two different producers. In plain black sleeve. Very Rare.
* Fr Glitterbest/Barclays (on Sex Pistols Records), 640.112 (BA 105), first main pressing. Tri/NOC. Black/white (fourth different) ps. Fairly Common.
* Fr Glitterbest/Barclays, 640.112, white

'Anarchy In The UK' – this French edition was issued in July 1977, seven months after 'Anarchy' was first released.

label test pressing. No ps. Very Rare.
* Fr Glitterbest/Barclays (on Sex Pistols Records), 640.112 (EA), reissue. Tri/NOC. Fourth different b/w ps, once again. Fairly Common.
* UK Virgin, VS 1431, Sept 92. Fifth different ps. Remastered. Common.

God Save The Queen/No Feelings

* UK A&M, AMS 7284, March 77. The b-side is from the July 76 *Spunk* demo session. Came in an A&M custom sleeve. Never officially released, since A&M terminated their contract on the 16th. The definitive Sex Pistols collectors item, 25,000 pressed and almost all immediately melted down. Approximately anything up to 100 escaped the pyromaniacs' clutches. Very Rare.
* UK A&M, AMS 7284. Super-rare white label test pressing.

God Save The Queen/ Did You No Wrong

* UK Virgin, VS 181, 27 May 77, first pressing of 50,000 copies. Royal blue labels with silver lettering on both sides. In ps. Common.
* UK Virgin, VS 181, second pressing. Royal blue labels, with white lettering on a-side and silver lettering on the b-(credits) side. In same ps. Common.
* UK Virgin, VS 181, third pressing. Royal blue labels; with white lettering on both sides. In same ps. Common.
* UK Virgin, VS 181. There is also a very limited issue in a plain blue jacket (no credits at all). Rare.

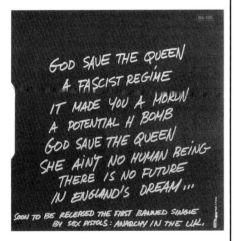

'God Save The Queen' – the reverse of this French sleeve is unique, featuring the lyrics of the first verse.

* UK Virgin VS 181, juke box edition. Royal blue labels; with silver lettering on both sides. NOC. Issued without ps. Common.
* UK Virgin, VS 181, promo copy. Features release date, 24 May, inscribed on label. In same ps. Rare.
* UK Virgin, VS 181, white label test pressing. No ps. Rare.
* Fr Glitterbest/Barclays, 640.106 (BA-105), NOC. With different back ps. Common.
* Fr Glitterbest/Barclays, 640.106 (EA), NOC. Reissued with different barcode. Same ps. Common.
* It Virgin, VIN 45009, b/w dragon/Virgin symbol labels, NOC. In same ps. Fairly Common.
* It Virgin, VIN 45009, promo labels. Rare.
* NI Virgin, 11308 AT, blue/white labels. NOC. In same ps. Fairly Common.
* WG Virgin, 11308 AT, b/w dragon/Virgin symbol labels. NOC. In same ps. Fairly Common.
* WG Virgin, 11308 AT, demo. In same ps. Rare.
* Sp Virgin, 11308A. Original classic black with red dragon/Virgin symbol labels. In different colour (b/w) ps. NOC. Fairly Rare.
* Sp Virgin, 11308A, blue/white labels. NOC. In b/w ps same as latter. Fairly Rare.
* Au Wizard, ZS 176, blue/greenish labels. In same ps. Fairly Rare.
* NZ Virgin, VS 181. In slightly different colour (purple) ps, carrying the customary NZ 'RTC' logo. Very scarce in this original ps format – since the main press run was issued without ps. With original sunken blue-sky Virgin labels. Rare.
* NZ Virgin, VS 181, white label test pressing. In slightly different colour (purple) ps. Very Rare.
* NZ Virgin, VS 181. Again with original blue/white labels. In purple 'festival' die-cut custom bag. Fairly Rare.
* NZ Virgin, VS 181. Third reissue in green/red labels. No ps. Fairly Common.
There were at least four NZ stock issues of 'GSTQ' alone – a subsequent pressing with blue/white 'sky' labels features 1979 copyright credits.
* Jp Nippon Columbia, YK 90 AX, inner includes Jap lyrics. NOC. First different ps. Inner is b/w. Rare.
* Jp Nippon Columbia, YK 90 AX, identical to the latter but the inner is blue/silver. Rare.
* Jp Nippon Columbia, YK 90 AX, promo. In same ps as Jap stock. Rare.
* SA Virgin, PD 1471, b/w dragon labels. In same (PD 1471) ps. Very Rare.

The ultra-rare Mexican pressing of 'God Save The Queen'. Note the Spanish title.

* Bz Virgin, 6079.202, plays at 33rpm. In totally different ps. Very Rare.
* Bz Virgin, 6079.202, promo. In (stock) ps. Very Rare.
* Mx Virgin, S-106 (VS-181). Titled 'Dios Salve à la Reyna'/'No Te Hice Mal'. Features beautiful white picture labels. NOC. In same (S-106) ps. Very Rare.
* Tu West, W8. In 'Punk Rock' banner (slightly different colour) ps. Very Rare.

God Save The Queen (EP)

* Th Express Songs, EXP 0330. An EP which also features Bryan Ferry's 'Tokyo Joe', the Ramones' 'Sheena Is A Punk Rocker' and Boz Scaggs. Splendid item. In slightly different ps to the UK 'GSTQ' sleeve, and c/w is white. Very Rare.

Pretty Vacant/No Fun

* UK Virgin, VS 184, 1 July 77, first pressing. Blue/white labels. The initial batch (20,000 units) of this pressing were rush released without the ps; however, free pic sleeves were subsequently issued. Common.
* UK Virgin, VS 184, second pressing. With green/red labels. In same ps. Common.
* UK Virgin VS 184, juke box edition. NOC. Issued without ps. Common.
* UK Virgin, VS 184, with mispressed labels. In same ps. Fairly Common.
* UK Virgin, VS 184, white label test pressing. In same ps. Fairly Rare.
* Fr Glitterbest/Barclays, 640.109 (BA 105), NOC. British back sleeve becomes the front ps for this pressing, but the back ps

Clockwise from top left: 'Anarchy In The UK' – coupled with 'Stepping Stone', this is the edition released in Dec 80 as part of the Sex Pack; 'Anarchy In The UK' – reverse of the 1992 reissue ps; 'Anarchy In The UK' – original Dutch pressing with gun logo; the famous 'God Save The Queen' A&M 45; 'Anarchy In The UK' – original West German release. 'Anarchy In The UK' – original Belgian logo'd ps.

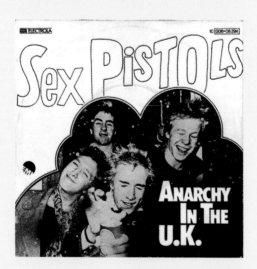

Above: 'God Save The Queen' – the original controversial picture sleeve. Far left: 'God Save The Queen' – original Brazilian 'spray can' ps. Left: 'God Save The Queen' – original Japanese insert (reverse) with the lyrics translated into Nipponese.

640 109

Right: 'Pretty Vacant' – the original British pressing released within exactly five weeks of 'God Save The Queen'. Above: the reverse of the ps featuring two buses on their respective journeys to 'nowhere' and 'boredom'.

(which states 'on Sex Pistols Records') is totally unique. Common.

* Fr Glitterbest/Barclays, 640.109 (EA), NOC. Reissued with different price code. Same ps. Common.
* Fr Glitterbest/Barclays, 640.109. White label test pressing. No ps. Very Rare.
* It Virgin, VIN 45011, b/w dragon/Virgin symbol labels. NOC. In same ps. Fairly Common.
* It Virgin, VIN 45011, white label promo. With three-page colour press release/biography and photo. Rare.

Some of the Italian stock units came with the above biography/photo kit, in which case be prepared to pay more.

* NI Virgin, 11331 AT, blue/white labels. NOC. In same ps. Fairly Common.
* WG Virgin, 11331 AT, again with those b/w dragon/Virgin symbol labels. NOC. In brighter colour ps. Also note: the reverse of the jacket on all other issues is white (buses/logos) on a black background, whereas this pressing is the reverse. Fairly Common.
* Gr Virgin/Phonogram, 2097 942. Limited

edition pressed for promotional purposes. In black die-cut bag. Beautiful b/w labels. Rare.
* Gr Virgin/Phonogram, 2097 942, white label test pressing. Super rare. Issued without ps. Very Rare.
* Au Wizard, ZS 184, bluish labels. In

'Pretty Vacant' – the Japanese edition with logo'd titles.

same ps. Fairly Rare.
* NZ Virgin, VS 184, original sky-blue/white labels. In completely different ps, carrying the customary NZ 'RTC' logo. Very hard to find in this original ps format, since the main press run was issued without ps. Rare.
* NZ Virgin, VS 184, again in original blue/white labels. In purple 'festival' die-cut custom bag. Fairly Common.
* NZ Virgin, VS184. Third reissue in green/red labels. No ps. Fairly Common.
* Jp Nippon Columbia, YK 94 AX. In same ps. With 'Denon' stickers on labels and back ps. NOC. Rare.
* Jp Nippon Columbia, YK 94 AX (AX 458 95), promo. In same ps. NOC. Rare.
* SA Virgin, PD 1470, b/w dragon labels. Issued without ps. Rare.

Pretty Vacant/Submission

* US Warner Bros, WBS 8516, 78, b/w labels. NOC. The front of the ps is a picture of John Reid – MD of EMI Records – with his eyes blanked out! Fairly Common.

* Ca Burbank/Warner Bros, WBS 8516 (VAA 7565 S), 78. Issued without ps. With beautiful colour palm tree labels. Approx. 500 pressed. NOC. Rare.

Pretty Vacant (Stereo)/ Pretty Vacant (Mono)

* US Warner Bros, WBS 8516, 78, promo, b/w labels. NOC. In same ps as the latter stock edition. Sleeve claims the reverse is 'Submission' although it's 'Vacant' (mono). Fairly Rare.

'Pretty Vacant' – this Canadian pressing features Warner Bros' 1970s 'Burbank palm trees' label.

Pretty Vacant (EP)

* Th Express Songs, EXP 0342. Another South East Asian EP which also includes the Jam, the Saints and Dave Edmunds. Front ps shows the Jam. Very Rare.

Pretty Vacant

* UK Chaos, APOCA 4, 85, unreleased white label test pressing. Black vinyl. Only twenty made, all individually numbered. Issued without ps. Very Rare.
* Jp VAP, 00119-00 (E-7497). One-sided, red vinyl, promo-only, stereo flexi. Issued without ps. Johnny is credited on the label as 'Rotton'. Given out free with the first batch of the Japanese *Mini Album*. Very Rare.

Holidays In The Sun/Satellite

* UK Virgin, VS 191, 14 Oct 77, first pressing. With blue/white labels. In ps. Common.
* UK Virgin, VS 191, 14 Oct 77, first pressing. With blue/white labels. Subsequently issued in a plain white jacket. Common. *Reid's artwork was based on an ad by a Belgian Travel Company, who subsequently threatened court action. The sleeve was eventually banned and is considered slightly rare, copies going for as much as £10. However, bear in mind there were at least 50,000 issued in the superb picture sleeve.*
* UK Virgin, VS 191, second pressing. In green/red labels. Some still made available in the banned ps. Common.

* UK Virgin, VS 191, second pressing. In green/red labels. Mostly issued in the plain white sleeve. Common.
* UK Virgin VS 191, mispressed labels: 'Holidays In The Sun' is stated on both sides, though the record actually plays the correct tracks. Rare.
* UK Virgin, VS 191 (matrix: VS 191 A1 / VS 191 B1), white label test pressing. Issued without ps. Rare.
* UK Virgin, VS 191 (matrix: VS 191 A2 / VS 191 B2), white label test pressing. Issued without ps. Rare.
* Fr Glitterbest/Barclays, 640.116/BA 105. This first pressing titled the b-side as 'Satellite Kid'. Tri/NOC. With b/w labels. In same ps except it additionally states 'nice sleeve'. Fairly Common.
* Fr Glitterbest/Barclays, 640.116/BA 105. The b-side is correctly retitled 'Satellite'. NOC. With b/w labels. In same French ps. Common.
* Fr Glitterbest / Barclays 640.116 / EA. Same ps as the latter French pair except the price code is 'EA' (not 'BA 105'). Common.
* NI Virgin, VS 191, blue/white labels. In same ps. Fairly Common.
* WG Virgin, 11643 AT, blue/white labels. NOC. In same ps. Fairly Common.
* It Virgin, VIN 45013, b/w labels. NOC. In first different ps. Rare.
* It Virgin, one-sided promo only. Issued without ps. Rare.
* Au Wizard, ZS 191. In pink 'festival' die-cut custom sleeve. Fairly Common.
* NZ Virgin, VS 191. Original blue-sky labels. In purple 'festival' die-cut custom bag. Fairly Common.
* NZ Virgin, VS 191. Reissued with green/red labels. No ps. Fairly Common.
* Jp Nippon Columbia, YX 97 AX. Includes inner with both English and Japanese lyrics. NOC. In same ps. Fairly Rare.
* Jp Nippon Columbia, YX 97 AX, promo. Came with lyrics. In same ps. Rare.

Holidays In The Sun/ (The Motors) Dancing The Night Away

* It Virgin, JB 125/VIN 45013/45012. Special jukebox promo-only edition. In plain pale blue die-cut custom sleeve. NOC. Fairly Rare.

'New York' – this French release was the only 45 to feature the track (as a b-side to 'Submission').

Holidays In The Sun (EP)

* Th Super Hits, SP 1011, Oct 77. Came in a spectacular unique colour picture sleeve which was taken in Virgin's Portobello yard. It's one of the 'wall shots', where Johnny has a quiff and Sid's fly is open! Yet another super rare Thai four-track EP which also features Status Quo's 'Rockin' All Over The World'; Santa Esmeralda and Leroy Gomez's 'Don't Let Me Be Misunderstood' and Rokotto's 'Boogie On Up'. Very Rare.

Submission

* UK Virgin, VDJ 24, one sided. Given out free with first 50,000 copies of *Never Mind The Bollocks*. With blue/white labels. Issued without ps. Common.

Lentilmas – A Seasonal Offering To You From Virgin Records

* UK Virgin/Lyntone, LYN 3261, Dec 77. Xmas message from Virgin given free to the music press. 33rpm, one-sided promo flexi in ps. Some issued with Xmas card. Very Rare.
* UK Virgin/Lyntone, LYN 3261, Dec 77. More were issued without the Xmas card. Very Rare.

Submission/New York

* Fr Glitterbest/Barclays, 640.137 (BA-105), Oct 77. NOC. In different ps to any other release. French only issue. Common.
* Fr Glitterbest/Barclays, 640.137 (EC), NOC. Same ps. Common.

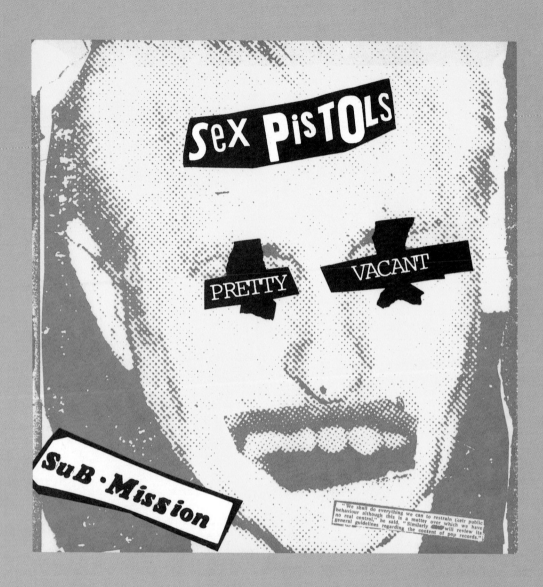

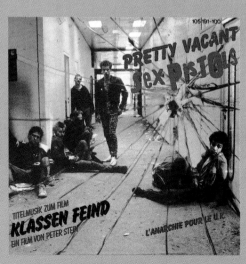

Above: 'Pretty Vacant' – the American release's sleeve is actually a picture of John Reid (MD of EMI Records) with his eyes blanked out! Right: 'Pretty Vacant' – the 1992 reissue with controversial artwork attacking the next generation of royalty. Far right: 'Pretty Vacant' – with a still from the German movie Klassen Feind on the picture sleeve.

nice sleeve

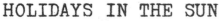

HOLIDAYS IN THE SUN

Above: 'Holidays In The Sun' – the original, subsequently banned British picture sleeve. Far left: 'Holidays In The Sun' – the original Italian ps used a live stage shot. Left: 'Holidays In The Sun' – coupled with 'My Way', this is the ps for the edition released in Dec 80 as part of the Sex Pack.

No One Is Innocent/ My Way

* UK Virgin, VS 220, 30 June 78, first pressing. Double a-sided release. With b/w labels. In (gloss) ps. Common.
* UK Virgin, VS 220, second pressing. With black/cream labels. In same (matt) ps. Common.
* UK Virgin, VS 220, silver labels. In same ps. Common.
* UK Virgin, VS 220, reissued in 83. In same ps. NOC. Common.
* UK Virgin, VS 220, mispressing: plays 'My Way' and The Motors' 'Airport'. In same ps. Fairly Rare.
* UK Virgin, VS 220, yet another mispress: plays Magazine's 'Shot By Both Sides' instead of 'No One Is Innocent'. In same ps. Fairly Rare.
* UK Virgin, VS 220, white label test pressing. In same ps. Fairly Rare.
* Fr Glitterbest/Barclays, 640.145 (BA-105). 'My Way' becomes the main side, whilst the b-side is re-titled 'Cosh The Driver' (aka 'No One Is Innocent'). This first batch was mispressed: a small quantity – c.5000 – incorrectly credited Sid with the aforementioned c/w. NOC. In same ps, except the b-side is upside down. Fairly Rare.
* Fr Glitterbest/Barclays, 640.145 (BA-105). As the latter except the b-side ('Cosh The Driver') is credited to Biggs. Fairly Common.
* Fr Glitterbest/Barclays, 640.145 (EC). As the latter except the price code (EC) on the cover is different. Fairly Common.
* Fr Glitterbest/Barclays, 640.145 (BA-105). 'My Way' is still the main side but the flip-side CTD is correctly credited to 'A Punk Prayer By Ronnie Biggs'. NOC. In same ps as latter French issue. Common.
* Fr Glitterbest/Barclays, 640.145, white label test pressing. Issued without ps. Fairly Rare.
For the record: most (possibly all) of the French pressing incorrectly credit Biggs as Briggs.
* It Virgin, VIN 45018, blue/white labels. NOC. In first different ps. Rare.
* NI Virgin, 15707 AT, blue/white labels. NOC. In different colour ps. Fairly Common.
* WG Virgin, 15707 AT, blue/white labels. NOC. In same ps. Common.
* Gr Virgin/Phonogram, 2097961. Limited edition pressed. In second different ps. Collector's take note: the a-side is billed *à la* the 12"er 'The Biggest Blow'. With beautiful white Virgin emblem (stock) labels. Very Rare.

* Gr Virgin/Phonogram, 2097961, white label test pressing. Same (Greek stock) ps. Very Rare.
* Jp Nippon Columbia, YK 109 AX. Inner sleeve with both English and Japanese lyrics. NOC. In same ps. Fairly Rare.
* Jp Nippon Columbia, YK 109 AX, promo. With inner sleeve, etc. In same ps as stock issue. Rare.
* Au Wizard, ZS 190, some in Wizard company sleeve, most issued without ps. Fairly Common.
Some copies are available with a promo or demo stamp, but they are all fakes as Wizard never pressed any promos at all.
* Au Virgin, VS 220 (MX 194285). In same ps. Fairly Common.
Some of the stock editions have 'sample record' stamped on their sleeves.
* Au Virgin, VS 220 (194 284/5), white label promo. In same ps. Fairly Rare.
* NZ Virgin, VS 220, original blue/white labels. Without ps. Fairly Rare.
* NZ Virgin, VS 220, green/red labels. Without ps. Fairly Common.
* NZ Virgin, VS 220, demo. Without ps. Very Rare.
Ronnie Biggs takes vocals on front, while Sid sings on flip.

Something Else/Friggin' In The Riggin'

* UK Virgin, VS 240, 23 Feb 79, first pressing. Original b/w labels. The ps has Sid with swastika on T-shirt. Common.
* UK Virgin, VS 240, second pressing. With green *Swindle* labels. In same ps. Common.
* UK Virgin, VS 240, mispressing, plays 'Silly Thing' on side one, although it incorrectly claims 'Something Else'. With green *Swindle* labels. In same ps. Fairly Common.
* UK Virgin, VS 240, white 'A' label test pressing. Some in ps, most issued in black die-cut bag. Fairly Rare.
* UK Virgin, VS 240, white label test pressing. Yet another mispress: plays 'Who Killed Bambi?' on b-side. Without ps. Fairly Rare.
* Fr Glitterbest/Barclays, 640.159 (BA 105). In same ps, but without the circle and swastika on the front of jacket (different to Italian edition). NOC. Fairly Common.
* It Virgin, VIN 45023, green *Swindle* labels. In same ps, but has black circle masking out the swastika (different to French edition). NOC. Fairly Common.
* WG Virgin, 100404, green/red labels.

NOC. In same ps. Common.
* Au Wizard, ZS 305, bluish labels. Issued without ps. Fairly Common.
* NZ Virgin, VS 240, green/red labels. In same ps. Fairly Common.
Sid's vocals on a-side, with Steve on flip-side accompanied by Ten Pole Tudor.

Silly Thing/ Who Killed Bambi?

* UK Virgin, VS 256, 30 Mar 79, bright purple *Swindle* labels. In ps. Common.
* UK Virgin, VS 256, white label promo. In same ps. Fairly Rare.
* Fr Glitterbest/Barclays, 640.160. The a and b-sides are reversed. NOC. In same ps. Paul Cook takes vocals on 'Silly Thing' on this French pressing! Fairly Common.
* WG Virgin, 100504-100, green/red labels. NOC. In same ps. Common.
* Au Wizard, ZS 311, bluish labels. Issued without ps. Fairly Common.
* NZ Virgin, VS 256, red/green labels (*not* green/red). With different colour b-side ps. Fairly Common.
Steve Jones sings on the a-side – although it's Paul Cook who sings lead vocals on the double album version – and the b-side is performed by Ten Pole Tudor.

The c/w of the Nipponese-only issue of 'Silly Thing'/'Something Else' featured the lyrics in English!

Silly Thing/ Something Else

* Jp Nippon Columbia, YK 122 AX. Inner with English lyrics. NOC. In ps. Fairly Rare.
* Jp Nippon Columbia, YK 122 AX, promo. In same ps with lyrics. Rare.

Silly Thing/Anarchy In The UK

* Pl Virgin, VV 45009 ES, blue/white labels. In unique Sid cartoon-ps. Rare.
* Pl Virgin, VV 45009 ES, reissued with ugly green/red labels. In same ps. NOC. Rare.

C'mon Everybody/God Save The Queen (Symphony)/Watcha Gonna Do About It?

* UK Virgin, VS 272, 22 June 79, first pressing with yellow *Swindle* labels. In gloss ps. Common.
* UK Virgin, VS 272, second pressing. The labels have a lower centre but are otherwise the same. In same matt ps. Common.
* UK Virgin, VS 272, third pressing. With standard green/red Virgin labels. In same matt ps. Common.
Some copies of the British pressings were issued in a hi-gloss ps, with the same pics.
* UK Virgin, VS 272, white label test pressing. Issued without ps. Fairly Common.
* Fr Echantillon, test pressing dated 29 Oct 80. Fairly Rare.
* WG Virgin, 100 791 100, green/red labels. NOC. In same ps. Common.
* NZ Virgin, VS 272. In same ps. Common.
* Au Wizard, ZS 313, bluish labels. Some in Wizard company sleeve, most issued without ps. Fairly Common.
Sid sings on the a-side; the b-side is courtesy of the original Pistols line-up.

Don't be misled by the title – this is actually the Nipponese-only issue of 'Silly Thing' and 'Something Else'.

The Swindle *label was used extensively on Pistol product for numerous releases in the late 70's / early 80's.*

The Great Rock 'N' Roll Swindle/Rock Around The Clock

* UK Virgin, VS 290, 5 Oct 79, dark pink *Swindle* labels. Initially issued in an AMEX (credit card) ps. Inevitably, American Express heard the news and complained. It was subsequently withdrawn *à la* 'Holidays', but there were at least 80,000 units released in this full ps format. Common.
* UK Virgin, VS 290. Some featured an extended phone call version which included twenty seconds of lawyers talking on a telephone. With same labels and sleeve as above. Fairly Common.
* UK Virgin, VS 290, mispressed b-side features the Doors. In same ps. Fairly Rare.
* UK Virgin, VS 290, white 'A' label promo. In same ps. Fairly Common.
* UK Virgin, VS 290, white label test pressing. Without ps. Fairly Rare.
* NI Virgin, 100 916 100. In same ps. Common.

* WG Virgin, 100 916, green/red labels. NOC in same ps. Common.
* WG Virgin, 100 916 100, green/red labels. NOC. In totally different front ps to any pressing, also note the front ps cat. no. is three digits longer. Fairly Rare.
The b-side is performed by Ten Pole Tudor. Some trivia: in all cases the back ps is the same, divided into a dozen sections depicting passed-away icons . . . starting with Sid, they are, clockwise: Janis Joplin, Bruce Lee, Jim Morrison, 'Mama' Cass Elliot, James Marshal Hendrix, the revolutionary Che Guevara, Brian Jones, Moon the Loon, Eddie Cochran, Elvis Presley and Marc Bolan. The significance? 'Rot Around the Clock'.

You Need Hands/God Save The Queen (Symphony)

* Fr Glitterbest/Barclays, 640.161 (BA 105), June 79. NOC. In same ps. Common.
The a-side was credited to Malcolm McLaren.

41

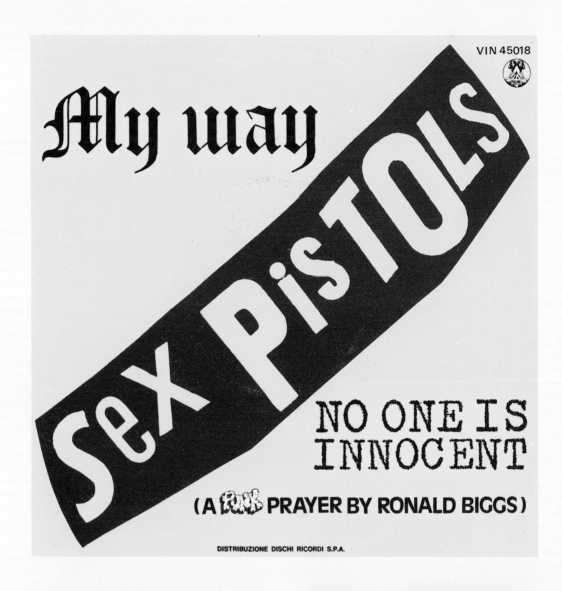

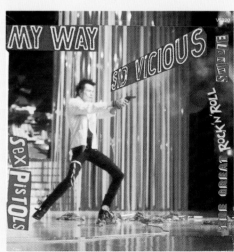

Above: 'My Way'/'No One Is Innocent' – this Italian pressing was issued in a unique sleeve a la Bollocks. Right: 'No One Is Innocent' – 'great train robber' Ronnie Biggs performs vocals and appears on the front of this British picture sleeve. Far right: 'My Way' – the reverse side of the British ps featured a shot from the then forthcoming Swindle flick.

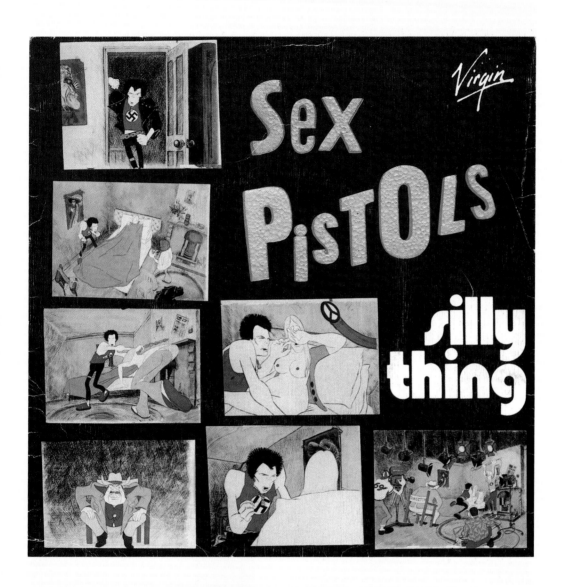

Above: 'Silly Thing' – this is a unique and very rare Portuguese 45. The b-side is 'Anarchy In The UK' Far left: 'Who Killed Bambi?' – although this is the b-side of a Pistols single ('Silly Thing') 'Bambi' was actually performed by Ten Pole Tudor. Left: 'Silly Thing' – Steve Jones takes vocals on this British pressing.

640.162

ANARCHIE POUR L'U.K.

SEX PISTOLS

From The Film THE GREAT ROCK 'N' ROLL SWINDLE

This French version of 'Anarchy', played on an accordian, was released in 1979 and features Jerzimy on vocals.

God Save The Queen (Symphony)

* Fr Glitterbest/Barclays, 640/161 (BA 105). June 79. NOC. In same ps. Common. The a-side was credited to Malcolm McLaren.

Anarchie Pour L'UK/ Anarchy In The UK

* Fr Glitterbest/Barclays, 640.162 (BA 105), Mar 79. NOC. Dave Goodman credited for production on b-side. In ps. Common. *Jerzimy on vox.*

Stepping Stone/ Pistols Propaganda

* UK Virgin, VS 339, June 80, yellow *Swindle* labels. The initial pressing had a card (solid paper) ps. Common.
* UK Virgin, VS 339, second pressing had a paper-thin ps, otherwise the same. Common.
* UK Virgin, VS 339, mispressed a-side plays Ian Gillan's (of Deep Purple/Gillan fame) 'Sleeping On The Job'. In same ps. Fairly Common.

* UK Virgin, VS 339. Another mispressed b-side plays the Doors. In same ps. Fairly Common.
* UK Virgin, VS 339. Third mispressing, this time it's the a-side: features the band's cover version of the Who's 'Substitute'. In same ps. Fairly Common.
* UK Virgin, VS 339, white label promo. In same ps. Fairly Common.
* UK Virgin, VS 339, white label test pressing. In same ps. Fairly Common.
* WG Virgin, 102 142 100, green/red labels. NOC. In same ps. Common.
* WG Virgin, 102 142 100, demo. In same ps. Fairly Rare.
* Au Virgin, VS 339 (MX 194 286/7), green/red labels. In same ps. Common.
* Au Virgin, VS 339 (MX 194 286/7), white label promo. In same ps. Fairly Common.
* NZ Virgin, VS 339, green/red labels. In same ps. Common.
* NZ Virgin, VS 339, green/red labels. Jukebox edition in Polygram b/w die-cut custom bag. NOC. Common.
* NZ Virgin, VS 339, demo. In same ps. Fairly Rare.

The original line-up is on the a-side while BBC announcer John Snagge provides a voiceover on the flip side.

Pretty Vacant/ L'Anarchie Pour L'UK

* WG Virgin, 105 191 100, with silver labels. NOC. In ps. Fairly Common.

Pistols Pack (Sex Pack)

* UK Virgin SEX 1-6, Dec 80. All came in same pic sleeves as original releases except 'Holidays' and 'Stepping Stone'. The entire set comes in a fold-out plastic wallet and was in a limited edition of 40,000. Fairly Common.
'God Save The Queen'/'Pretty Vacant' 'Holidays In The Sun'/'My Way'/'Something Else'/'Silly Thing'/'C'mon Everybody'/'The Great Rock'N'Roll Swindle'/'(I'm Not Your) Stepping Stone'/'Anarchy In The UK'/'Black Leather'/'Here We Go Again'
* Fr Virgin 102 720. Sleeve nos. are SEX 1-1, 1-2, etc. All in same picture sleeves as UK edition. Rare.
* Fr Echantillon 1-6. Test pressings of the latter. Features handwritten labels. Very Rare.

Pistols Box Set

* Gr Virgin, VG 8008-013, 87. Reissue of *Sex Pack*. Again in same pic sleeves. Fairly Rare.

Anarchy In The UK/ No Fun

* UK Virgin, VS 609, Oct 83, b/w labels. In black bag with title credits on the back. Common.
* UK Virgin, VS 609 92 U1, white label test pressing. In same ps. Fairly Common.
* Au Virgin, VS 609. In same ps. Common.
* Au Virgin, VS 609, stamped demo. In same ps. Common.

Submission/ No Feelings

* UK Chaos, CARTEL 1, Dec 84. In yellow wax, with ps. Common.
* UK Chaos, CARTEL 1. In pink wax, with same ps. Common.
* UK Chaos, CARTEL 1, white label test pressing. In standard black vinyl. Issued without ps. Supposedly only twenty made. Rare.
The pair of colour waxes were issued in a limited edition of 4,175 in total. The tracks are

studio outtakes from the July 76 session. Note: cat. no. on the back ps is Chaos DICK 1.

Suburban Kid/ Don't Give Me No Lip Child/(I'm Not Your) Stepping Stone/ Submission

* Jp VAP, 35162-00, 33rpm. In plain white VAP custom sleeve. This single was a free-bie included with the Japanese album *Better Live Than Dead*. Common.
* Jp VAP, 35162-00, white label test pressing. Common.

Pretty Vacant/ I Wanna Be Me

* Fr Spiral Scratch, SCRATCH 4 (APOCA 4), Jan 89. Presented free with Issue Four of *Spiral Scratch*. The reverse is actually 'Seventeen' and not 'I Wanna Be Me'. Issued without ps. Common.
These are outtakes from the July 76 session.

Sid Vicious And Friends: 'Don't You Gimme No Lip'/ 'I'm Not Your Stepping Stone'

* Fr Spiral Scratch SCRATCH 7, Jun 89. Free with *Spiral Scratch*. No ps. Common.

Anarchy In The UK/(Various Artists)

* UK Spiral Scratch, SCRATCH 201, March 91. Also includes the Users' 'I'm In Love With Today'/Sick Things' 'Bondage Boy'/the Killjoys' 'Recognition'. Issued without ps. Once again, this was presented exclusively with the Aug 90 issue *Spiral Scratch*. Common.
*UK Spiral Scratch, SCRATCH 201, white label test pressing. Issued without ps. Common.

Anarchy In The UK

* Pd K 3. Special Polish postcard flexi-disc. In nice white jacket ps. Unique 33rpm item. Supposedly limited edition of 50 copies issued exclusively for Polish Pistols collectors. Features the common 'Not For Sale!' warning. Fairly Rare.

God Save The Queen

* Pd. Postcard. 5" flexi-pic disc. Limited edition of 1,000 in envelope. Fairly Rare.

No Fun

* Pd. Polish Postcard flexidisc. Limited edition of 1,000 in envelope. Fairly Rare.

Liar

* Ru Budkon 2277. 6" red, Russian-only flexi-disc. Issued in ps with Russian sub-titles on front. Fairly Common.
* Ru Budkon 2277. 6" transparent, Russian-only flexi-disc. Issued in ps with Russian subtitles on front. Fairly Common.

Stepping Stone

* Ru Budkon, 2481. 6" green, Russian-only flexi-disc. Issued in ps. Fairly Common.
* Ru Budkon, 2481. 6" yellow, Russian-only flexi-disc. Issued in ps. Fairly Common.

No Fun

* Ru Budkon, 2482. 6" red, Russian-only flexi-disc. Issued in ps. Fairly Common.
* Ru Budkon, 2482. 6" brown, Russian-only flexi-disc. Issued in ps. Fairly Common.

Be A Man, Kill Yourself

* Ru Budkon, 2558. 6" green, Russian-only flexi-disc. Issued in ps. Slightly rarer than the other Soviet issues in that the credit is mispelled as 'Sexx Pistols'. Fairly Common.

Submission

* Ru Budkon, 2990. 6" transparent, Russian-only flexi-disc. Issued in ps. Fairly Common.
* Ru Budkon, 2990. 6" yellow, Russian-only flexi-disc. Issued in ps. Fairly Common.

Pretty Vacant /No Feelings

* UK Virgin, VS 1448, Nov 92. The ps is Princess Diana on front accompanied by Fergie on the back! Common.

Pretty Vacant/Buddies

* UK Virgin VUS 113 (7243 8 93692 7 4), Aug 96, live from Finsbury Park, London. Pressed on silver vinyl with matching silver labels. Black ps. Common.

Sex Pistols/ The Ugly EP

* US Man's Ruin MR 053, Feb 97. Orange/black 'Sex Pistols – Pretty Vacant' letter logos. Common.
* US Man's Ruin MR 053, Feb 97. Pink/black 'Sex Pistols – Pretty Vacant' letter logos. Common.
The first release from the Punk Hall Of Fame series. Features unreleased 'Vacant' demo from Clapham Studios 76. B-side has two tracks from Toronto band the Ugly. In fold-open colour card jacket.

Sex Pistols/ The Sofisticatos EP

* US Man's Ruin MR 056, 97. Features demo version of 'No Feelings'. B-side has two tracks from the Sofisticatos. In fold-open colour card jacket. Common.

Sex Pistols/ The Curse EP

* US Man's Ruin MR 090, 98. Features demo version of 'Problems'. B-side has two tracks from the Curse. In fold-open colour card jacket. Common.

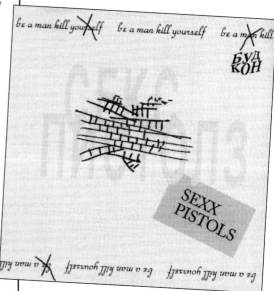

This retitled Russsian release of 'Belsen Was A Gas' misspells 'Sexx' Pistols.

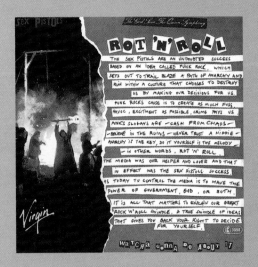

Top left and right: 'You Need Hands' – three years before 'Buffalo Girls', Malcolm released this cover of the Max Bygraves 'classic' in France on the Glitterbest/Barclays label; centre left: 'C'mon Everybody' was actually a three-track EP, also featuring 'God Save The Queen' and 'Watcha Gonna Do About It?' – the reverse of the ps (centre right) shows a pic from the Swindle flick. Bottom left: 'Friggin' In The Riggin'' – this still is from the animated sequences of The Great Rock'N'Roll Swindle; the front of the French ps, (for 'Something Else' – bottom right) was censored, with Sid's offending swastika removed.

Above: 'Stepping Stone' was a very early Pistols recording of a Monkees song. Far left: 'Black Leather' was a unique addition to the Dec 80 limited-edition Sex Pack. Left: 'Rock Around The Clock' – the ps was divided into a dozen sections, displaying dead icons from Che Guevara to Sid.

PiSTOLS
12" SINGLES

Anarchy In The UK/ I Wanna Be Me

* Fr Glitterbest/Barclays, 740.501 (Ba 171), June 77, original pressing. In b/w glossy ps. Fairly Common.
* Fr Glitterbest/Barclays, 740.501 (G), reissued with a different price code. In b/w glossy ps. Fairly Common.
* Fr Glitterbest/Barclays, 740.501. Third pressing reissued without any price code. In b/w matt ps. Fairly Common.
* Fr Glitterbest/Barclays, 740.501, reissued in a creamy off-white/black ps. This pressing features an additional cat. no. on the labels: yBarcx 84.860/l. Common.
* Fr Enchantillon, one-sided test pressing release. Without ps. Fairly Rare.

Though the French were seven months late releasing 'Anarchy', they were the only ones to retain the original coupling (b-side 'I Wanna Be Me') on 12" format.

God Save The Queen/ Did You No Wrong

* NZ Virgin, VS 181 12, 77. In nice pale blue Virgin custom die-cut jacket. Fairly Common.

Pretty Vacant/No Fun

* NZ Virgin, VS 184 12, 77. In pale blue Virgin custom die-cut jacket. Fairly Common.

Holidays In The Sun/ Satellite

* NZ Virgin, VS 191 12, 77. In pale blue Virgin custom die-cut jacket. Fairly Common.

No One Is Innocent (A Punk Prayer By Ronald Biggs)/My Way

* NZ Virgin, VS 220 12, 78. In pale blue Virgin custom die-cut jacket. Fairly Common.
* NZ Virgin, VS 220 12, demo stamp (only). In pale blue Virgin custom die-cut jacket. Fairly Common.

The Biggest Blow (A Punk Prayer By Ronald Biggs)/My Way

* UK Virgin, VS 220 12, 30 June 78. The b-side features a Ronnie Biggs interview with Steve and Paul. In a limited edition of 20,000 copies. In b/w ps. Also note: unlike subsequent pressings, the labels on this special issue feature a small emblem of the twin Virgin ladies. Fairly Common.
* UK Virgin, VS 220 12, standard issue. In same ps. Common.
* UK Virgin, VS 220 12, white label test pressing. In plain white jacket with title. Rare.

* Au Wizard, ZS 12 190, July 78. In piss-coloured wax. Includes insert. In same ps. Fairly Rare.
* Au Wizard, ZS 12 190, standard black vinyl. Fairly Common.
* Au Wizard, AZ 12 190. Identical to the latter except catalogue prefix is 'AZ' not 'ZS'. Fairly Rare.
* Jp Nippon Columbia, YB 7003 AX. Includes banding and lyrics. In same ps. Rare.
* Jp Nippon Columbia, YB 7003 AX, promo. Includes banding and lyrics. In same ps. Very Rare.

The UK pressings are double a-sided while the Aussie, Nipponese and NZ 'No One Is Innocent' issues are a/b-sided respectively. 'No One Is Innocent' ('The Biggest Blow') was originally titled 'God Save The Sex Pistols' and is also known as 'Cosh The Driver'. In any case it's Ronald Biggs on vocals.

The ersatz Pistols perform on a raft on the river.

The c/w ps of the Japanese version of 'No One Is Innocent'. Note the 'obi.' (yellow banding) used in the Nipponese market to promote other releases by the record company.

(I'm Not Your) Stepping Stone/ Pistols Propaganda

* NZ Virgin, VS 191 12, 80. In pale blue Virgin custom die-cut jacket. Fairly Common.

Anarchy In The UK// EMI/No Fun

* UK Virgin, VS 609 12, Oct 83. In black sleeve with credits on back. Common.
* UK Virgin, VS 609 12, white label test pressing. Issued without ps. Fairly Common.
* Au Virgin (EMI), VS 609 12. Fairly Common.
* Au Virgin (EMI), VS 609 12, promo. Fairly Rare.
* NZ Virgin, VS 609 12. Fairly Common.
* NZ Virgin, VS 609 12. Due to a factory error the labels are out of sync, and a 'For Promotional Use Only – Not For Resale' sticker was assigned to the sleeve. Fairly Rare.
* Mx Virgin, SL 7099 (105.419). Titled: 'Anarquia En El Reino Unido'/'Sin Diversion'/'EMI'. Fairly Rare.

All of the above foreign 12"s have similar jackets to the UK release.

Submission

* UK Chaos, CARTEL 1, 8 Oct 84. One-sided promo 'A' label. In white die-cut jacket. Common.

Submission/ Anarchy In The UK

* UK Chaos, CARTEL 1T, Dec 84. In green wax, with ps. Fairly Common.
* UK Chaos, CARTEL 1T, Dec 84. In clear wax, with same ps. Fairly Common.
* UK Chaos, CARTEL 1T, Dec 84. In white wax, with same ps. Fairly Common.
* UK Chaos, CARTEL 1T, Dec 84. In blue wax, with same ps. Fairly Common.
* UK Chaos, CARTEL 1T, Dec 84. In red wax, with same ps. Fairly Common.
* UK Chaos, CARTEL 1T, Dec 84. In yellow wax, with same ps. Fairly Common.
Note: label catalogue is 'CARTEL 1', whilst

back ps catalogue is 'EXPORT 1'.
* UK Chaos, EXPORT 1T, Dec 84. In clear wax, with same ps. Fairly Common.
* UK Chaos, EXPORT 1T, Dec 84. In white wax, with same ps. Fairly Common.
* UK Chaos, EXPORT 1T, Dec 84. In yellow wax, with same ps. Fairly Common.
* UK Chaos, EXPORT 1T, Dec 84. In red wax, with same ps. Fairly Common.
* UK Chaos, EXPORT 1T, Dec 84. In blue wax, with same ps. Fairly Common.
* UK Chaos, EXPORT 1T, Dec 84. In green wax, with same ps. Fairly Common.
* UK Chaos, EXPORT 1T, Dec 84. In pink wax, with same ps. Only 500 pressed. Fairly common. *Both label and back ps cat. nos. are 'EXPORT 1'.*
These tracks are the studio outtakes recorded between 13 and 20 July 76. The entire release consisted of approximately 12,000 copies. Note the pink wax edition was only made available via the second batch.

Pretty Vacant

* UK Chaos, 85, promo. Only six pressed. Very Rare.

Anarchy In The UK (Live)/(Bollock Bros) Return Of The Vampire

* Fr McDonald Bros JOCK 1201, 86. In ps. Common.
* Fr Echantillon (McDonald Bros JOCK 1201), white label test pressing. Issued in black die-cut jacket. Labels are different from stock edition. Common.

The first 'semi-legal' Pistols release – 'Submission' coupled with 'Anarchy', issued by Chaos Records in November 1984.

Clockwise from this page: painting of Sid by Dee Dee Ramone, 2000; 'We're the Flowers in the Dustbin . . .' Warner Bros. US promo poster for the Bollocks LP, 1977; original promo poster for 'God Save The Queen', 1977.

We're the flowers in the dustbin
We're the poison in your human machine
We're the future
Your future

SL-7099

SEX PISTOLS

ANARCHY IN THE U.K.
ANARQUIA EN EL REINO UNIDO
WARNER BROS MUSIC LTD./GLITTERBEST LTD.

no fun
SIN DIVERSION.
WARNER BROTHERS MUSIC LTD.

EMI
WARNER BROTHERS MUSIC LTD./GLITTERBEST LTD.

PRODUCIDO POR
CRIS THOMAS O BILL PRICE
A EXCEPCION DE (*) DAVID GOODMANN

Virgin
(P) 1983 VIRGIN RECORDS LTD. HECHO EN MEXICO POR BERTELSMANN DE MEXICO,S.A.
Av. DE LAS FUENTES 41-A 4o. PISO. TECAMACHALCO EDO. DE MEXICO
MIEMBRO ACTIVO DE AMPROFON EL DISCO ES CULTURA

This is the backsleeve of the rare Mexican three-track EP issued in October 83. Note the dual (English and Spanish) titles.

Sex Pistols Talk

* 10": UK SEX, 10, July 95. Interview on marble-colour vinyl. Limited edition of 500 issued in plain pvc bag. Fairly rare. *This is the Pistols' first standard 10".*

Sex Pistols 100 Club Press Conference

* UK SEX 1 LP, May 96. Reformation announcement and interview recorded live 18 March 96. Picture disc. Common.

Sid Vicious Heritage EP

* Fr Barclays/Glitterbest (BA 171) 740.509, March 79. Tracks: 'My Way'//'Something Else'/'C'mon Everybody'. In nice full-colour ps. Fairly Rare.
* Fr Barclays/Glitterbest 740.509. Ultra-scarce white-label test pressing, featuring only one track per side. No ps. Very Rare.

Interview Disc

* UK (cat./ matrix no. 0026) 86. Limited edition pic disc. Interviewed in 78. Fairly common.

Interview Disc

* UK 86, without any cat. no. except the matrix, which is RD PD 18. Picture disc release. Fairly Common.
* UK Tell Tale Series. A similar pic disc to the latter, except the interview is shorter and the picture is not as good quality. Fairly Common. *The above two releases are from the 1977 Rock On Radio 1 interview. Some of both pressings were issued in nice white die-cut jackets showing the actual picture disc(s).*

Sex Pistols Interview

* UK, without any cat. no. except the matrix which is SP A/B. In white die-cut jacket. Common.

The Original Sex Pistols Live EP

* UK Castle Communication, ARCHIVE/TOF 104, Aug 86. Tracks: 'Anarchy'/'I'm A Lazy Sod'//'Vacant'/'Substitute'. Live 76 club, Burton On Trent, 24 Sept 76. A limited edition of 5,000. In ps. Common.
* UK Castle Communication, TOF 104, white label test pressing. Issued in plain white sleeve. Supposedly only four made. Rare.

The Original Pistols The Early Years Live

* UK Receiver, REPLAY 3012, 90. Limited edition in blue wax. Tracks (all live): 'Anarchy'/'Vacant'// 'Liar'/ 'Dolls'. Issued in nice yellow/black ps. Features 'Limited Edition Coloured Vinyl' sticker on cover. Common.

Pretty Vacant/No Feelings (demo)// Satellite (demo)/ Submission (demo no.1

* UK Virgin, VST 1448, Nov 92. In ps. Common.

This handwritten handbill by Malcolm is in a pastiche Dickensian style. It was produced for the Christmas day show on the 1977 'Never Mind The Bans' tour, at a Huddersfield childrens home – hence the reference to Oliver Twist.

debris and with burning torches play rock 'n roll to the screaming delight of the frenzied pissing pogoing mob. SHOUTING AND SPITTING 'anarchy' one of these gangs call themselves the SEX PISTOLS. This true and dirty tale has BEEN CONTINUING THROUGHOUT 200 years of teenage anarchy and so in 1978 there still remains the SEX PISTOLS. Their active Extremism is all that, they come about because that's what WHAT COUNTS to JUMP RIGHT OUT of the 20th CENTURY AS FAST YOU R CENTURY possibly can in order to CREATE an environment that you can TRUTHFULLY RUN WILD IN

Oliver Twist.

This page: Never Mind The Bollocks poster, 1977. *Opposite page: this cartoon strip, originally featured in the UK music press, was reproduced on the American promo poster for* Never Mind The Bollocks, *1977.*

PISTOLS ALBUMS

Never Mind The Bollocks, Here's The Sex Pistols

* UK Virgin, V 2086, 28 Oct 77, original blue/white Virgin labels. Without the titles on the back sleeve. The album has eleven tracks: 'Holidays In The Sun', 'Liar', 'No Feelings', 'God Save The Queen', 'Problems'/'Seventeen', 'Anarchy In The UK', 'Bodies', 'Pretty Vacant', 'New York', 'EMI'. Producers: Chris Thomas (at that time, highly respected for his work with Roxy Music, the Beatles and Floyd's *Dark Side* . . .) and Bill Price (worked with Mott the Hoople and more recently produced BAD alongside Mick Jones). The track listings on labels are timed. Glen credited with 'EMI'. Fairly Rare.
This initial batch made it to the USA, as the US edition was not released until 4 Nov. The Very Rare US import includes a sticker reading 'ANOTHER IMPORT ALBUM FROM JEM'.
* UK Virgin, V 2086 – as above except back sleeve correctly states eleven tracks. Fairly Common.
The above two albums came in a limited edition of 50,000 and included a one-sided 7" single, 'Submission' Virgin VDJ 24, and a collage poster, the entire package sealed with an orange sticker, the former entry being the first batch of this pressing; quantity a mere 1,000. The poster is rare.
* UK Virgin, V 2086, white label test pressing. Rare.

* UK Virgin, V 2086, white label test pressing which has dots to enable someone to 'fill in the blanks' (write in the tracks by hand). Very Rare
* UK Virgin, V 2086, first (main) pressing of 200,000. Features original 'sky' labels and is without the titles on the back sleeve. Sid is wrongly credited with 'EMI'. Fairly Common.
Four permanent changes from this pressing onward: (1) 'Submission' appears on the album; (2) the labels state twelve tracks, in different order: 'Holidays', 'Bodies', 'No Feelings', 'Liar', 'GSTQ', 'Problems'/ 'Seventeen', 'Anarchy', 'Submission', 'Vacant', 'NY', 'EMI'; (3) tracks on labels are not timed; (4) production credits state: Chris Thomas or Bill Price.
* UK Virgin, V 2086, second pressing. Same as first pressing, but the sleeve correctly lists twelve tracks. Common.
* UK Virgin, V 2086, third pressing. Same as the first, except the back cover states eleven tracks (incorrectly neglects 'Submission'). Common.
One more permanent change from this pressing onward: Glen is correctly credited with 'EMI'.
* UK Virgin, VP 2086, Jan 78, pic disc. Initially pressed for export only. Comes in large pink die-cut jacket. Fairly Rare.
Picture discs exported to the US featured a JEM import sticker on cover.
* UK Virgin, V 2086, fourth pressing. Same as third – cover without 'Submission'. Common.
Another permanent change from this pressing

onward is the introduction of Virgin's bland green/red labels.
* UK Virgin, V 2086, fifth pressing. Same as the fourth, but cover correctly states twelve tracks. Common.
* UK Virgin, V 2086, sixth pressing. Same as fifth, but 'No Feelings' is misspelled on the label as 'No Fellings'. Fairly Common.
* UK Virgin, V 2086, seventh pressing. Same as fifth pressing but back sleeve claims eleven tracks. 'Belsen Was A Gas' is wrongly listed while 'Liar' is stated twice. Common.
* UK Virgin, OVED 136, 85, eighth pressing. Mid-price issue. Same as seventh pressing except for the cat. no. Includes mid-price inner advertiser. Common.
* UK Virgin, OVED 136, ninth pressing. Same as the eighth, except it has a barcode on the top of the back cover. Common.
* UK Virgin, OVED 136, tenth pressing. Same as the ninth, except it has Virgin's current cream/grey labels. Features the correct twelve tracks on back cover. Common.
* UK Virgin 7243 8 42802 1 5 (LP CENT 20), 17 Feb 97. One-off, direct metal master pressing on 180-gram vinyl. With silver/red 'EMI 100 - 1997 The First Centenary . . .' sticker on cover. Features original Virgin blue-sky labels. In a heavy duty jacket, but only eleven tracks on back sleeve. (As usual, 'Submission' is left out.) Common.

* Fr Glitterbest/Barclays, 940.553, 77, original pressing. This edition was imported into

the UK marginally ahead of the British release. The tracks are in identical order to its early UK counterpart: eleven tracks on platter, labels and back sleeve. With nice b/w labels. Fairly Rare.

* Fr Glitterbest/Barclays, 941.001 (B), second pressing. In similar pink/green sleeve to the American/Canadian pressings. Labels and vinyl list the full twelve track, back sleeve lists eleven. The front ps is unique to any release of *Bollocks*, featuring additional reverse pink type on cover, stating 'Includes the unreleased "Submission"'. With nice b/w labels. Easily the rarest of all three French pressings. Fairly Rare.

* Fr Glitterbest/Barclays, 941.001 (BA 213), third pressing. In blank pink back cover. Like the subsequent UK pressings this issue features the full twelve tracks, albeit in uniquely different order. With standard French b/w labels. Fairly Common.

Watch you don't pay too much for this pressing on account of its blank back sleeve – it's only a reissue.

* Fr Virgin, 202984 (PM 252), fourth pressing. Virgin finally issue their own release of *Bollocks* in France. The sleeve is standard yellow/pink, but the French have replicated the mispressed British sleeve design: 'Liar' is listed twice whilst 'Belsen Was A Gas' is wrongly stated. Fairly Rare

* Fr Virgin 70057. Reissue. Cover states eleven tracks. Fairly Common.

Other slight discrepancies on the French labels are: (1) producers Thomas and Price, while credited on both sides for subsequent pressings, were only mentioned on the b-side; (2) the times allocated to most of the tracks conflict with those on other pressings; (3) Matlock is mispelled on all track credits as 'Mattlock'.

* WG Virgin 25 593 XOT, original pressing. Includes beautiful green labels with two Virgin symbols. Back cover states only eleven tracks – 'Submission' is omitted, though it appears on the album. Fairly Rare.

* WG Virgin 25 593-XOT, second pressing. Green/red labels. Fairly Common.

* WG Virgin, 25 593 270, third pressing. Green/red labels. Collectors note: the back sleeve catalogue number on this pressing is 25 593-270, while the labels read 25 593 XOT. The print on the bottom back cover is slightly different from the second pressing. Fairly Rare.

* WG Virgin, 25 593 270, fourth pressing. As per the third pressing except for the following two differences: both the sleeve and

the labels are in a high-gloss finish; there is a b/w barcode sticker on the back sleeve, reading 'OVED 136 SEX PISTOLS'. Fairly Common.

Completists note: on most of the West German pressings 'Anarchy' is mispelled as 'Anarchy In The UX', Glen Matlock is misspelled on all songwriting credits as 'Maflock', and Sid is incorrectly co-credited with 'EMI'.

* It Virgin, VIL 12086. In original blue/white snake/twin emblem labels. Some copies featured a 'Rotten promo sheet' insert. Labels and back cover state twelve tracks. Fairly Rare.

* It Virgin, VIL 12086, second pressing. Standard green/red Virgin labels. Labels and back cover state twelve tracks. Fairly Rare.

* It Virgin VIL 12086, third pressing. Standard green/red Virgin labels. Back cover states only eleven tracks — 'Submission' is omitted, though it appears on the album. The front sleeve also features an additional 'PUNK' emblem. Fairly Rare.

* NI Virgin, 25098 XOT, original issue. With beautiful green labels featuring two Virgin symbols. Initial pressings featured a b/w

'Geef Voor New Wave' sticker on the front cover. Fairly Rare.

* NI Virgin, 25098 XOT, second pressing. Sleeve is high quality gloss. The labels on this LP are unique in that all the other releases with the more recent Virgin labels (UK and foreign) are green/red whereas these are red/green. Labels correctly state twelve tracks. Back cover lists eleven tracks (neglects 'Submission'), similar to some of the UK pressings. Fairly Common.

* NI Virgin, 25098 XOT, third pressing. Identical to the second, except the sleeve has a drab matt finish. Fairly Common.

*Gr Virgin/ Phonogram, 2933710. This was the first variation from a set of three. In yellow front/pink back jacket. Came with the beautiful original blue/white Virgin labels featuring the twin virgins. Rare.

* Gr Virgin/Phonogram, 2933710, white label test pressing. Very Rare.

* Gr Virgin/Phonogram, 2933710, second pressing. Features green labels with same pair of twin virgins. Again in the standard yellow/pink sleeve. The most common of the

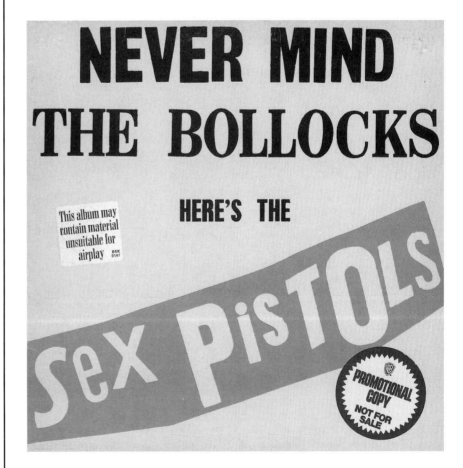

Warner Bros. US promotional edition. Note the b/w warning sticker.

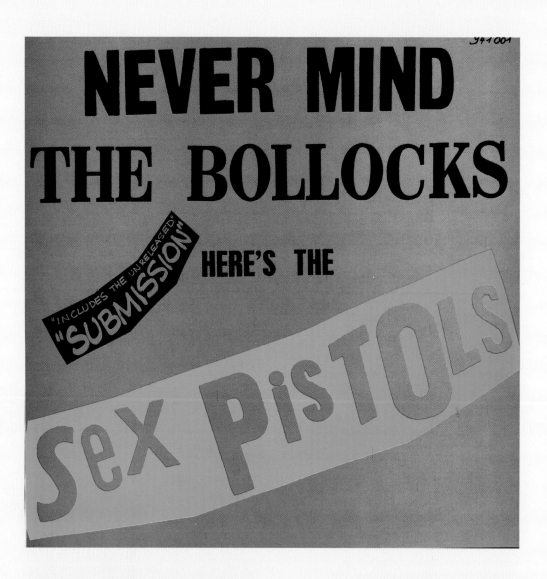

Above: Never Mind The Bollocks – *the rarest of the French pressings. Glitterbest/ Barclays were determined to out-perform Virgin in the UK by including 'Submission'. Bottom left: the picture disc was issued three months after the standard vinyl edition, pressed solely for the export market. Bottom right: the original Japanese issue with the wide splatter-patterned obi. (banding).*

Above: The Great Rock'N'Roll Swindle *double album, released in the wake of the band breaking up.* Bottom left: *the back sleeve of the French edition features a unique newspaper collage.* Bottom right: *this single album package, featuring scenes from* Swindle *on its back sleeve, was released to coincide with the movie in May 1980.*

three initial Greek pressings. Fairly Rare.
* Gr Virgin/Phonogram, 2933710, third pressing. Once again, this pressing features the twin virgins on green labels, though this time the sleeve changes to pink/purple on front and green on back. This pressing is slightly rarer than the latter. This is the third and final variation on the initial Greek pressings. Features a two-page Greek press release. Rare.
* Gr Virgin/Phonogram, 2933710. As the latter pressing except without the press release. Rare.
There was also an early Greek pressing (one of the initial three) which featured the same label on both sides. However, the record played perfectly.
* Gr Virgin, 062 VG 50.009/MT 10990, c.82, fourth pressing. Standard Virgin stock reissue. In yellow front/pink back sleeve. With standard green/red labels. Fairly Rare.
* Gr Virgin, 062 VG 50.009 (A/A 10990), fifth Greek pressing. Features standard cream/grey labels. Initial copies had the 'Value – Virgin – Value' sticker on the front cover. Fairly Common.
* Gr Virgin, 062 VG 50.009 (A/A 10990). Some of the latter Greek pressings had a mispressed a-side label: it is completely out of place and runs right out onto the vinyl! Fairly Rare.
* Sp Virgin, 25593E. The back cover states twelve tracks. The lettering sequence of 'Submission' on the cover is slightly different to the UK issues. Fairly Rare.
* Pl Virgin VV-33.012V, with green/red labels. With correct twelve tracks on labels and back sleeve. Some copies included a free badge. Fairly Rare.
Collector's note: Sid was incorrectly co-credited for 'EMI' on almost all of the continental European releases, even the subsequent and recent reissues!

* US Warner Bros, BSK 3147, first pressing. In different colour cover: front is pink, back is green. Same tracks as the UK main pressing except 'GSTQ' and 'Problems' are reversed. Includes blue/white pic inner which states 'Made in USA'. With nice white labels. The back sleeve states only eleven tracks, though a sticker was added – prior to shipping – which credits the missing track 'Submission'. Basically a limited edition run. Fairly Rare.
* US Warner Bros, BSK 3147, authentic white label test pressing. Rare.
* US Warner Bros, BSK 3147, promo issue. Same as initial stock run: with nice white labels, 'Submission' sticker on back sleeve,

and inner ps, etc. With two promo stickers on cover: 'This Album May Contain Material Unsuitable For Airplay – BSK 3147' and 'WB – Promotional Copy – Not For Sale'. Includes label copy sheet. Rare.
* US Warner Bros, BSK 3147, second pressing. Same as first pressing except: (1) 'Submission' is on cover; (2) inner sleeve is replaced by plastic inner with WB logos; (3) tracks are timed; and (4) labels are cream. Fairly Common.
* US Warner Bros, BSK 3147, third stock pressing. Identical to second pressing except the labels are dyed brown and inner sleeve is included. Common.
* US Warner Bros, BSK 3147, fourth stock pressing. As third pressing except: (1) without some of the printed credits on labels; (2) six WB logos are lightly imprinted on the labels; (3) the disc is in a transparent plastic bag without the logos; (4) labels are cream. Common.
* US Warner Bros, BSK 3147, fifth pressing. Identical to fourth issue except the back cover has the modern barcode on top of back. Common.
* US Warner Bros/Columbia House. The sleeve is a deep cherry luminous pink with green lettering. With standard b/w labels like the other WB issues. The back sleeve states 'Manufactured by Columbia House under license'. With barcode on back cover. Limited pressing. Fairly Rare.
* Ca Warner Bros, BSK 3147, original stock issue. With Canadian inner sleeve. 'Submission' is missing from back cover. Rare
* Ca Warner Bros, BSK 3147, promo. With same inner. Once again, 'Submission' is missing from back cover. Very Rare.
* Ca Warner Bros, promo-only pink and green vinyl edition, extremely scarce. Very Rare.
* Ca Warner Bros, BSK 3147, second pressing. With same inner. Back cover states 'Submission'. With small maple tree on back cover. Fairly Rare.
* Ca Warner Bros, BSK 3147, third pressing. As second but with different label indents and featuring a plain white inner bag. Fairly Rare.
* Ca Warner Bros, BSK 3147, fourth pressing. As the second/third pressings but, once again, different label indents plus a standard plastic bag inner. Fairly Rare.
Another slight difference in these Canadian pressings and their US counterparts is that the former feature two different cat. nos. – the Canadian sleeve's spine and inner ps both incorrectly read KBS 3147, while their labels correctly state BSK 3147.
* Mx Ariola/Virgin, LA 142, 79. With beautiful

original twin Virgin colour labels, printed in Spanish. Includes small Ariola box on front cover, and back sleeve excludes 'Submission', although it's on the album. Rare.
* Mx Ariola/Virgin, LA 142, promo. Rare.
* Bz Virgin, 710 8362, 78. With original twin virgins on red labels. Rare.
* Bz Virgin, 710 8362, 78, promo stamped. Rare.
* Bz RCA/Virgin, 104.8362, 86. With green/red labels. The back cover is orange and lists eleven tracks (neglects 'Submission'). Fairly Rare.
* Bz RCA/Virgin, 104.8362 (710 8362), 86, gold leaf promo stamp on back cover. Includes two red stamps on front plastic outer and promo comic strips. With green/red labels. Sleeve as latter reissue stock pressing. Fairly Rare.
* Ar RCA/Ariola/Virgin, TLP 60169 (V2086), 86. Once again, this features the usual wrong track listings on c/w ('Belsen Was A Gas', etc.) With red labels on both sides. Tracks on labels are in both Spanish and English. Fairly Rare.
* Ar Virgin, TLP 60169, 86, promo. Fairly Rare.
* Uy Virgin, 100008/1. Mispressed sleeve. Fairly Rare.
Practically all of the subsequent South American pressings were issued in the common 'Belsen' mispressed sleeve.

* Au Wizard, ZL 225, bluish Wizard labels. Initial issues had an A4 flyer advertising all punk rock/new wave pressings to date of issue. Fairly Rare.
* Au Wizard, ZL 225, promo. Though Wizard never issued any *genuine* Pistols promo editions, this limited quantity featured an information pack/promo biog, etc. Rare.
* Au Virgin (EMI), V 2086, reissue. With insert. Fairly Rare.
* Au Virgin, V 2086 (MX 194222/3). With green/red labels. Fairly Common.
* Au Virgin, V 2086 (MX 194 222/3), white label promo. Features gold promo stamp on back sleeve. Fairly Rare.
* Au/NZ Virgin, V 2086. In standard black vinyl. Features new cream/grey Virgin labels. Fairly Common.
* Au/NZ Virgin, V 2086. In red vinyl. Features new cream/grey Virgin labels. Fairly Common.
* Au/NZ Virgin, V 2086. In blue wax. Features new cream/grey Virgin labels. Fairly Common.
* Au/NZ Virgin, V 2086. In green wax. Features new cream/grey Virgin labels. Fairly Common.
These latter four were issued by Virgin in the Autumn of 90, with the back covers in a much

With the disintegration of the U.S.S.R. Bollocks *finally made it to the Russian market in 1993. This is the reverse of the sleeve and is totally different to any other.*

darker shade of pink to the previous editions.
* NZ Virgin, V 2086. With original overseas twin-virgins logo on green labels. The sleeve retains the original black spine. Very Rare.
* NZ Virgin, V 2086. With green/red labels. As usual, the back sleeve neglects 'Submission' although it's on both the label and disc. Fairly Rare.

* Jp Nippon Columbia, YX 7199 AX, original issue. Includes insert with lyrics in both English and Japanese. With wide banding and lovely navy blue labels. Very Rare.
The lyrics are grossly inaccurate though hilarious: '. . . I look around your house, you got nothing here still, I think you're in a bind when you're dead on a hill, That's why you play your drawers . . .'
* Jp Nippon Columbia, YK 7199 AX, promo. Includes same inner and banding as stock. Very Rare.
* Jp Victor Musical Industries Inc./Virgin, VIP 6986, 82, reissue. With green/red labels. The cover correctly states twelve tracks. With normal size banding: smaller and different to the original Japanese issue. With insert. Fairly Rare.
* Jp Victor Musical Industries Inc./Virgin, VIP 6986, 82, white label promo. With red/white promo sticker on sleeve. Features banding and insert as VMI/VIP stock. Rare.

* Jp Virgin, 25 VB-1068 (32VD-1011), 82, stock issue. With banding and insert. Fairly Rare.
* Jp Virgin, 25 VB-1068 (32VD-1011). With green/red promo labels and narrow banding. Includes four-page insert with English and Nipponese lyrics, and b/w promo sticker on back. Fairly Rare.
* Jp Virgin Japan, VJL 110, 88, fourth Nipponese stock pressing. From the Best Selection 30 series. Unusual yellow labels with black print. With banding and insert. Fairly Rare.
* SK Nippon Columbia, YX 7199 Ax, 78. In the same sleeve as the first Nipponese pressing. Includes white labels with the album title misprinted as *God Save The Queen* in black lettering, and crediting the band as 'the Sex Postols' (the name is spelled correctly on the cover). Though this pressing hails from 1978, it is highly likely to be a bootleg pressed in the Philippines. Very Rare.
* Ru Anton, 00273/00274 (ATR 30059/60), 93. In different sleeve to any other: green border, with Russian writing; c/w: has pic of HM QE II and track titles in both Russian and English. Fairly Rare.

* SA Virgin, ML 4147, 77. Original b/w labels with girls and dragon. Rare.
* SA CCP/Virgin/EMI Brigadiers VIR (L) 3010 (V 2086), 80. Reissue with green/red labels. Fairly Rare.
Completists take note: on this RSA pressing, 'No Feelings' is incorrectly credited to 'Jones/Cook/ Matlock/Vicious'.

The Great Rock 'N' Roll Swindle (double album)

* UK Virgin, VD 250, Feb 79. Features 25 tracks, with blue text from a handbill designed by Malcolm for the Pistols' Xmas day gig in 77 on back cover. Also includes a b/w inner which lists tracks. Inside g/f cover the tracks are listed in four boxes. Cover spine is white, with two stickers on front

cover promising 21 new tracks, and band members listed on back. The '21 new tracks' are (in alphabetical order): 'Belsen Was A Gas', 'Belsen' (live), 'Black Arabs', 'C'mon Everybody', 'Friggin' In The Riggin'', 'GSTQ (Symphony)', 'The Great Rock'N'Roll Swindle', 'EMI (Orchestra)', 'Johnny B. Goode', 'L'Anarchie Pour L'UK', 'Lonely Boy', 'Don't Give Me No Lip Child', 'Road Runner', 'Rock Around The Clock', 'Something Else', 'Silly Thing', '(I'm Not Your) Stepping Stone', 'Substitute', 'Watcha Gonna Do About It?', 'Who Killed Bambi?' and 'You Need Hands, while the 'four previously available' tracks were (alphabetically): 'Anarchy', 'I Wanna Be Me', 'My Way' and 'No One Is Innocent'. The b-side yellow label (on record one) is also unique to this pressing in that it does not feature the joke – 'Sorry About Incorrect Track Listing On Sleeve – It's Another Swindle!' – that occurred on all other UK stock issues. The labels state 'All Titles Published . . .'. Fairly Rare.
This 25-track edition was initially pressed in Jan 79. McLaren changed his mind after the first pressing and altered the track listing – hence this original pressing was to be destroyed. However, the threat of a French edition flooding the UK market one week prior to the domestic issue forced Virgin to act. 10,000 from this early batch were released the last week in February, while the label stuck to the originally scheduled release date (2 March 79) for the modified pressing. As well as the inclusion of 'Watcha Gonna Do?', another unique difference in this limited batch is that 'GSTQ (Symphony)' does not have the customary McLaren running commentary. This album changes hands for in excess of £60 – although its true value is actually closer to a quarter of this.
* UK Virgin, VD 2510, 2 March 79, second issue. The deletion of 'Watcha Gonna Do?' brings the track count down to 24. Features the blue text on back ps and the customary b/w inner. Inside g/f cover the tracks are listed in four boxes. Spine is white. With two stickers on front and back. Labels state 'All Titles Published . . .'. Fairly Common.
* UK Virgin, VD 2510, third pressing. Contains usual 24 tracks, but without the blue text credits. Includes b/w inner. Inside g/f cover lists tracks in two columns. Spine is red. With two stickers on front and back. Labels state 'All Titles Published . . .'. Common.
* UK Virgin, VD 2510, fourth pressing. 24 tracks, without blue text. Includes b/w inner. Inside g/f cover: tracks listed in two columns.

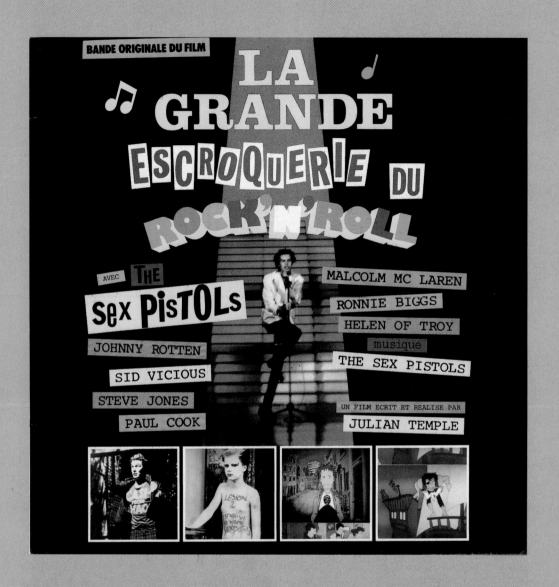

Above: the French soundtrack album was issued in a unique sleeve. Below: the inside of the Swindle double album contained a fuller selection of stills from the film.

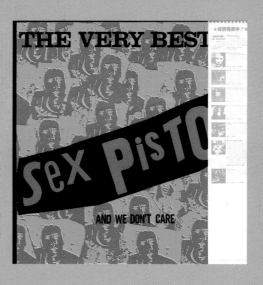

Above: the original New Zealand pressing of Some Product. *Bottom left:* Flogging A Dead Horse *was the British version of a Pistols 'greatest hits' compilation.* *Bottom right:* the Very Best of the Sex Pistols *was a Japanese-only compilation.*

Red spine, no stickers on sleeve. The labels state 'All Titles Copyright . . .'. Common
* UK Virgin, VD 2510, fifth pressing. With blue text on back ps, also has barcode on back cover. Common.
On the inside g/f of all the above British stock pressings, 'Watcha Gonna Do?' is wrongly listed – it is only available on the initial pressing. Subsequent to its deletion, Virgin still insisted in putting the '21 New Tracks' sticker on the sleeve. In some instances the correct sticker '20 New Tracks' was substituted, but these are on far fewer jackets than the former. Also, at least one of the latter pressings featured spoken overdubs on 'GSTQ (Symphony)'. Further editions featured a different sticker altogether: 'Includes the smash hits "Something Else", "C'mon Everybody" and "Silly Thing".'
* UK Virgin, VD 2510, promo. Very Rare.
* UK Virgin, VD 2510, white label test pressing. Sides three and four have handwritten labels and cover. Very Rare.
* Fr Matrixbest/Barclays rec 930101/02 (BA 613). This initial French pressing had unique pink and yellow labels. With different back ps (newspaper cuttings collage) and also features an unusual message inside g/f: 'All Johnny Rotten recording except "Belsen Was A Gas" was recorded in 1976.' Rare.
Entrepreneurial war news: once again it appears Edward Barclay tried to get the better of the more successful Branson when the platter was – yet again – released marginally ahead of its UK counterpart, thus prompting a rush release from Virgin to counteract the prospect of massive importing.
* Fr Matrixbest/Barclays 930101/02. White label test pressing. Very Rare.
* Fr Glitterbest/Barclays rec 930101-2 (BA 613), second main pressing. Again with the different back sleeve. With pink and yellow labels. Fairly Rare.
* Fr Virgin 300 278/9 (AE 202), third pressing and Virgin's first to go it alone. The word 'Sacem' appears on all four labels. Tracks are listed in four boxes. With blue text on back ps. Fairly Rare.
* Fr Virgin 60011 (PM 524), fourth pressing. With extra track, 'Watcha Gonna Do?'. Sacem on all four labels. Fairly Rare.
* It Virgin, AVIL 212510. Fairly Rare.
Collectors take note: Virgin also issued an export pressing primarily for the US which had an almost identical label no. (AVIL 21250) to the latter.
* WG Virgin, 300 279.406. The original pressing had German (only) copyright warning inside

labels. The labels also featured a small emblem of the twin female virgins. Fairly Rare.
* WG Virgin, 300 279.406. Second pressing features both German and English copyright/warning on labels. Again the labels have the twin virgins. Fairly Rare.
* WG Virgin, 300 279.406, third pressing. Also features German and English copyright warning on labels, but the twins emblem is dropped altogether. There is also a barcode sticker on the back sleeve which claims the mainland cat. no. VD 2510 – Sex Pistols. Fairly Common.
* WG Virgin, 300 279.406, fourth pressing. Identical to the latter except the barcode is embedded in the jacket. Fairly Common.
Most of the WG pressings have blue text on back sleeve and their label cat. nos. are different to that on the sleeves, 300 277/8. To make matters more complicated, there also exists a West German mispressing, which, three quarters of the way through 'No One Is Innocent', speeds up to 45rpm!!!
* Pl Virgin, VV 33010/11 DN. With yellow labels. Fairly Rare.
* Sw Virgin VD 2510, green/red labels. With story on back. Rare.
* Gr Virgin/Polygram, 2676.718 (50022/50023). With import UK sleeve. Apparently Virgin initially had a special 'export sleeve' (VD 2510) version for the Greek market (the actual platters are Greek). More than likely it was a joint venture between Virgin and Polygram, although the latter is not credited on the actual album. This one is the rarest of the Greek *Swindles*. Fairly Rare.
* Gr Virgin/Polygram, 2676.718. Another original Greek pressing. This one has all the correct details on its sleeve – Polygram's local address and contact numbers, etc. The labels and matrix numbers are identical on both pressings. Fairly Rare.
* Gr Virgin/EMI, 062 VG 50022/3 (A/A 12335). Third reissue with standard green/red labels. With blue story on back. Fairly Rare.
* Gr Virgin/EMI, 062 VG 50022/3 (A/A 12336). Fourth Greek pressing with the new cream/grey labels. With story of '200 years of teenage anarchy' on back – attributed to 'Oliver Twist', written by Malcolm. Fairly Rare.
Collectors note: the Greek pressings with cat. no. '062 VG 50022/3 (A/A 12336)' had a slightly different cat. no. on the spine, 'WG 50022 / 23', while the back ps read 'MT 12335/6'

* Au Wizard, ZL 237, 79. With beautiful, original, bluish 'Wizard' labels. Also came with

insert. Features Wizard logo on back ps. Fairly Rare.
* Au Wizard, ZL 237, 79. Issued in a multitude of different coloured waxes, with the Wizard logo on back ps. Very Rare.
These pressings were withdrawn and deliberately destroyed due to inferior sound quality. Colours included marble, blue, turquoise. Although there are at least twenty different variants, overall only a few of each exist.
* Au Virgin, VD 2510/MX 194 212 (2/3/4/5), reissue. With green/red labels. Also includes insert. Fairly Rare.
* Au Virgin, VD 2510/MX 194 212 (2/3/4/5), white promo labels. Features gold leaf promo stamp on back cover. Rare.
* NZ Virgin, VD 2510. Original issue with the RTC insignia on back of jacket. With yellow/pink labels. Also with a board-weight inner, not the customary paper. The labels are fairly unique in that they sneer, once again, at the buyer: 'This is not the correct playing order, it's all part of the Swindle.' Fairly Rare.
* Au/NZ Virgin (EMI), VD 2510. Labels state 'Manufactured by EMI in Australasia'. With standard green/red labels. Fairly Rare.
* Au/NZ Virgin (EMI), VD 2510. For the first time, the double album set is reduced to a single sleeve. With the same collage (high quality gloss) inner. Features new cream/grey Virgin labels. 'Aust Made' sticker on back ps. Fairly Rare.

* Jp Nippon Columbia, YB 7004-5, original. With banding and free poster. Rare.
* Jp Nippon Columbia, YB 7004-5, original promo. With banding. Also includes promo info sheets. Rare.
* Jp Victor Musical Industries Inc/Virgin, VIP 9911-2, reissue. In fold-open cover. Includes four-page insert. Rare.
* Jp Victor Musical Industries Inc./Virgin, VIP 9911-2, white label promo. With banding and insert, etc. Features red/white promo sticker on cover. Rare.

* Bz Virgin, 122.8003. Fairly Rare.
* Bz RCA/Ariola/Virgin, 122.8003 (772 8003), 87. With gold-leaf promo stamp on front ps, and four stamped promo labels. Each platter features the common green/red labels. Standard b/w insert. Nice item. Rare.
Alongside the Pistols on this album were: Ten Pole Tudor, Black Arabs, Jerzimy, Malcolm McLaren, Ronnie Biggs and the imbecilic 'Martin Bormann', aka Jim Jetter.

Some Product — Carri On Sex Pistols

* UK Virgin, VR 2, 27 July 79. With green/red labels. On this original pressing the labels are 'sunk' halfway out from the centre. With small white circular 'VR2 Sex Pistols R.R.P. £3.20' sticker on front cover. Tracks: 'The Very Name "Sex Pistols"', 'From Beyond The Grave', 'Big Tits Across America'/'The Complex World Of John Rotten', 'Sex Pistols Will Play', 'Is The Queen A Moron?', 'The Fucking Rotter'. Common.
* UK Virgin, VR 2, second pressing. The green/red labels are flat. Common.
* UK Virgin, VR 2. Reissued with bar code on back cover. With green/red labels. Common.
* UK Virgin, VR 2. Reissued with the new cream/grey Virgin labels. The custom barcode is on the back sleeve. Common.
* Fr Virgin, 205223 (AE 280). With green/red labels reading 'Sacem'. Fairly Common.
* NI Virgin, 200.786. With red/green labels. Fairly Common.
* It Virgin, VIL 12. With green/red labels and small ink stamp on a-side label. Fairly Common.
* Gr Virgin, 062 VG 50049. With green/red labels. Fairly Rare.
* Gr Virgin, 062 VG 50049. White label test pressing. Rare.

* Au Wizard, ZL 238. With nice bluish Wizard labels. The album wasn't pressed down-under till October. Fairly Rare.
* Au Virgin (EMI), V2. Fairly Rare.
* Au Virgin, V2 (MX 194230/1), white promo labels. With gold leaf promo stamp on back sleeve and 'This album includes lyric content which may be offensive to some members of the public' sticker. (However, label credits have swear words asterisked out!) Fairly Rare.
* NZ Virgin, VR 2, 79, first pressing. With warning in top left top corner: 'You Should Not Pay More Than $5.99 For This Record.' This issue was marketed by the RTC people who handled most of Virgin's material in New Zealand in the late seventies/early eighties, and is a hard-to-find original. With green/red labels. Fairly Rare.
* NZ Virgin, VR 2, 79. Reissued and marketed solely by Virgin, hence the different back sleeve credits. Without warning in top left top corner. Features green/red labels. Fairly Rare.
* Au/NZ Virgin, V2. Note the cat. no. is V2 not VR2. Features the new cream Virgin labels. Fairly Common.

Low cost compilation of interviews, radio adverts, etc, put together by John Varnom. Hear it for the Tubular Bells *extract.*

Flogging A Dead Horse

* UK Virgin, V 2142, Oct 79. Tracks: 'Anarchy', 'I Wanna Be Me', 'GSTQ', 'Did You No Wrong', 'Vacant', 'No Fun', 'Holidays'//'The Biggest Blow (No One Is Innocent)', 'My Way', 'Something Else', 'Silly Thing', 'C'mon Everybody', 'Stepping Stone', 'The Great Rock'N'Roll Swindle'. With green/red labels. Common.
The singles compilation that for one reason or another omits the eighth track on each side: 'Satellite' and 'Rock Around The Clock', which make for a full compliment of all the singles accompanied by their b-sides.
* UK Virgin, OVED 165, Apr 86. A mid-price issue. Features mid-price inner advertiser. With green/red labels. Common.
* UK Virgin, OVED 165. This latest reissue has the new cream/grey Virgin labels. Common.

* WG Virgin, 201.165, original pressing. Fairly Common.
* WG Virgin, 201.165. Reissue with Virgin logo in white lettering on back sleeve. Fairly Common.
* WG Virgin, 201.165 (270) (OVED 165). From Virgin's mid-price back catalogue. As the initial reissue but has an OVED/barcode sticker on back of sleeve. Common.
* It Virgin, VIL 12142, original pressing. With green/red labels. Features small blue ink stamp on the a-side label. Fairly Common.
* Sp Virgin, E 201 165, original issue. Features green/red labels. Fairly Common.

* Gr Phonogram, original issue. Either 300 or 500 pressed. Rare.
* Gr Virgin/Polygram, 2933 799. Note the misprinted cat. no. is 9933 799 on back of sleeve and 2933 799 on the actual label. Fairly Rare.
* Gr Virgin/Polygram, 2933 799, white label promo. Fairly Rare.

* SA Virgin, VIR(L) 3009. Green/red labels. Fairly Rare.

* Au Virgin (EMI), V 2142 (MX 194 232/3). With green/red labels. Fairly Rare.
* Au Virgin (EMI), V 2142 (MX 194 232/3), white label promo. Fairly Rare.
* NZ Virgin, V 2142. Fairly Rare.
* Au/NZ Virgin/EMI, OVED 165. With green/red labels. Fairly Common.
* Jp Victor Musicals Industries Inc./Virgin, VIL 6024, 83. In totally different ps to any other issues. Features full size fold-open inner that also acts as banding, via a flap that protrudes from inside the jacket. With green/red labels. Fairly Rare.
* Jp Victor Musicals Industries Inc./Virgin, VIL 6024, 83. Beautiful white promo labels. With red/white promo sticker on cover. The ps, inner and obi. are as stock edition. Fairly Rare.

Some Product was an anthology of interviews with the band.

Clockwise from top: US cardboard promo for The Great Rock'N'Roll Swindle *film; original German poster; original Spanish poster, under the title* Dios Salve A La Reina (God Save The Queen).

Above: US cardboard promo for *The Great Rock'N'Roll Swindle. Below: the original British cinema poster.*

* Ar Virgin, TLP 90085. Actually titled 'Castigando Un Caballo Muerto'. Fairly Rare.
* Ar Virgin, TLP 90085, promo. Fairly Rare.
This was positively the nadir of the 'scraping of the barrel syndrome'; most genuine fans felt Bollocks was already a 'greatest hits', considering that four tracks were widely available prior to its release. Some trivia: 'horse' correlates to 'heroin' according to old hippy lingo.

The Very Best Of The Sex Pistols (And We Don't Care)

* Jp Nippon Columbia (Flyover), YX 7247 AX, Dec 79. Includes booklet with group's history in Japanese. Also includes lyrics in both Japanese and English. Features standard banding. Tracks: 'Vacant', 'No Fun', 'Anarchy', 'I Wanna Be Me', 'GSTQ', 'Here We Go Again'/'The Great Rock'N'Roll Swindle', 'C'mon Everybody', 'Did You No Wrong', 'Black Leather', 'Satellite', 'Silly Thing', 'My Way'. Fairly Rare.
* Jp Nippon Columbia (Flyover), YX 7247 AX, promo. Includes inserts and banding. Rare.

The Great Rock'N' Roll Swindle (Soundtrack)

* UK Virgin, V 2168, May 80. Includes paper booklet. With sticker on front: 'V 2168 – Includes Free Book.' Tracks: 'GSTQ (Symphony)', 'The Great Rock'N'Roll Swindle', 'You Need Hands', 'Silly Thing', 'Lonely Boy', 'Something Else'/'Rock Around The Clock', 'C'mon Everybody', 'Who Killed Bambi?', 'No One Is Innocent', 'Anarchie Pour L'UK', 'My Way'. Rare.
The free booklet was an illustrated, twelve-page, tabloid-sized newspaper penned by novelist Michael Moorcock. It currently sells for £40-50. This newspaper subsequently surfaced as a book - see 'Pistols Publications'.
* UK Virgin, V 2168. An edition of 15,000 including a giant film poster. Labels state 'Published by Warner Bros Limited except . . .'. Fairly Common.
The poster sells for anything up to the ridiculous price of £300!
* UK Virgin, V 2168. Labels state 'All tracks copyright control except . . .'. Common.
* UK Virgin, OVED 234, Apr 89. With OVED sticker on back cover. Common.
* UK Virgin, OVED 234. This latest reissue has the new cream/grey Virgin labels. With the OVED sticker on back. Common.

* Fr Virgin, 202 521 (AE 260), 80. Actually titled *La Grande Escroquerie Du Rock'N'Roll*. Issued in a completely different sleeve to any other: Sid doing his classic Sinatra piece. Some had a free info book. With green/red labels. Very Rare.
This pressing was not only unique in regard to its sleeve, but it also marked a departure from the familiar Glitterbest/Barclays French issues: this was Virgin's first Pistols platter to be released in France.
* Fr Virgin, 70025 (PM/254), 81. Reissued with same ps, title and labels. Very Rare.
* It Virgin, VIL 12168. With 'Colonna Sonora Originale del Film Omonimo' title on bottom of front sleeve. Features small blue ink stamp on the a-side label. Fairly Rare.
* WG Virgin, 202 521. Fairly Common.
* Pl Virgin, VV-33.047 Y, green/red labels. Fairly Rare.
* Is General Music Co./Virgin, V 2168. Features red/white Hebrew writing on front cover. Also red (slightly different to UK) labels on both sides. The actual platter was made in the UK specifically for export. Fairly Rare.

* US Virgin, 722561. Fairly Common.
* Mx Virgin, LA 259 (82555). Titled *La Gran Estafa Rocanrolera*. Song names in Spanish, synopsis on back is also in Spanish. Beautiful white labels with colour pic on top half. Includes large red 'Rock De Los 80's' sticker on front cover. Rare.

* Au Virgin, (EMI) V 2168 (MX 194 224/5). Fairly Rare.
* Au Virgin, (EMI) V 2168 (MX 194 224/5), white label promo. With gold promo stamp on back sleeve. Fairly Rare.
* NZ Virgin, V 2168. Fairly Rare.
* Au/NZ Virgin, V 2168. With green/red labels. Fairly Common.

* Au/NZ Virgin, V 2168. Reissued with Virgin's new cream/grey labels. Fairly Common.

* Ph Virgin V 4610 (VD 2510). In totally different sleeve to any other: the front is the same as that of the double album, while the back is a unique collage accompanied by the song titles in a messy typeface. Very Rare.

* SA Virgin VIR(L) 3016. Fairly Rare.
See double album version for additional guest appearances.

Kiss This

* UK Virgin, V 2702, 5 Oct 92. A double 'Best Of' set in g/f sleeve. Features twenty tracks digitally re-mastered by the mainman Mr Lydon: 'Anarchy', 'GSTQ', 'Vacant', 'Holidays', 'I Wanna Be Me'/'Did You No Wrong', 'No Fun', 'Satellite', 'No Lip', 'Stepping Stone'/'Bodies', 'No Feelings', 'Liar', 'Problems', 'Seventeen'/ 'Submission', 'New York', 'EMI', 'My Way', 'Silly Thing'. Common.
* Bz Virgin, 168786489-1, 93. Fairly Common.

Never Mind The Bollocks, Here's The Sex Pistols / Spunk (This Is Crap)

Sid Sings was released the Xmas after Sid died, a compilation of tracks from Sid's solo NYC gigs in September/October 1978.

* UK Virgin, Jun 96. Limited issue on vinyl. Tracks: 'Seventeen', 'Satellite', '(No) Feelings', 'Just Me' ('I Wanna Be Me'), 'Submission',

'Nookie' ('Anarchy'), 'No Future' ('GSTQ'), 'Problems', 'Lots Of Fun' ('No Fun'), 'Liar', 'Who Was It?' ('EMI'), 'Looking For A Kiss (NY)', 'Problems', 'No Feelings', 'Vacant', 'Submission', 'No Feelings', 'EMI', 'Satellite', 'Seventeen', 'Anarchy', 'Holidays', 'Bodies', 'No Feelings', 'Liar', 'GSTQ', 'Problems', 'Seventeen', 'Anarchy', 'Submission', 'Vacant', 'NY', 'EMI (Unlimited Edition)'. Common

Filthy Lucre Live

* UK Virgin Records America Inc. VUSLP 116, 29 July 96. Live from Finsbury Park 23 June 96. With full colour inner sleeve. Tracks: 'Bodies', 'Seventeen', 'NY', 'No Feelings', 'Did You No Wrong', 'GSTQ', 'Liar', 'Satellite', 'Stepping Stone'/'Holidays', 'Submission', 'Vacant', 'EMI', 'Anarchy', 'Problems'. Common.
Die-hards note: Chris Thomas was brought in on production. American collectors take note: contrary to Virgin's new name, Virgin Records America Inc., there was no American pressing as such – the British issue was imported into the States and had a 'Marketed and Distributed by Caroline' barcode sticker placed on the back sleeve.

Sid Sings

* UK Virgin, V 2144, 7 Dec 79. With original Fender Stratocaster guitar-cum-swastika purple labels. With sticker on cover, inner sleeve and free poster. Tracks: 'Born To Lose', 'I Wanna Be Your Dog', 'Take A Chance On Me', '(I'm Not Your) Stepping Stone', 'My Way'/'Belsen Was A Gas', 'Something Else', 'Chatterbox', 'Search And Destroy', 'Chinese Rocks', 'I Killed The Cat'. Fairly Rare.
The poster is a shot of Sid sitting, winking, with a drink in his hand.
* UK Virgin, V 2144. Same as the latter pressing. With different poster, in a more limited quantity than other editions. Rare.
The poster is a street shot of Sid in a leather jacket, holding a knife.
* UK Virgin, V 2144. Same as the latter pair of pressings. With different poster, rarest of all editions. Very Rare.
The poster is a shot of Sid selling Pistols/Glitterbest memorabilia at a stall.
* UK Virgin, OVED 85, mid-price issue. With green/red labels. Common.

* UK Virgin, OVED 85, mid price. With current cream/grey Virgin labels. Common.
* WG Virgin, 201.249 (320/96 642), original WG issue w/original purple/white labels, inner, original twin virgin emblem on back sleeve and original b/w 'Sid Vicious *Sid Sings*' sticker on front sleeve. Fairly Rare.
* WG Virgin, 201.249 (320), reissue. With small b/w 'Sid Vicious *Sid Sings*' sticker on cover, green/red labels and an OVED 85 series sticker/barcode applied to back sleeve. Fairly Common.
* Pl Virgin, VV-33.029 V. With green/red labels. Fairly Rare.
* Gr Virgin/Polygram, 2933.800, limited edition. With sticker on jacket; original pressing had a Polygram inner sleeve ad. As with many of the other Greek pressings, the sleeve was imported by Polyram and hence the jacket cat. no. is identical to its British counterpart (V 2144). Fairly Rare.
* Gr Virgin, 2933.800, white label test press. Rare.
Completists take note: the pair of Greek pressings are titled Sid Vicious *as opposed to* Sid Sings.
* Au Virgin, V 2144, white label promo. With gold stamp on back cover. Fairly Rare.
* NZ Virgin, V 2144. This original limited edition appeared in a superb gatefold jacket. The inner fold-out is exactly the same as the standard inner sleeve. This pressing also features unique white labels differing from any British pressing. With pink sticker listing tracks on front cover. Rare.
* NZ Virgin, V 2144. With same unique white labels and pink sticker, plus genuine RTC inner sleeve. Fairly Rare.
* Jp Virgin, VIP 6987. The labels are identical to the original UK issue. The sleeve states, 'Made In Japan, Licensed by Virgin, England, 1981.' With banding, etc. Rare.
* Jp Virgin, VIP 6987, white label promo. With banding, lyric sheet and promo symbols sticker on sleeve. Very Rare.
The entire Sid Sings *scam was conceived, orchestrated and executed by John Varnom (see* Some Product*) and John Tiberi - a.k.a. Boogie, the Sex Pistols' roadie/tour manager whom Sid regarded as 'the fifth member of the band' - at Max's Kansas City, NYC, where Sid played four gigs on 7, 28, 29 and 30 Sept 78 (backed by Mick Jones, Jerry Nolan, Arthur 'Killer' Kane and Steve Dior). Boogie recorded several live tapes from these shows and these became SS.*

PiSTOLS
POSTERS

FiRST SiNgLE EMI 2566

Opposite page: original promo poster for 'Anarchy In The UK', 1976. This page: Anarchy In The UK zine published by Glitterbest in newspaper format for the Anarchy tour.

You won't pick up an original commercial poster from the Pistols' heyday for less than £100. (Not to be confused with the flimsy reissues, or the recent abundance of glossy Sid Vicious junk.) If you're after the original billboard posters, you'll just have to dig a whole lot deeper into your pockets, as these are now going from £300 upwards. It's a savagely expensive hobby, considering there's in excess of £25,000 worth listed here alone!

Original 'God Save The Queen' banner, 1977.

I've tried to value them as accurately as possible, taking as yardsticks recent auctions (if anything, I've undervalued some of the auction prices), collector's shops in London and mail-order dealers. With all that said, don't be surprised to pick up a rare poster for a fraction of its value in some backstreet record shop!

Not included in these listings: (1) the usual shit that dealers refer to as 'posters', e.g. front covers of magazines, centrespreads, music papers, newspapers and flyers; (2) the 'one-offs' sold at recent auctions, e.g. screenprints and artwork autographed by Pistols designer Jamie Reid. Poster titles are given in bold where available – however, many are untitled so a description is given in normal type. Origin and year of manufacture are stated where known. Sizes are approximate, though most are either A: 60" x 40" (large), B: 40" x 30" (standard), or C: 30" x 20" (small). The absolute minimum size for entry to this section is tabloid A3: 11.7" x 16.5".

Concert Promos

* **Watford College** (23 Jan 76, Splendid gun-shaped poster designed by then Bromley Contingent member Steve Severin (subsequently of Siouxsie and the Banshees), yellow/red, C, Very Rare.
* **100 Club, Tuesday in May** (Thames boat trip shot, Sid in his 'vive lé rock' T-shirt), b/w, B, Fairly Common.
* **Sex Pistols 100 Club July 6th, also Damned** (free with *London's Outrage* box set), Leo Posters (reissue), b/w, B, Common.
* **Slaughter and the Dogs/Sex Pistols, Tuesday, 20th July, 1976, Lesser Free Trade Hall, Manchester** (strictly speaking, it's a Slaughter promo poster), pink/black, B, Very Rare.
* **London's Outrage** (original 100 Club poster) UK, Very Rare.
* **Barbarellas, Birmingham, 14 Aug 76**, Very Rare.
* **Club de Chalet**, **Paris, 3 Sep 76** (also known as *Naked Boy*), 50 printed in the UK for the French gig. Very Rare.
* **Punk Festival, 100 Club, Sep 76**, blue, A3, Very Rare.
* **Anarchy In The UK/Punk Special** (100 Club, Monday 20 Sept 76, also bills the Clash, Subway Sect and Siouxsie and the Banshees), the boys packed into a phone box: same classic shot as the *Pistols Party* bootleg cover, b/w, C, Rare.
* **Cleopatra's, Derby, Sep 30th 76; Didsbury College, Manchester, Oct 1st 76; and Priory Ballroom, Scunthorpe, Oct 2nd 76**, classic shot of original line-up crushed into a single phone box – not to be confused with the latter, A3, Very Rare.
* **Sex Pistols – Technical College, Dundee Oct 12th 76**, fly poster, Very Rare.
* **Queens Hall, Dunstable Concert – 21 Oct 76 – £1.10**, limited edition of 50, UK, b/w, A3. Very Rare.
* **It's Anarchy In The UK Tour Starring** (Derby 4 Dec 76, also the Damned, Johnny Thunders' Heartbreakers and the Clash), green/red/black, C, Fairly Rare.
* **Anarchy In The UK**, 10 Dec 76, the Charlton Theatre, Preston, 29" x 21", Very Rare.
* **Glasgow Apollo Dec 15th 76** (valuable item – gig cancelled as part of the authori-ties' backlash after the Grundy incident), EMI, pink/black, C, Very Rare.
* **Anarchy In The UK Tour** (special guests: the Damned, JT's Heartbreakers and the Clash), also gives single-release and tour dates – which were cancelled except for Dec 6, 9 and 21, b/w, C, Fairly Rare.
* Red/white, C, Fairly Common.
* **Anarchy In The UK - Civic Hall, Guildford, 19 Dec 76**, (scarce, since the gig was subsequently cancelled), dayglo-pink print on black, 2' x 3', Very Rare.
* **Electric Circus, Manchester, Sun 19th/First Single EMI 2566** (flag with 'Anarchy' logo), colour, A, Fairly Rare.
* B, Fairly Common.
* **Anarchy In The UK Tour** (Plymouth 21 Dec 76), C, Very Rare.
* **Anarchy In The UK Tour – Sex Pistols – Damned – Johnny Thunders And The Heartbreakers – With Special Guests The Clash** (gig promo for the 400 Ballroom, Torquay, Wed 22 Dec 76), C, Very Rare.
* **Sex Pistols/Kevin Ayers – Paradiso club, Amsterdam**, features Pistols logo, colour, C, Very Rare.

* **The Spots, Club Lafayette, Friday 19th August** (from the secret British tour of sum-

British government anti-litter campaign poster – mid eighties.

mer 77, where the Pistols played under a welter of pseudonyms), Aug 77, B, Very Rare.

* **Britain's Premiere Mystery Group – 'Acne Rebble' 26 Aug. 8-1** (from the 'secret gigs' tour), orange/black, 20" x 15", Very Rare.

* **Brunel University, Uxbridge, 16 December 77** (double-sided gig promo poster for last UK tour), b/w, A3, Very Rare.

* **Nikkers Club** (promo for scrapped 19 Dec 77 gig), b/w, C, Very Rare.

* **Never Mind The Bans – Dec 24 Cromer Links Pavilion**, (rare double-sided gig promo poster for last UK tour, featured inside g/f in *Swindle* LP), b/w, A3, Very Rare.

* **Never Mind The Bans ('Sex Pistols Will Play')**, UK reissue, yellow/black, B, Fairly Common.

* **Brunel University**, Uxbridge, 16 Dec 77. Rare double-sided gig promo poster for last UK Tour – original item, b/w, A3, Very Rare.

* **Huddersfield, Xmas 1977**, another rare double-sided gig promo poster for last UK tour – original item, b/w, A3, Very Rare.

* **Lund Ae Stora Salen, Sweden, 21st January 78** (promo poster for one of the Scandinavian dates intended to follow up the fated US tour), colour, A3, Very Rare.

* **Sex Pistols – 24.1.78** (promo for Markthalle, Hamburg, West Germany, subsequently cancelled due to band's demise), Very Rare.

Concert Promos – The Rebirth

* **Messila Goes Space 20-22.6.96** (first gig from the World Tour, June 96, Finland), B, colour, Rare.

* **Finsbury Park 23rd June 96**, A, Common.

* **Sex Pistols - The Filthy Lucre Tour – Dublin Point Depot**, Thursday 18 July 1996, A, Very Rare.

* **Sex Pistols – Massive Attack – The Filthy Lucre Tour – Milano Arena Spettacoli**, Colour, B, Fairly Rare.

* **Never Mind The Sex Pistols, Here Comes The Filthy Lucre** – Sonntag 14 Juli 1996 (promo for German gig), b/w shot of Johnny singing into microphone with fist raised in air, band name and other info in red and white lettering, 23" x 33". Fairly Rare.

* **Never Mind The Sex Pistols, Here Comes The Filthy Lucre Tour – July 31 – Red Rocks** (promo for the Red Rocks, Denver, Colorado gig, 31 July 1996), octagonal poster, 14" x 16", Fairly Rare.

* **Sex Pistols at the Dallas Music Complex** (2 August 1996), resembles two bar codes with images set behind – handsigned in gold

ink by the artist Emek, with original signed concert flyer, 21" x 30", Fairly Rare.

* **Goldenvoice Presents – Sex Pistols – Gravity Kills Goldfinger** (22 Aug Universal Ampitheatre – 23 Aug the Palladium), by the artist Coop in a limited edition of 700, colour, B, Very Rare.

* **Never Mind The Sex Pistols** (Japanese promo flyer/mini-poster for Japan 96 gig), colour, C, Common.

Pistols Platter Promos

* **Anarchy In The UK** (Union Jack/EMI 2566: promo for first single), colour, A, Rare.

* B, Very Rare.

* C, Rare.

* **Anarchy In The UK – 'The Art of Jamie Reid'** (Union Jack – reissue), GB Posters LPO 378, colour, B, Common.

* **God Save The Queen, A&M** (single promo), B, Very Rare.

* UK Virgin (single promo), colour, B, Very Rare.

* UK Virgin (as the latter except it's a flimsy reissue), colour, B, Common.

* UK, blue/yellow, B, Fairly Common.

* Blue/white, B, Common.

* Blue/silver, B, Common.

* Original French promo poster, white on black background, 'on Sex Pistols Records' – with safety pin through HM's nose! C, Very Rare.

* Original promo poster, black on white background (with swastika eyes and safety pin through the Queen's mouth!), Spanish(?), C, Very Rare.

* As the latter, with swastika and pin, except now stating: 'God Save The Queen – A Fascist Regime'. UK, C, Very Rare.

* **Pretty Vacant** (two buses: Nowhere/Boredom), b/w, A, Rare.

* B, Very Rare.

* C, Fairly Rare.

* Pink 'Vacant' logo at bottom, with fabulous Thames riverboat shot of band live and Sid with holes in trousers (original came folded with thicker white border and on superior heavy paper), b/w, B, Common.

* Latter reissued on flimsy paper – otherwise identical, b/w, B, Common.

* **Dance To The Sex Pistols** ('Vacant' promo, square pics), b/w/grey, B, Fairly Rare.

* **Holidays In The Sun** – 'Keep Warm This Winter, Make Trouble' (single promo, vague pic of people on beach), Virgin VS 191, b/w with yellow logos, B, Fairly Rare.

There are two variations on the latter: an original gloss and a reissued matt.

* Same as single cover, Virgin VS 191, colour, B, Very Rare.

* **Never Mind The Bollocks, Here's The Sex Pistols** (UK album promo, as sleeve), colour, B, Fairly Rare.

* Original fly poster for Virgin window fronts, AA (9' x 6'), Very Rare.

* A, Fairly Common.

Original black and white 'God Save The Queen' poster, 1977.

SEX PISTOLS

NEW SINGLE

pretty vacant

 **NEVER TRUST A HIPPIE**

 **BELIEVE IN THE RUINS**

 **CASH FROM CHAOS**

 **THE ONLY NOTES THAT MATTER ARE THE ONES THAT COME IN WADS**

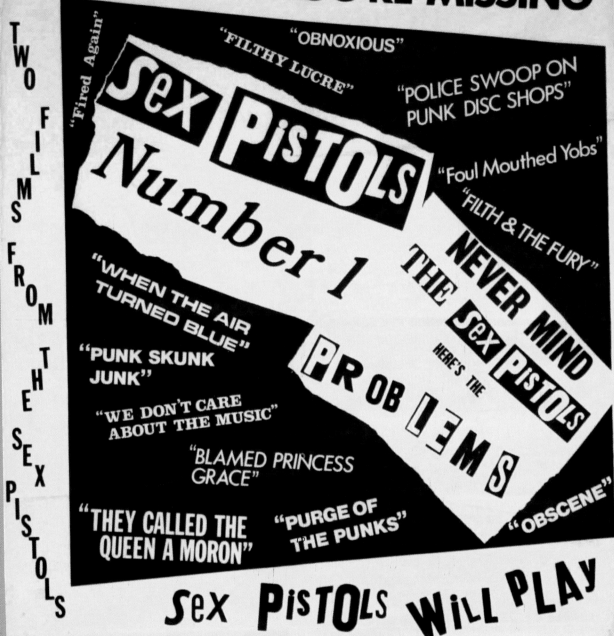

This page: an incredibly rare poster for the Pistols' first film Sex Pistols Number 1, 1977.

Opposite page: the original 'Pretty Vacant' promo banner (top). Below: the original Swindle soundtrack promo banners.

Original 'Holidays In The Sun' promo poster, 1977.

* Dayglow colour, Very Rare.
* Cut-up collage of track titles, initially came free with the album, colour, B, Very Rare.
* Promo for album on the Swedish Sonet label, 17" x 13", Very Rare.

The following five posters were issued by Warner Bros in the US to promote the début album:

* **Never Mind The Bollocks, We've Got The Sex Pistols** (Warner Bros), green fold-out poster, US Oct 77, unusual size: 13" x 36", Rare.
* **Never Mind The Bollocks, Here's The Sex Pistols – We're The Flowers In The Dustbin . . . ,** (Warner Bros/Careers Music Inc. promo), pic of Johnny with inset of da boyz out for a stroll and verse from 'GSTQ', US Oct 77, colour, B, Very Rare.
* **We're The Future** (WB), Sid line-up, live shot, US Oct 77, Very Rare.
* **Never Mind The Sex Pistols, Here's The Bollocks** – an abundance of shots of Her Majesty's head with safety pin stuck through her lips! US Oct 77, green/colour, B, Very Rare.
* **Never Mind The Bollocks, Here's The Sex Pistols,** (original WB promo poster – splendid cartoon strip of the Pistols' rise and rise – designed by MJS), US Oct 77, C, Very Rare.
You can easily verify if you have the original US edition: the bottom features a small pic of the cover of the American album.

* **Sex Pistols** (Euro-reissue of the latter without the album pic and title, otherwise identical), colour, C, Rare.
This was the cover that re-emerged courtesy of the Nashville *bootleg album.*
* **Punks** (centrespread free with *Record Mirror,* 7 May 77 – including the Pistols, Clash, Damned, Jam and Stranglers), colour, C. Fairly Common.
* **Sex Pistols** (centrespread free with *Record Mirror,* 9 July 77), colour, C, Fairly Rare.
* **Sex Pistols** (*Record Mirror,* 22 Oct 77, centrespread cartoon) – preceded both the US and subsequent European promotional poster editions, C, colour, Fairly Rare.
* **Sex Pistols** (*Record Mirror,* 28 Jan 78), spectacular full-colour collage as centrespread, C, colour, Fairly Rare.
* **No One Is Innocent – A Punk Prayer by Ronnie Biggs** (Matrixbest single promo), June 78, b/w, C, Fairly Rare.
* **Cosh The Driver** (single promo – large picture of Biggs), June 78, b/w, C, Very Rare.
* **Something Else,** colour, B, Very Rare.
* **Investors Review** (magazine cover shot of boys as 'Young Businessmen of the Year', *Swindle* double album promo), b/w, B, Fairly Common.
* Credit Card (*Swindle* promo, as withdrawn 7" ps), black/green, B, Fairly Rare.
There are two variations of the latter: an original gloss and a reissued matt.
* C, Fairly Rare.

* **Young Flesh Required** (similar to the latter), Virgin, black/green, B, Fairly Rare.
* **Silly Thing/Who Killed Bambi?** (7" promo, large pic of 'Bambi'), colour, B, Fairly Rare.
* **C'Mon Everybody,** fabulous full-colour shot of Sid all messed up (set against a white background), B, Very Rare.
* As the latter except set against a green background – rarest of the two, B, Very Rare.
* **Some Product - Carri On Sex Pistols** (album promo, same pic as cover), colour, C, Fairly Rare.
* **Some Product** (plastic coated, mounted promo poster), 12" x 16", Fairly Common.

The following five posters were issued by Virgin to promote Some Product *in Britain. All are separate glossy promo posters, extremely limited editions, and are now very hard to find.*
* **Some Product – Rotten Bar** (pic of some putrid ugly bastard), b/w, C, Very Rare.
* **Some Product – Gob Ale,** Very Rare.
* **Some Product – Piss Lemonade,** Very Rare.
* **Some Product – Fatty Jones,** Very Rare.
* **Some Product – Chelsea Hotel,** Very Rare.

* **Flogging A Dead Horse** (album promo, pic of girl with ice cream) colour, B, Fairly Rare.
* **The Great Rock'N'Roll Swindle** (soundtrack promo), B, Fairly Rare.
* **Young Flesh Required – The Great Rock'N'Roll Swindle** (plastic coated, mounted promo poster for the single), credit card, 12" x 16", blue, Fairly Common.
* **The Great Rock'N'Roll Swindle** (plastic coated, mounted promo poster for the album), basically reproduces logo, 12" x 16", b/w, Fairly Common.
* **Submission/No Feelings** (*Mini Album* sleeve), colour, B, Common.
* **Never Trust A Hippy** (album promo, with track listing), colour, B, Common.
* **Never Trust A Hippy – Sex Pistols Bootleg Album Available Now** (b/w live shot w/yellow border), colour, B, Common.
* **Anarchy In The UK Live!** (album promo), hazy live shot of group: Johnny pointing mike to a member of the audience, red/blue/white, B, Common.
* **Kiss This/Trondheim 21-7-77** (large billboard promo), colour, A, Common.
* **Kiss This,** C, with track listing, Common.
* **Kiss This** (CD inlay-cum fold-out collage poster), track listing on reverse, colour, C, Common.
* **Anarchy In The UK** (free with 'Anarchy' 92 CD single), collage of pics, colour, C, Common.
* **Kiss This** (double-sided Aussie promo

poster), colour, 19" x 19", Common.
* **Sex Pistols – The Collection** (free with Aussie LP of the same name), b/w with yellow logos, C, Common.
* **Pretty Vacant** ('LP out July 15'), June 96, grey, B. Common.
* **Pretty Vacant**, A, Common.
* **Filthy Lucre**, grey/red, A, Common.
* **Filthy Lucre**, C, Common.
* **Sex Pistols – Filthy Lucre Live** (US edition has additional black/yellow logo at bottom and is slightly longer), C, Common.

Movie Promos

* **Who Killed Bambi?** (movie poster featuring original intended title of film – pic is of dead deer with arrow in neck), colour, B, Very Rare.
* **The Great Rock'N'Roll Swindle** (movie promo poster free w/ s/t album V 2168), cartoon of band and cohorts on ship, with 'Ltd Edition at £3.99 Includes Free Colour Poster' emblem, colour, B, Rare.
* As the latter except rolled in poster tube for commercial sale, without 'Ltd Edition' emblem, colour, B, Rare.
* Again as the above except smaller – 33" x 25" – and much rarer since it was never issued in large quantities. Also of better quality, with superior colour contrast. Easily identifiable, via its 'Advertising Viewing Committee' stamp, this is the front-of-house cinema

Some Product – Carri On Sex Pistols *promo poster, featuring 'Gob Ale', 1979.*

The destination of the buses said it all for the youth of 1977.

poster normally kept under glass, easily the rarest of the last three. Colour, C, Very Rare. *These latter three posters are fetching in excess of £100, which is ridiculous given that 15,000 alone were issued free with the OST album.*
* Italian promo for film, collage of pics, nice 'n' glossy, completely different to any other version and includes Sting. Colour, B, Very Rare. This poster is fetching well in excess of £150, as it was withdrawn when Sting hit the jackpot with the Police at the time of issue.
* Film poster will all titles and credits in French, colour, A, Very Rare.
* As above, C.
* Fold-out back sleeve of the tabloid novel that tied-in with the movie, pic is of John and Paul playing live, with two insets of Paul and Steve, b/w, C, Fairly Rare.
* **The Great Rock'N'Roll Swindle Official Souvenir Poster** (collage of pics), features Sid and Nancy strutting their stuff in the streets of Paris, c/w is a full-sized shot of Sid riding motorbike, colour, C, Fairly Rare.
* **The Great Rock'N'Roll Swindle** (free poster given out with Japanese Nippon Columbia double album), colour, C, Rare.
* **The Great Rock'N'Roll Swindle** (plastic coated, mounted promo poster for the film), pirate Pistols hanging out of boat, 12" x 16", red/white, Fairly Common.
* **The Great Rock'N'Roll Swindle** (promo for the late American release, same as the cover of the front of the British double album), US,

Warner Bros, Nov 92, colour, 24" x 24", Fairly Common.
* **The Punk Rock Movie** (promo for Don Letts' classic documentary), Sept 77, 12" x 8", Fairly Rare.
* **D.O.A. – A Right Of Passage** (promo for American Pistols/punk documentary), US Apr 81, colour, B, Rare.

Some Product *promo poster, bearing the legend 'Sex Pistols Sales Conference This Way (Or This Way)', 1979.*

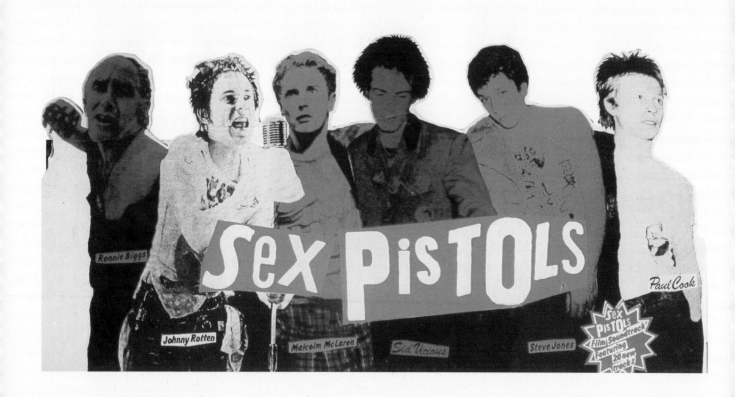

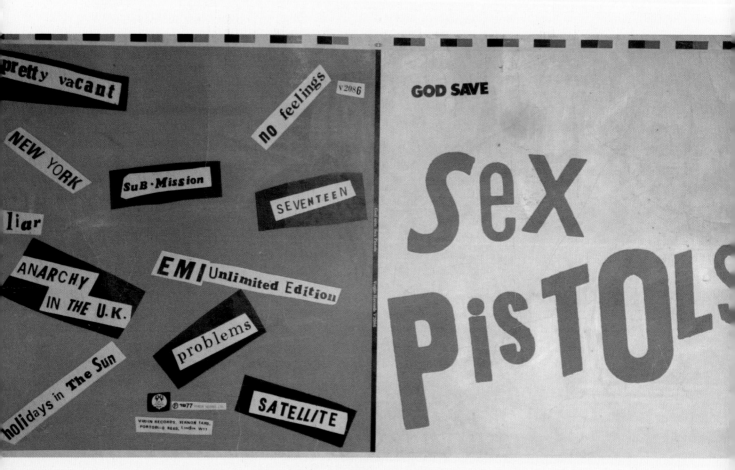

Top of opposite page: original cardboard cut-out promo used in cinema foyer for The Great Rock'N'Roll Swindle, *1980. Below: original artwork for* Never Mind The Bollocks *cover that was never used.*

Above: rare original 'Vicious Burger' promo poster for 'C'Mon Everybody', 1979. Below: Kiss This *cardboard promo, 1992.*

CD • TAPE • 2 LP + LTD EDITION CD DOUBLE PACK

Bootleg of the original black and white 'Anarchy In The UK' tour poster.

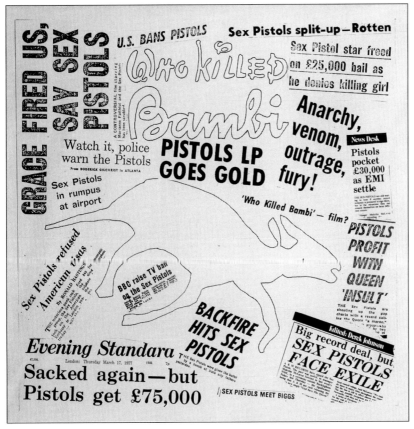

Above: original 'God Save The Queen' artwork, 1977. Below: original Swindle artwork, 1978.

Clockwise from bottom left: unreleased variation on the 'Vicious Burger' promo for 'C'mon Everybody', 1979; original promo poster for the 'Silly Thing'/'Who Killed Bambi?' double A-side, 1979; Sid and Nancy movie poster, 1986; bootleg poster for the cancelled Derby date on the 1976 Anarchy tour; Swindle Australian movie poster; original Italian poster for Swindle movie, 1980; US promo poster for punk movie D.O.A., 1981.

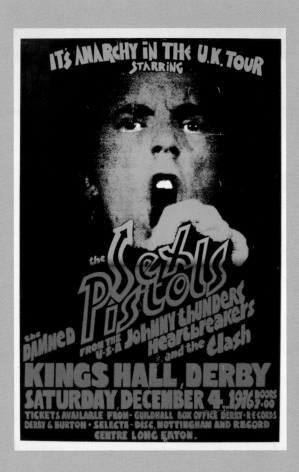

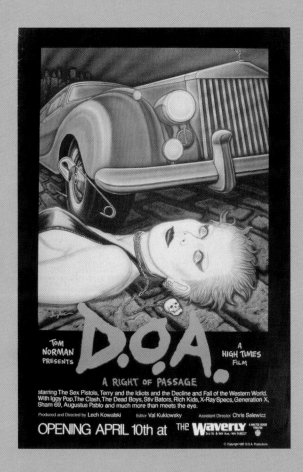

'Sex Pistols Bulletin' promo poster, 1977.

* **Cop Killer** (Italian movie with John Lydon, aka *Order Of Death*), 84, B, colour, Fairly Rare.

Live Shots

* **Sex Pistols** (London Posters no. 425, 78), live on stage, Sid topless, colour, B, Fairly Rare.
* The latter issued in the US by Glitterbest Inc/One Stop Posters no. 468, 78, colour, B, Fairly Rare.
* Another live shot, this time Sid wearing his leather jacket, similar to latter, Pace 8P/3226, colour, B, Fairly Rare.
* Reissued with white 'Sex Pistols UK Tour 77' logo, Minerva 68266 90, b/w, B, Common.
* Another live shot, this time Johnny with arm

in air, Pace, colour, B, Fairly Rare.
* **Anarchy In The UK** (massive Thames riverboat shot), b/w, A, Common.
* **Sex Pistols – I Wanna Be Me** (original group line-up with pink logo), b/w, B, Common.
* **Sounds – 30 Years Of Live Rock Souvenirs,** (live shot of Johnny, with Sid in background), b/w, Common.
* **Last UK Show Xmas Day 77** (free with *Sounds*' 'Top 100 Singles Of All Time') colour, B, Common.
* **Sex Pistols** (London Posters no. 519, 78), collage of individual members playing live, colour, A, Fairly Rare.
* The latter issued in the US by Glitterbest Inc/One Stop Posters no. 479, 78, colour, A, Fairly Rare.
* Collage poster, b/w, framed, with Johnny Rotten's signature, b/w, B, Very Rare.
* **The Sex Pistols: NME Classics** (free, came folded in *NME*, 13 Apr 91), c/w Happy Mondays from 85, b/w, C, Common.

Miscellaneous Posters

* **Let It Rock,** (Malcolm's original emporium), 72, b/w, A3, Very Rare.
* **Sex Pistols Kings Road,** C, Very Rare.
* **And We Don't Care** (vintage original line-up shot), b/w with red logos, B, Fairly Common.
* **Pistols Shock USA!** (main pic is Vicious goofing around in his cowboy t-shirt, also has inserts), b/w, A, Common.
* B, Common.
* **Pistols Shock USA** (the Stars 'n' Stripes, with Sid inset), colour/b/w, B, Common.
* **Evening Standard: 'Sex Pistols Sacked Again With £75,000'** (billboard for newspa-

per), March 77. b/w, B, Very Rare.
* **Evening News: 'I Hate Britain'** (billboard for newspaper), Dec 77. red/b/w, C, Very Rare.
* **Evening News: 'Sex Pistols Fans In US Riot'** (billboard promo), Jan 78. red/b/w, C, Very Rare.
* **The Sun**, billboard promo featuring a leering Johnny Rotten, C, Very Rare.
* **Sex Pistols Bulletin** (newspaper collage, EMI 2566), b/w, C, original is on heavy duty paper, Rare.
* Larger quantity issued on flimsy material, otherwise identical, b/w, C, Fairly Common.
* B/w live shot centrespread free with LA mag *Slash* vol. 1, no. 4, Sept 77, Fairly Common.
* Unique centrespread b/w poster of Sid – issued free with *Slash* vol. 2, no. 6, June 79, C, Fairly Common.
* Classic centrefold, full-colour poster *a la* the *Fuck USA* boot album cover, issued free with *Hit Parade* mag no. 167, June 78, colour, Fairly Common.
* **Fuck Forever** (EMI), early sixties style pic of seductive woman, nice item, b/w, C, Fairly Rare.
* Red/b/w, B, Fairly Common.
* Bright green, Fairly Common.
* Bright orange, Fairly Common.
* Bright orange, with collage on back, Fairly Common.
* Green lettering set on black/white/pink background by Jamie Reid, *Splash* no. 8112, 90, B, Common.
* **Sunday Newspaper Advert**, UK, Fairly Rare.
* **We Stock Sex Pistols**, yellow/black, 7" x 40", Fairly Rare.
* Collage of Jamie Reid's designs for numerous Pistols sleeves and posters, limited edition, Reflex Posters Ltd/Assorted Images Ltd, 83, colour, B, Fairly Common.
* **Sex Pistols File** (book cover), colour, B, Common.
* **Omnibus Press' Top 50 Rock and Pop Books,** promo poster, includes Johnny Rotten, colour, B, Common.
* **RIP January 1987**, classic shot of boys spraying tin of Carlsberg, but with Sid superimposed over Glen and Johnny inset at bottom, b/w, B, Common.
* The latter reissued in UK, cat. no. R604, b/w. common.
* **New Wave**, collage of artists including Johnny Rotten, Devo, Bowie, Blondie,

The boys perform on the ill-fated Thames riverboat trip, 7 June 77.

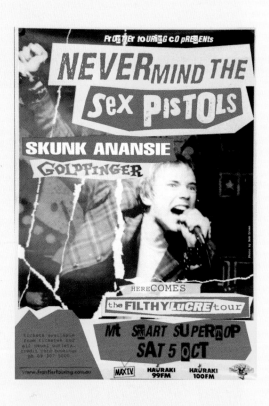

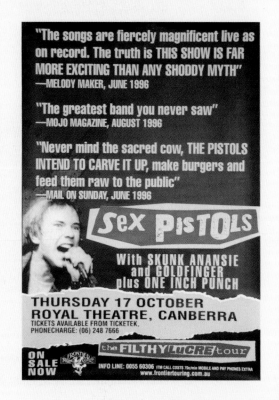

Clockwise from top left: promos for the Filthy Lucre tour, 1996 – Tokyo, 22 November; Mount Smart Supertop, New Zealand, 5 October; Canberra, Australia, 17 October. Bottom left: Sid Sings promo poster, 1979. Opposite page: composite of newspaper headlines on the Pistols, giving prominence to the accusation 'Knifes Girlfriend', 1980.

One of the two original 'Pretty Vacant' promo posters (the other features the buses destined for 'Nowhere' and 'Boredom'), 1977.

Costello, B52s, Clash, Talking Heads, no. 3515, 24" x 36", Common.
* **Anarchy In The UK 92**, A, Common.
* **Teenage Kicks**, UK Polygram, promo poster for various artists CD, collage of artists' names (including the Pistols, Costello, Bow Wow Wow, Undertones, X-Ray Spex), B, Common.
* **Sex Pistols Retrospective**, free poster with initial copies of book of same name, June 96, Common.
* **Sex Pistols**, Player, 12/96, C, colour, Common.

John Rotten, Esq.

* Big O B58, C, Fairly Rare.
* Superb shot, posing in suit and tie with microphone in one hand and glass of lager in other, UK 78, Big O B224, colour, C, Fairly Rare.
* Swedish Tour promo poster, full colour close-up (adorned in safety pins, hair dyed reddish orange), Rex Features 77, Colour, B, Rare.

* Arms in cruciform, wearing 'Destroy' T-shirt, US, b/w, C, Fairly Common.
* Singing (head only), low resolution but a superb original item, yellow/red, C, Rare.
* Singing live in the USA (accompanied down the left-hand side by three smaller pics of him smoking and laughing), b/w, B. Common.
* **I Wanna Be Me** (Johnny), B, Common.
* **No Fun** (singing with eyes squinted), b/w with pink logo title, B, Common.
* **No Fun** (singing with eyes squinted), b/w with yellow logo title, B, Common.
* Sitting in corner of room with arms folded inside a straitjacket, Italian fold-out from *Rockstar-UNO* magazine no.3, Dec 80, the back has details on all (five!) members of band, b/w/grey, B, Rare.

The following six posters were all from one series published by Young Blood in the mid-eighties. All are untitled, authentic b/w shots c.76 and all were quickly deleted.
* Posing in safety pins, b/w, C, Fairly Common.

* Singing into mike, in classic black bondage jacket, b/w, C, Fairly Common.
* Full shot, holding mike, wearing T-shirt and tie, with Paul on drums behind him, b/w, C, Fairly Common.
* Snarling, playing piano, b/w, C, Fairly Common.
* Posing in French beret and bondage jacket, b/w, C, Fairly Common.
* Live group shot (also includes Glen and Steve), taking off jacket, b/w, C, Fairly Common.
* Sid line-up group shot: out walking, Steve in Mackintosh, classic Rotten pose. B/w, C, Fairly Common.
* **New Wave RIP**, wearing 'New Wave RIP' logo with arms stretched out — *Trouser Press*'s first poster-print, originally entitled *The Suicide of New Wave*. Colour, C, 18" x 22", Fairly Rare.
In addition to the latter commercial issue, there were 50 autographed posters given out to readers in TP no.23. Very Rare.
* Tulsa, USA 87, C, Fairly Common.

* **Johnny Rotten – Wessex Studios 76**, sitting at piano, Cult Images, 90, Common.
* Crucified on cross, b/w, B, Common.
* Also in large size, b/w, A, Common.

The Classic 'Wall' Posters

* Sid with big holes in trousers, chain around waist and holding a twirler in front of his face, Big O B301, colour, B, Fairly Rare.
* With yellow 'Security' sign on wall behind Steve, Big O B298 80, colour, B, Fairly Common.
* Reissue of the latter, Dutch, Zamania RO 029, 84, colour, B, Common.
* Reissued again, this time as Rebel Rock RA 029, 85, colour, B, Common.
* **Sex Pistols (**Canadian, Big Foot No. 405), with orange band logo, Sid with tin of Fanta, Johnny looking away from camera, b/w, B, Common.
* **Sex Pistols**, red band logo, identical to latter, b/w, B, Common.
* **Anarchy In The UK (**issued by Splash), red 'Anarchy' logo, b/w, B, Common.
* **Discography (**Anabas AA 404, 89), Johnny sneering, with arms folded, while Sid has a problem with his thumb – also lists albums, singles, etc. Colour, B, Common.
* **Sex Pistols (**Masterpiece Enterprises 1185, 86), black band logo, same shot as latter, colour, B, Common.
* **Smash Hits/Sex Pistols 1977** (free with issue no. 22 of pop magazine), C, Fairly Common.
All of the above are basically the same, originating from the photo session where Johnny wears his teddy-boy suit throughout.

Poster Mags

* **New Wave News – With The Sex Pistols** no. 1, 77. Burchill-assisted poster-cum-magazine from the heyday, focussing on the boys, opens out into a spectacular pic of original line-up playing live, Johnny bent over in his usual demonic stance, Steve wearing a pair of cords! Rare.
* No. 2, 77. Unique shot of Johnny standing in a corner wearing punk suit, looking pissed off. Fairly Rare.
* No. 3, 77. The usual shots of da boyz. Fairly Rare.
* No.4, Autumn 77. Another original poster of Johnny wearing dark glasses, standing against a wall in his black bondage suit, holding a bottle. Fairly Rare.
* **Total Punk** 77. Aussie poster mag featuring a giant poster of Johnny smirking obnoxiously in his blue 'holy mohair'. Rare.
* **Punk Star Monthly Special** 77. Pistols, Clash and Stranglers. Fairly Rare.
* **Star Monthly – Sex Pistols Wanted** no.9, 77. Individual profile on front, opens out into two different 'wall' shots, one full, one half-size. The latter uniquely catches Johnny with arms dramatically outstretched. Fairly Rare.
* **Punk**, Byblos Publishing, Sept 77. Folds out into a massive Pistols poster. Colour, 36" x 24", Fairly Rare.
* **Sex Pistols Punk Rock Special** 77. Original line-up posing on stairs; the other side has three different shots of the lads. Fairly Rare.
* **Oh Boy**, Sept 77. Girls' mag including 'Wild Pistols Pin-Up', colour, 16" x 12", Fairly Common.
* **Poster** no. 2, 78, Runaways cover, back is Shaun Cassidy – centrespread is unique full-colour shot of Pistols, European, C, colour, Fairly Rare.
* **Ripped and Torn** no. 3, late Feb/March 77, Johnny pin-up came free with fanzine, Fairly Common.
* **Johnny Rotten**, fold-out centre-spread free with Californian mag *Back Door Man* no. 14, March/Apr 78, b/w, C, Fairly Common.
* **D.O.A. The Official Film Book** no. 1, Apr 81, Punk Publications Inc, superb full-colour centrespread of Pistols live in America, Fairly Rare.
* **The Punk Scene**, fold-out poster mag of the Pistols, Fairly Rare.

El Sid Himself

* **From Beyond The Grave**, Sid in coffin, same pic as cover of *Heritage* EP, colour, B. Rare.
* **Sid Vicious (**Pace 93/P3243), singing, holding bottle of Harp, colour, B, Fairly Common.
* **Sid Rules OK – Vicious Chain Saws Ltd** (UK Media & Graphics Creations/Communications Vectors No. 10 of Series A, 1979), superb shot of Sid with chainsaw, on heavy cardboard paper, colour, C, Fairly Rare.
* **The Sid Vicious Family Album**, Virgin Sept 80. The actual book in poster format, only one in existence, given away in *Sounds* promotional competition. Very Rare.
* **C'mon Everybody**, snarling in leather jacket, playing guitar, b/w, B, Common.
* **Sid Vicious (**Virgin V 2144), free with *Sid Sings* LP, sitting, winking, with a glass in his hand, colour, C, Common.
* **Sid Vicious (**Virgin V 2144), also free with *Sid Sings* LP, wearing leather jacket in street, holding a knife - rarer than latter, colour, C, Fairly Common.
* **Sid Vicious (**Virgin V 2144), also free w/*Sid Sings* LP: a shot of Sid selling Pistols/ Glitterbest memorabilia at a stall – the rarest of the three editions, colour, C, Rare.
* **In Memoriam**, (Anabas AA 273), Sid in leather jacket, supposedly only 200 printed, b/w/grey, B, Common.
* **Sid Sings**, not to be confused with the two different posters that came with the LP, this is the same shot as the cover (Sid holding a green bottle), colour, B, Common.
* **Drugs Kill**, promo for album, Sid sitting on bed toking, b/w, A, Common.
* Canada, First Productions, b/w, B, Common.
* W/ thick white border, UK, b/w, B, Common.
* Reissued in UK, cat. no. R644, b/w, Common.
* 'Wall' shot (Splash), in Mac with tin of Fanta, b/w, B, Common.
* **Undermine Their Pompous Authority** (Athena 311001), Sid surrounded by dot-to-dot numbers, colour, B. Common.
* **1957-1979** (Anabas AA 403, 89), smiling, scratching back of head, colour, B, Common.
* **My Way**, promo for the *Great Rock'N'Roll Swindle* movie, original laminated poster with yellow border, C, Rare.
* Matrixbest Productions, b/w with yellow

The rarest of three promo posters issued for the Sid Sings *album, 1979.*

Above: original Seditionaries t-shirt, 1977. Below: large foldout promo cloth for US Never Mind The Bollocks, 1977.

Opposite page – top left and right: front and back of original US Warner Bros. promo t-shirt, 1977. Bottom left and right: gold disc awarded to the Pistols for 500,000 sales of Never Mind The Bollocks, 1987; platinum disc awarded for 1,000,000 US sales of the same, 1992.

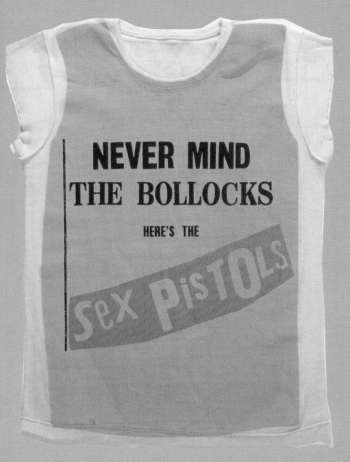

logos, B, Fairly Common.

* C, Common.

* **Sid Vicious Sex Pistols** (Enterprises 1224, 87), topless, solemn, playing bass (possibly at Winterland), masterpiece. Colour, B, Common.

* Sid drinking, rubbing eye at the A&M press conference, b/w, C, Fairly Common.

* Sid on drums for 'Suzie and the Banshees' at the 100 Club, 20 Sept 76, b/w, C, Fairly Common.

* Sid grinning in studded leather jacket, drinking, b/w, C, Fairly Common.

The above three posters were issued by Young Blood in the mid-eighties.

* Two shots (Anabas AA 378, 88), one drinking from a Cossack vodka bottle, colour, B, Common.

* **Sid** (Athena, 89), multi-colour glossy, main pic on bike plus inset with gun, B, Common.

* **Sid** (Athena, 89), multi-colour glossy, playing guitar, B, Common.

* **Vicious Punk**, original item, classic shot of Sid looking wasted, crouching beside a 'big dipper' amp in leather jacket, b/w, C, Rare.

* **Sid Vicious no. 1**, USA, 87, C, Fairly Common.

* Sid playing guitar, USA, 87, b/w, C, Fairly Common.

* Sid playing guitar, USA, 87, first 1,000 signed and numbered by photographer, b/w, B, Fairly Common.

*Collage of Sid pics (no.139 – possibly US, 89), 24" x 34", Fairly Common.

* Sid playing bass (NM P66, possibly US), 24" x 34", Fairly Common.

* Sid smiling, chain around neck, limited numbered edition of 3,000, b/w, C, Fairly Rare.

* Sid posing in wrist band and open leather jacket, similar to latter, b/w, C. Fairly Rare.

* **Sid looking melancholic, picking nose, the best shot I've ever seen of him, spotted in a rare record store in Haight Ashbury, SF, and begged from the shop owner for a princely 50 bucks! B/W, C, Rare.**

* Acupuncture shop, 12th May 93, large billboard poster with full shot of Sid, yellow/black, A, Common.

* Sid sitting, looking at camera, accompanied down the right-hand side by three smaller pics of him playing bass, b/w, B, Common.

* **Sex Pistols – Complete Fucking Anarchy (UK Live Wire Posters)**, picture of Sid playing bass with Union Jack in the background, colour, B, common.

* **Sid Vicious – Submission** (Howard Jeman, 96), two pics of Sid: one playing bass, the

Poster used to promote a Jamie Reid art exhibition, 1977.

other shooting-up. B/w/red, B, Common.

The Real Romeo And Juliet

* **The Real Sid And Nancy**, album promo with two insets at bottom, b/w, C, Common.

* **Love Kills NYC**, backstage at Brunel University, 16 Dec 77, Sid holding beer can, looking at Nancy, b/w, C, Common.

* With two additional insets, b/w, C, Common.

* **Sid And Nancy/Chelsea Hotel** (logo), standing beside Phil Lynott's toilet in Cricklewood!!! B/w, C, Common.

* As latter except without 'Chelsea Hotel' logo, b/w, B, Common.

* Sid winking with arm around Nancy, both in front of *Bollocks* poster, b/w, A, Common.

* B, Common.

* Handcuffed together in front of *Bollocks* poster, b/w, B, Common.

* **Sid And Nancy** (Anabas AA 379, 88), as latter, but w/colour border, B, Common.

The Shitty Imitators

* Colour, A, Common.

* Colour, B, Common.

* MCA, yellow/black, C, Common.

* Embassy Home Entertainment (long, narrow full-colour pic of Oldman/Webb), colour, 12" x 40", Common.

* A, Common.

* B, Common.

* C, Common.

* **Ogni Generazione** (Italy), giant pic of Gary Oldman and Chloe Webb, colour, A, Fairly Rare.

* Oldman/Webb (Big Foot, Canada), b/w, B, Common.

* **Sid And Nancy – Love Kills**, Oldman and Webb, former pointing to camera, 24" x 24", Common.

* **Sid And Nancy**, French promo poster for the movie, colour pic on red/b/w background, very large – bigger than A-format, Rare

Unusual Posters

* **The Great Rock'N'Roll Swindle** film poster (large/framed) – Very Rare.

* **The Great Rock'N'Roll Swindle** fold-open cardboard poster (Virgin) — Fairly Rare.

* **Sex Pistols Fuck Forever** original silk-screened poster, used for exhibition by Jamie Reid – Fairly Common.

* **Dickens/Oliver Twist** poster, given out at only one live concert on Xmas day 77 (for these and other superb rare poster illustra-

tions, consult Jamie Reid's book *Up They Rise*) – Very Rare.

* Six original posters from the film, 2' by 6', all in bright fluorescent colour: *The Great Rock'N'Roll Swindle*, 'They Swindled Their Way To The Top', 'The Only Notes That Matter Are The Ones That Come In Wads', 'Believe In The Ruins', 'Cash From Chaos' and 'Never Trust A Hippy' – Very Rare.

* Cartoon strip in colour, poster sized, mounted on card, framed and glazed, autographed by all – Very Rare.

* **Charcoal Drawing of Johnny Rotten** by Bradford John Salamon, 24" x 20" – Very Rare.

* Sid Vicious promo poster for the tracks 'Born To Lose', 'Something Else', 'My Way' and 'I Killed The Cat' – Very Rare.

PiSTOLS

SEMI LEGAL ALBUM RELEASES

Above: the Japanese gatefold of The Swindle Continues. *Bottom left:* The Best of the Sex Pistols Live *is from the famous 76 Club, Burton-on-Trent gig. Right: like a lot of the semi-legals,* Where Were You in 77? *also made it to picture disc.*

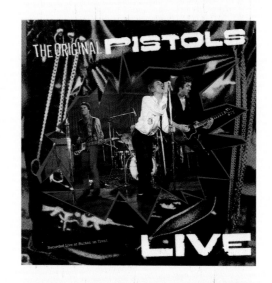

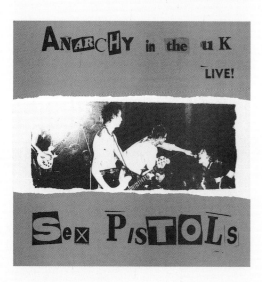

The Mini Album (centre right), 1985, opened the floodgates for the subsequent flurry of semi-legal releases – such as The Original Pistols Live (top right and left), the latter edition of which came with a freebie 12" interview disc. Some semi-legals were deliberately mistitled. Anarchy In The UK Live! (bottom left) was actually a recording of a gig at the Happy House in Stockholm, Sweden.

No other band rivals the Sex Pistols when it comes to releases of dubious origin. After gross exploitation courtesy of Virgin in the late seventies, 84 saw the corrupt 'Land Of Hope And Glory' (credited to the Pistols, but really recorded by producer Dave Goodman's imposter band the *Ex* Pistols), as well as the demo cut of 'Submission' in 7" and 12" formats and an abundance of colour vinyls.

The forerunner of the spate of 'semi-legal' albums is *The Mini Album* (Jan 85), with sales exceeding 50,000. It's a good album, unlike most of the subsequent releases, which are both spurious and dodgy in terms of sound quality; ironically, the boots are superior in most cases.

According to Pistolphile Mark Woodley, if they originate from Italy and carry the 'SIAE' stamp on the back then royalties are forwarded to the Sex Pistols. The bottom line is that as long as there's a market these people will continue to dump their merchandise. In fact, Dave Goodman claims that Glen and Paul are fully aware of the products, even to the extent of assisting him in re-recording the material.

The Mini Album
* UK Chaos, APOCA 3, Jan 85. Studio outtakes recorded between 13 and 30 July 76 and produced by Dave Goodman. Tracks: 'Submission', 'Seventeen', 'Satellite'/'I Wanna Be Me', 'Anarchy', 'No Feelings'. Previously only available on the bootlegs. Common.
* UK Chaos, APOCA 3. In white wax. Fairly Common.
* UK Chaos, APOCA 3. Mispressed b-side features a single track at 45rpm from HM band Bon Jovi's Ritchie Sambori. Fairly Common.
* UK Chaos, APOCA 3, white label test pressing. Fairly Common.
* UK Chaos, MINI 1. Fairly Common.
* UK Chaos, AMPL 37, Jan 86. Picture Disc. Fairly Common.
* NI Anthler, ANTHLER 37, Jan 86. Picture Disc. Same tracks but 'Vacant' replaces 'I Wanna Be Me'. B-side pic is a live shot of the band. Fairly Common.
* NI Anthler, ANTHLER 37. Picture Disk. Same as other Anthler pic disc except b-side pic is of a girl in an office full of Pistols memorabilia. Limited Edition. Fairly Common.
* US Restless, 72257- 1, Aug 88. With different labels to both the UK and Japanese pressings. With Restless plastic inner advertiser. Also with large blue/black sticker on

front cover. Common.
* Ca Enigma/Restless DI-72257-1. Also features the same large sticker as the US edition. Common.
* Ar Continen CCP 859, 91. With unique yellow labels. Collectors note: the sleeve logos, track titles, etc, are light gold, a different colour to any other edition. Fairly Rare.
* Jp Chaos, APOCA 3 (VAP 35155-20), Dec 85. Features different labels and wide banding which includes info on the 'Vacant' freebie inside. Features 'Vacant', a one-sided promo-only red wax flexi-disc. Includes fold-open sheet with lyrics in both English and Japanese. Also features the group's history in Japanese. Very Rare.
* Jp Chaos, APOCA 3 (VAP 35155-20). As the latter except the banding is slightly narrower and there is no freebie single. Fairly Rare.
* Jp Chaos, APOCA 3 (VAP 35155-20), white label promo. With obi. (as latter) and insert. Rare.

The Original Pistols - Live
* UK Receiver, RRLP 101, June 85. Live from Burton on Trent, 24 Sept 76. Features eleven tracks: 'Anarchy', 'I Wanna Be Me', 'I'm A Lazy Sod' ('Seventeen'), 'Dolls'('NY'), 'No Lip', 'Substitute'/'Liar', 'No Feelings', 'No Fun', 'Vacant', 'Problems'. Common.
* UK Receiver, RRLP 101, white label test pressing. Includes press review promo insert. Without cover. Fairly Common.
* UK Receiver, RRLP 101. Reissue of original. Includes interview 12". With two small stickers on front sleeve. Fairly Common.
* UK Receiver, RRLP 101. As the latter (with free 12" and sticker), but with a b/w sleeve. Fairly Common.
* UK Receiver, RRLP 102, Nov 85. Actually titled *After the Storm*. Side one has four demo tracks from the New York Dolls, recorded in 72, while side two has four tracks from the original Pistols' 76 club, Burton on Trent gig (as above). Common.
* UK Fame, FA 41 31491, July 86. Budget reissue in a different cover. Common.
Little known fact: Fame is an EMI offshoot!
* Completists take note: there is another pressing from Fame, which is identical to the latter in every aspect, except the bars on the b-side label are offset. Common.
* UK Demon, APKPD 13 American Phonograph International, July 86. Picture Disc. Features six tracks. Fairly Common.
* UK Dojo, DOJO LP 45, Nov 86. Yet another reissue in yet another different ps. Also features an extra track, 'Submission'. Tracks are

rearranged. Common.
* UK Dojo, DOJO LP 45, white label test pressing. Supposedly only seven made. In plain white sleeve. Fairly Rare.
* UK Dojo, DOJO LP 45, white label test pressing. With mispressed tracks. Once again, supposedly only seven pressed! In plain white sleeve. Fairly Rare.
* Sp Vemsa, VLP 349 (PDI 30.1900) (B-15-273-1989). With beautiful green labels. Fairly Common.
* NZ Jayrem/Receiver, RRLP 101, 86. Features nice labels. Fairly Rare.

Live Worldwide
* Bg Konexion, KOMA 788017, Aug 85. An anthology of tracks from various gigs. Side one includes snippets of John Lydon's *Juke Box Jury* TV appearance. It also features a live PIL version of 'Anarchy' (from Channel 4's *Tube*, 28 Oct 83). Tracks: 'I Wanna Be Me', 'Anarchy', 'Vacant', 'No Feelings', 'No Lip', 'Submission'/'Stepping Stone', 'Satellite', 'No Fun', 'Substitute', 'Problems', 'GSTQ'. Common.

Never Trust A Hippy
* UK Hippy HIPPY 1, Sept 85. Yet another live compilation, most of this LP is from the Beach Disco Halmstad, Sweden, 15 July 77 gig. Tracks: 'GSTQ', 'Anarchy', 'Seventeen', 'Vacant', 'Problems', 'Liar'/'NY', 'No Feelings', 'Stepping Stone', 'Satellite', 'Substitute'. Common.
* UK Hippy HIPPY 1, also on pic disc. Common.
* Jp, promo-only pic disc. Fairly Rare.

Anarchy In The UK Live!
* UK UK, UK 1, Sept 85. Live at the Happy House, Student Karen, Stockholm, 28 July 77. The last three tracks on side two are live at Winterland, San Francisco (last performance), 14 Jan 78. Tracks: 'Anarchy', 'I Wanna Be Me', 'Seventeen', 'NY', 'EMI', 'Submission'/'Problems', 'GSTQ', 'Vacant', 'Belsen', 'Bodies', 'Holidays'. Common.
* UK UK, UK 1, 30 May 89, reissue in a darker pink sleeve. Also the inner (standard blank) sleeve is black. Contains release date sticker on back cover. Common.
* UK UK, UK 1 PD, first 2,000 limited edition pic disc. Common.
* Jp, promo-only pic disc release. Fairly Rare.

The Best Of The Sex Pistols Live
* UK Bondage, BOND 007, Nov 85. Side one is live at the 76 club, Burton-On-Trent, 24 Sept 76. Side two is live at Winterland, SF,

This unique 1992 German semi-legal release was originally intended by Warner Bros to be a US follow-up album to Bollocks.

14 Jan 78. Tracks: 'Submission', 'Liar', 'Substitute', 'No Feelings', 'No Fun', 'Vacant', 'Problems'/'GSTQ', 'I Wanna Be Me', 'Seventeen', 'New York', 'EMI', 'Belsen', 'Bodies', 'Holidays'. Common.
* UK Bondage, BOND 007 PD, limited edition of 2,000 pressed on picture disc: one side is pic of Johnny, c/w Sid. Fairly Common.

Where Were You In 77?
* UK 77, 771, Nov 85. Live at the Village Hall, Newport, Wales, 23 Dec 77. Tracks; 'No Future', 'Lazy Sod', 'Looking For A Kiss' ('NY'), 'EMI', 'Bodies', 'Belsen', 'Holidays', 'No Feelings'/'Problems', 'Vacant', 'Nookie' ('Anarchy'), 'No Fun', 'Submission', 'Liar'. Common.
* UK 77, 771 PD, Nov 85, limited edition of the first 2,000 available on pic disc. Fairly Common.
This album incorrectly lists 'Substitute', which does not appear. It's also one of two unique non-bootleg releases.

Power Of The Pistols
* UK 77, 772, Nov 85. Live at the Beach Disco, Halmstad, Sweden, 15 July 77. The last four tracks on side two are live at the Great Southeast Music Hall, Atlanta, GA, 5 Jan 78 (their first US performance). Tracks: 'Anarchy', 'I Wanna Be Me', 'Seventeen', 'NY', 'EMI', 'No Feelings'/'Vacant', 'GSTQ', 'Bodies', 'Submission', 'Holidays', 'Problems'. Common.
* UK 77, 772, Nov 85, also on pic disc. Common.

Pig Dog Interview 1977
* UK PD 1, Oct 84. Pic disc. Fairly Rare.
* UK, black vinyl, white label test pressing. Reputedly only four made! Very Rare.

Limited Edition
* UK PIC 007, Apr 86. A reissue pic disc of The Best Of The Sex Pistols Live. Tracks: 'Submission', 'Liar', 'Substitute', 'No Feelings', 'No Fun', 'Vacant', Problems'/

'GSTQ', 'I Wanna Be Me', 'Seventeen', 'NY', 'EMI', 'Belsen', 'Bodies', 'Holidays'. Fairly Common.
* UK PIC 007. Mispressing of the above pic disc, features a small black stripe across bottom on side one. Fairly Rare.
* UK PIC 007. Another mispressing of the pic disc saw the Pistols on one side, while c/w is Kate Bush on both picture and disc. Supposedly only two or three escaped. Very Rare.

Last Concert On Earth
* Bg Konexion, KOMA 788025, Feb 86. I've tried in vain to track down this LP. It should be noted that this cat. no. surfaces on a later release, Sid Vicious With Johnny Thunders And The Heartbreakers Live At CBGBs, NY.

Last Show On Earth
* Fr McDonald, JOCK LP 1, Feb 86. Side one features demo tracks from 76 while side two is Sid Vicious: Drugs Kill. Tracks: 'More Feelings'('No Feelings'), 'PVC (Wants To Be Me)' ['I Wanna Be Me'], 'Rotten (Was A Lazy Sod)' ['Seventeen'], 'Underwater Secrets' ('Submission'), 'Anarchy For The USA', 'I Love You (Sputnik)' ['Satellite']/'C'mon Everybody', 'Chatterbox', 'Born To Lose', 'Sid Vicious Speaks', 'Take A Chance With Me'. Common.
* Fr Echantillon/McDonald, JOCK LP 1. White label test pressing from 20/10/86. Common.

10th Anniversary Album
* UK McDonald Bro. Corp, JOCK LP 3, 22 Aug 86. Contains seven live tracks (mistitled and in wrong order) from the 76 Club concert. Tracks: 'Sigue Sigue Sex Pistols' ('Satellite' demo), 'UK Disorder' ('Anarchy'), 'Lip Child', 'This Is Brainwash' ('I Wanna Be Me')/'It's Not Funny' ('No Fun'), 'For People Like Us (There Is No Order)' ['Problems'], 'Oh So Pretty' ('Vacant'), 'Underwater Secrets'. Common.
* UK McDonald, JOCK LP 3, white label test pressing. Issued in a proof sleeve. Common.

The Sex Pistols
* UK JOCK BOX 1, Jan 87. A six album box-set: (1) Last Show On Earth/Sid Vicious: Drugs Kill; (2) The Filth And The Fury; (3) 10th Anniversary Album; (4) Sid Vicious: The Real Sid And Nancy; (5) Italian Demos; (6) No Future USA.. Came with a 24-page booklet featuring credits, etc. Rare.
* UK JOCK BOX 1, six test pressings of the latter box set. Rare.

Interview Picture Disc
* UK Music And Media, SP 1001, Feb 88. A

pic disc issue. Common.

Better Live Than Dead

* US Restless, 72255-1, May 88. Live at the 76 Club, Burton On Trent, UK, 24 Sept 76. With large yellow sticker on front cover, also includes Restless plastic inner advertiser. Tracks: 'Liar', 'Substitute', 'No Feelings', 'No Fun', 'Vacant', 'Problems', 'Anarchy'/'I Wanna Be Me', 'I'm A Lazy Sod', 'Suburban Kid' ('Satellite'), 'No Lip', 'Stepping Stone', 'Submission'. Common.
* Ca Restless, 72255-1. Fairly Common.
* Jp VAP, 35161-25. Features banding and inner sheet that contains both English and Japanese lyrics. Also with cardboard inner separator, small 'returns' card and a four-track 33rpm 7" single of 'Suburban Kid' ('Satellite' – VAP 35162-00). Fairly Rare.
* Jp VAP, 35161-25, white label test pressing. Includes a four-track white label 7" single. Also features the customary Nipponese banding and lyrics. Rare.
8 Jp VAP, 35203-25, reissue. Features and inner. Excludes 7" single. Fairly Rare.

It Seemed To Be The End Until The Next Beginning

* UK McDonald, JOCK LP 12, Jun 88. Common.

The Swindle Continues

* US Restless, 72256-1, Aug 88. Side one is the Sex Pistols (76 demos), while side two is various tracks by the Ex Pistols – i.e. not the actual Sex Pistols. However side two includes the rare Pistols track 'Understanding' (billed

as 'Judging Minds'). Features a large orange sticker on the front sleeve and the Restless inner advertiser. Tracks: 'GSTQ', 'Problems', 'Vacant', 'Liar', 'EMI', 'NY', 'No Fun', 'Anarchy'/'Here We Go Again', 'Silly Thing', 'Dancing On The Dole', 'Anarchy', 'Revolution In The Classroom', 'Judging Minds', 'Sex On 45', 'The Swindle Continues'. Common.
* Jp VAP Includes, 35204-5-45, 88. A double pic disc in a g/f jacket. Features banding and lyrics, inner, etc. Quite a unique pressing. Rare.
* Jp VAP Includes, 35204-5-45, 88, promo with stamps in grooves of actual wax. Once again, double pic disc format in g/f jacket, with banding and lyrics, inner, etc. Also features a promo sticker on back. Very Rare.
* Ar Continen CPP 903. With unique green labels. Collector's note: the album title on the spine and labels is *La Estafa Continua*. Fairly Rare.

Re the previous four: platter no.1 is from the Jan 77 Goosebury and Wessex Studios Oct 76 sessions; no. 2 is the Ex Pistols. The sleeve pics include a classic rare shot of Johnny singing in his white sports jacket, probably from Sweden. Definitely one of the finer semi-legal releases, a must-have Nipponese issue.

We've Cum For Your Children (Wanted: The Goodman Tapes)

* US Skyclad (Sick), SEX 6, 88. Basically various demos, live tracks and tele-appearances. Includes an A4 advert for the US video *Buried Alive*. Note the sleeve is Canadian. Tracks: 'McLaren TV Show Interview', 'Suburban Kid', 'Here We Go Again', 'No Lip', 'No Fun', 'Vacant'/'Revolution In The Classroom', 'GSTQ', 'Bill Grundy Interview', 'Unlimited Supply' ('EMI'), 'Anarchy', 'Submission'. Common.

Dave Goodman pinched the title from an early Dead Boys album.

God Save The Sex Pistols

* Bg Konexion, KOMA 788031, 88. Another live anthology from the UK and America. The back cover features an extensive Sex Pistols chronology. Tracks: 'Introduction', 'GSTQ', 'I Wanna Be Me', 'Seventeen', 'NY', 'EMI', 'Bodies', 'Belsen', 'Holidays'/'No Feelings', 'Submission', 'Satellite', 'Problems', 'Vacant', 'Anarchy', 'Liar', 'Closing Credits'. Common.

Live And Loud (Official Bootleg)

* UK Link, LP 063, Feb 89. Live at Winterland, San Francisco, 14 Jan 78. This first 500 were numbered and appeared on green wax. Tracks: 'Seventeen', 'NY', 'EMI', 'Belsen', 'Bodies', 'Holidays'/'No Feelings', 'Problems', 'Vacant', 'Anarchy', 'I Wanna Be Me', 'GSTQ'. Fairly Common.
* UK Link, LP 063. This next 1,000 were pressed on pink/marble wax. Rare.
* UK Link, LP 063, standard black vinyl edition. Common.
* UK Link, LP 063, white label test pressing on orange wax. No cover whatsoever! Fairly Common.

Paul and Glen are rumoured to have assisted with this release.

Pirates Of Destiny

* US I Swirled, BALL X (72310-1), March 89. contains various live tracks, interviews and excellent remixed studio tracks from the Wessex Studios session. Issued in a classic g/f jacket. Pressed on white wax with pink streaks. The sleeve is Canadian and features an import sticker for the US market. Tracks: 'Lydon Speaks', 'No Feelings', 'Lazy Sod', 'The GLC Councillor Comments On Punk', 'Problems', Medley ('Anarchy', 'Vacant', 'GSTQ'), 'Australian TV Ad', 'Vacant' (Backing Track), 'I Wanna Be Me', 'McLaren Talks . . .', 'Schools Are Prisons'/'McLaren Gabs . . .', 'Lydon Chats . . .', 'A Brief Woodstock Baby', 'Substitute', 'No Lip', 'Stepping Stone', 'Johnny B.Goode', 'Roadrunner', 'Watcha Gonna Do?', 'A Brief Through My Eyes', 'Lazy

The US semi-legal release We've Cum For Your Children. *Compiler/producer* Dave Goodman, *took the title from an early Dead Boys album.*

Cash From Chaos *featured a combo of studio outtakes and live material.*

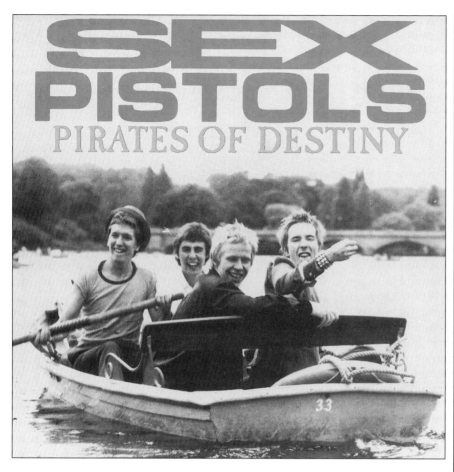

Pirates of Destiny *featured outtakes, live material and some unusual interview snippets.*

Sod'. Common.
* US I Swirled, BALL X (72310-1). As the other pressings except for that it was pressed on pink wax. Common.
Dave Goodman and his Ex-Pistols cronies were behind this album of demos and interviews. It has Johnny doing a cover of the Creation's 'Through My Eyes'! There was a single taken from this album titled 'Schools Are Prisons' and credited to the Ex Pistols. Memo to triviaheads: BALL X = Bollocks; also I Swirled Records = IceWorld = Goodman's American video label.

Anarchy Worldwide
* UK Specific, SPAW 101, 3 May 89. Side one contains studio outtakes while side two is live at the Happy House, Sweden, 28 July 77 and at Winterland, SF, 14 Jan 78 (all tracks are rearranged). Features release date sticker on back cover. Tracks: 'Seventeen', 'Satellite', 'No Feelings', 'I Wanna Be Me', 'Submission', 'Anarchy'/'Vacant', 'Holidays', 'EMI', 'Belsen', 'Problems', 'GSTQ'. Common.

* UK Specific, SPAW 101PD, 91, limited edition of 2,000 pressed on pic disc. Fairly Common.

Cash From Chaos
* UK Specific, SPCFC 102, 3 May 89. Side one contains studio outtakes while side two features more live material – including two tracks from the above Happy House concert. With 'Have You Got Pistols Awareness ?' sticker on front and release date sticker on back. Tracks: 'GSTQ', 'Problems', 'Vacant', 'Liar', 'EMI', 'NY'/'Seventeen', 'Anarchy', 'Satellite', 'No Feelings', 'Belsen', 'Submission'. Common.
* UK Specific, SPCFC 102, also available on pic disc. Common.
Such is the professionalism of the latter two albums that acronyms are now being used for the catalogue numbers – excellent sleeves though!

No Future UK
* UK Receiver, RRLP 117, Sep 89. At last the infamous bootleg *Spunk* finally gets a (semi-) legitimate release. Tracks: 'Vacant', 'Seventeen', 'Satellite', 'No Feelings', 'I Wanna Be Me', 'Submission', 'Anarchy', 'Anarchy' (different version)/'No Fun', 'GSTQ', 'Problems', 'Vacant', 'Liar', 'EMI', 'NY'. Common.

Party Till You Puke
* WG Disc De Luxe, TTE 005 (LC 7706), 89. From Wessex Studios, London. Tracks: 'EMI', 'Submission', 'Satellite', 'No Feelings', 'Seventeen'/'Bodies', 'NY', 'Liar', 'EMI' (second version), 'Submission' (second version). Common.

The Collection
* Au Telmak, TMAK 174. An Aussie-only release, issued in a g/f sleeve containing lyrics and a collage of early pics of the group. Most pressings featured a free poster. Basically an anthology of different recordings. Tracks: 'GSTQ', 'Problems', 'Vacant', 'Liar', 'EMI', 'Pills', 'Here We Go Again', 'Silly Thing', 'Stepping Stone'//'Dancing On The Dole', 'McLaren Interview', 'Submission', 'Seventeen', 'Suburban Kid', 'I Wanna Be Me', 'Anarchy', 'No Feelings', 'Substitute'. Fairly Rare.

Live At Chelmsford Top Security Prison
* US Restless, 7 72511-, June 90. The sleeve is Canadian and has an import sticker on cover for US importation. Tracks: 'Satellite', 'Submission', 'Liar', 'No Fun', 'Vacant', 'Problems'/'I Wanna Be Me', 'Lazy Sod', 'NY', 'No Lip', 'Stepping Stone', 'Substitute', 'Anarchy In The Prison', 'Did You No Wrong'. Common.

Live At Chelmsford Top Security Prison *gave the fans some rare live material.*

The inside gatefold of the Pretty Vacant *double album featured the original line-up peering down the staircase of the EMI building. It was a parody of the Beatles' debut LP,* Please Please Me, *for which the cover pic was taken at the same location.*

This set was recorded live on 17 Sept 76. The album features the encore as well as the actual gig and was re-recorded by 'session men' (supposedly UK Subs man Alan Lee and Glen Matlock were brought in on the remix). It's long been common knowledge that Dave Goodman recorded this concert, and it's the only previously unreleased legitimate(?) vinyl material since Where Were You In 77?. *This leaves us to ponder whether Dave has the 'Tax Exiles' gig on tape.*

Pretty Vacant

* UK Receiver, RRLD 004, 10 June 91. Double album. Disc one is *No Future UK?* while disc two is *The Original Pistols*. Comes in a g/f jacket that folds out with superb centre-spread shot of the original four looking down the staircase at EMI – *à la* the Beatles' famous shot for the cover of *Please Please Me*. John Tobler tops the whole thing off with the Pistols' turbulent rise and fall on the sleeve notes. Tracks; 'Vacant', 'Seventeen', 'Satellite', 'No Feelings', 'I Wanna Be Me', 'Submission', 'Anarchy', 'Anarchy' (different version)/'No Fun', 'GSTQ', 'Problems', 'Vacant', 'Liar', 'EMI', 'NY'//'Anarchy', 'I Wanna Be Me', 'I'm A Lazy Sod', 'Dolls', 'No Lip', 'Substitute'/'Liar', 'No Feelings', 'No Fun', 'Vacant', 'Problems'. Common.
* UK Receiver, RRLD 004, double album, white label test press promo. In proof sleeve which consists of separate card pieces, otherwise same ps, but including a 'Product Information Sheet' with release details, etc. Fairly Rare.

Anarchy In The USA (Features Sid Vicious)

* Ge M.B.C., SPV 008-60321, 92. Tracks: 'No Feelings', 'PVC (Wants To Be Me)',

'Rotten (Really Was A Crazy Sod)' ['Seventeen'], 'Under Water Secrets', 'Bill Grundy Interview', 'C'mon Everybody', 'Search And Destroy', 'Malcolm's Interview'/'Anarchy In The USA', 'Satellite', 'The Off Again', 'Finsbury Park Kid', 'No Lip', 'Something Else', 'My Way', 'Revolution'. Common. *Released in the cover of the much rumoured/vaunted* Anarchy In The USA *that WB were strongly tipped to release in the wake of the band's disintegration in March 78. Other than that it's basically more muck from McDonald.*

Introspective: Sex Pistols

* UK Baktabak, MINT 5008, Apr 92. Common.

God Save The Queen

* US JOCK LP A/B (matrix only). A pic disc. No track listing whatsoever! Common. *This pic disc is also known as* Destroy *on account of the cover picture which features Johnny wearing his 'Destroy' logo T-shirt.*

Sid Vicious Albums

Love Kills NYC

* Bg Konexion, KOMA 788020, Nov 85. Tracks: 'Chinese Rocks', 'I Wanna Be Your Dog', 'Stepping Stone', 'Belsen'/'Something Else', 'More Lip' ('No Lip'), 'Search And Destroy', 'Sid's Way'. Common. *Bad quality compilation of tracks from the Max's Kansas City gigs.*

Drugs Kill

* Fr McDonald, JOCK LP 1, Feb 86. Side two is the Sex Pistols: *Last Show On Earth*.

Tracks: 'C'mon Everybody', 'Chatterbox', 'Born To Lose', 'Sid Vicious Speaks', 'Take A Chance With Me'/'More Feelings', 'PVC (Wants To Be Me)', 'Rotten (Was A Lazy Sod)', 'Underwater Secrets ', 'Anarchy For The USA', 'I Love You (Sputnik)'. Common.
* Fr McDonald, JOCK LP 1, white label test pressing. Common.
Another bad quality mix of the Kansas gigs, also includes a studio track and an interview.

Live At The Electric Ballroom, London

* UK McDonald Bros. Corp., JOCK LP 2, 22 Aug 86. Tracks: 'C'mon Everybody', 'Stepping Stone', 'No Lip', 'I Wanna Be Your Dog'/ 'Belsen', 'Chatterbox', 'Tight Pants', 'My Way'. Common.
* UK McDonald JOCK LP 2, white label test pressing. In proof sleeve. Fairly Common.
Recorded on 15 Aug 78, where the line-up was billed as the Vicious White Kids, this was a farewell gig from Sid (leaving for NYC) . . . the gig itself was titled 'Sid Sods Off', and featured Sid on vocals, Glen Matlock on bass, Steve New on guitar, Rat Scabies on tubs, and girlfriend Nancy on backing vocals.

R.I.P. (Punk Never Forgets)

* UK (without cat. no., matrix: MPO Ritchie 1). Limited edition pic disc release of the 'Sid Sods Off' gig. Tracks: 'C'mon Everybody', 'Stepping Stone', 'No Lip', 'I Wanna Be Your Dog'/'Belsen', 'Chatterbox', 'Tight Pants', 'My Way'. Fairly Common.

This dubious Vicious/Cochran release was quickly withdrawn.

The reverse of the Vicious/Cochran LP attempted to compare the similarities of the two artists. Sadly, excepting their ages when they died, there were NONE!

The Real Sid And Nancy

* UK McDonald, Bros. Corp. JOCK LP 4, 22 Aug 86. Reissue of *Love Kills NYC* in a totally different sleeve. Tracks: 'Chinese Rocks', 'I Wanna Be Your Dog', 'Stepping Stone', 'Belsen'/'Something Else', 'No Lip', 'Search And Destroy', 'My Way'. Common.
* UK McDonald, JOCK LP 4, white label test pressing. In proof sleeve. Common.

('Sid Vicious V Eddie Cochran') Battle of the Rockers

* UK McDonald Bros. Corp. JOCK LP 6, Dec 86. Subsequently withdrawn. Fairly Rare.
* UK McDonald rec JOCK LP 6, white label test pressing. In proof sleeve. Fairly Rare.
Featuring four tracks each from Sid and Eddie Cochran, all studio except Sid's 'Search And Destroy'. The remaining tracks by Sid are 'Something Else', 'My Way' and 'C'mon Everybody'. In classic sleeve, with photos of Sid and Eddie opposing each other and biographical material to show they both died at the age of 21.

(Sid Vicious with Johnny Thunders and the Heartbreakers) Live At CBGB's, New York

* Bg Konexion, KOMA 788025. Really live at Electric Ballroom, 15 Aug 78 and not at CBGB's, and hence does not feature Thunders whatsoever. The spine of the sleeve states: (Sex Pistols – *Harry Munk*)/(Sid Vicious –

Drugs Kill). Tracks: 'C'mon Everybody', 'Stepping Stone', 'No Lip', 'Doggy Ways'/'Belsen', 'Chatterbox', 'Tight Pants', 'My Way (Sid's Way)'. Common.

(The Vicious White Kids featuring Sid Vicious) Live At The Electric Ballroom August 15 1978

* UK de-Lorean, STR LP 601, 91, white wax. Splendid full colour live shot on front sleeve and potted biography on back, littered with inaccuracies. Tracks: 'C'mon Everybody', 'Stepping Stone', 'No Lip', 'I Wanna Be Your Dog', 'Belsen'/'Chatterbox', 'Tight Pants', 'Something Else', 'My Way'. Common.
* UK de-Lorean STR LP 601, red wax. Common.
* UK de-Lorean STR LP 601, pink wax. Common.

This popular Athena poster of Sid brought anarchy to the high street in the 1980's. Note the stamp of approval (bottom right) by the late Anne Beverley.

PISTOLS
PIRACY ON THE HIGH SEAS

The Sex Pistols certainly have their share of illicit recordings: for a band who played only 130 live gigs, almost 40 are readily available on tape, yet only ten of these have materialised onto vinyl! *Spunk* has been rebooted again and again over the past 21 years, in almost twice as many variations. Some collectors may be content with one edition, while completists will be out to obtain all versions. However, while some of the reissues only differ marginally in presentation, there are others re-pressed in beautiful deluxe jackets, e.g. the two Swedish gigs available on vinyl, which were released in at least six superb, completely different sleeves.

How to use this catalogue:
The title is generally lifted from the label, spine or front of the jacket – in that order. Where an additional title exists on the sleeve, this is also given (in brackets), since some mail order dealers sell them under this title. Country of origin and date of release are stated where known. The catalogue number is taken from the sleeve or the label. The matrix

number is what you see etched into the vinyl at the end of a record, also known as run-off grooves. Remember: unlike legitimate wax, bootlegs are, for obvious reasons, quite hard to trace, and misinformation is in some cases inevitable!

Bootleg Albums
Spunk
* Studio outtakes released in UK in Oct 77. Cat. no. (label): Blank BLA 169. Matrix: BLA 169 lyn 4732 MAX. Sleeve: deluxe purple/white gun illustration. Deluxe gun labels with track listing, also states 'Published by White Bitch, produced by P. Dickerson (P) 1977'. Tracks: 'Seventeen', 'Satellite', 'Feelings (No)', 'Just Me' ('I Wanna Be Me'), 'Submission', 'Nookie' ('Anarchy In The UK')/'No Future' ('God Save The Queen'), 'Problems', 'Lots Of Fun' ('Pretty Vacant'), 'Liar', 'Who Was It?' ('EMI'), 'New York' ('Looking For A Kiss'). The actual band are credited as 'Spunk'. Rare.
Initially released without the sleeve in a rush to beat Never Mind The Bollocks *to the*

shops.
Reviewed in both Sounds *29 Oct 77 and* Zig Zag *no. 78, Nov 77. Unfortunately it's been rebooted in literally dozens of formats.*
* In blue/white deluxe (*No Future UK?*) jacket. Fairly Common.
* Also in blue/white deluxe (*No Future UK?*) sleeve, which folds open and lists twelve correct tracks (not fifteen). Features additional sleeve cat. no: A Rocky Schultz Production B.L.A.N.K. 000. Fairly Common.
* In plain white jacket (my copy has 'Sex Pistols – No Future' sprayed in silver on front). Fairly Common.
* There is also a copy similar to latter with 'Sex Pistols – No Future' logo in a multi-colour stencil. Fairly Common.
* Reissued in a white sleeve with 'Sex Pistols' silver logo stamped on front and featuring the original gun labels. Matrix: BLA 169. Fairly Common. There is also a copy of the latter with blank white labels.
* Also available in a b/w deluxe (*Smilin' Ears – Venezuela*) sleeve, despite not being a Venezuelan release. Fairly Rare.

No Future UK? *was a reboot of* Spunk *and featured three additional tracks. Aka* Spunk II *and* Son of Spunk.

* Issued with deluxe black gun labels. Fairly Common.
* A US copy is available with navy blue labels. Cat. no. BLA 169. Sleeve: blank white. Fairly Common.
* Another US copy which features the original *Spunk* labels. Came in a white jacket with attached live shot taken from the US 'We're the Flowers in the Dustbin . . .' 78 promo campaign. Fairly Common.
* In plain white jacket, with two small logos on top of cover: (left) 'Sex Pistols, No Future UK', in red; and (right) 'Blank Records Quality First', in blue. Fairly Common.
* Rebooted in America with cat. no. (sleeve): TAKRL 929 and matrix: MSD 929 A/B. Came in a b/w deluxe sleeve; front: b/w with song titles scattered; back: a big loada bullshit from the Amazing Kornyfone Record Label. Monique D'ozo yellow labels with a pic of a woman on each side. Fairly Rare.
This album is often referred to as The Sex Pistols.
* There is also another issue in a white jacket with attached orange/black classic pic of the lads playing live. Cat. no. f-bla 169. Matrix: BLA (a) (169 b). Labels: (b/w); a-side is pic of group live, b-side has 'Anarchy In The UK' logo. Fairly Rare.
* Also a copy issued in a white jacket with two attached green/black pics of Johnny. Labels: same as latter. Matrix: BLA (a) (b). Sleeve claims fifteen tracks, but the actual album has only twelve. Fairly Common.
* There is also a mispressed edition which plays Patti Smith live. Features original *Spunk* labels. Fairly Rare.

* Rebooted as *Smilin' Ears – Venezuela (The Filth And The Fury).* Cat. no. 7706. Matrix: SE 7706. Sleeve: b/w deluxe newspaper cover story. Labels: orange with track listing. Copies exist with a slightly different matrix: SE 7706 DREK (A). Fairly Rare.
* Rebooted as *The Life And Times Of The Sex Pistols (1976 Demos).* Matrix: SPIT A. Sleeve: white jacket with wraparound b/w ps. Labels are blank white. Fairly Rare.
* Rebooted on the continent as *Spunk II.* Features extra tracks: 'Vacant', 'Anarchy' (different version) and 'No Fun'. Cat. no. GD 001/002. Sleeve: blank white. Labels: blank. This album is also known as *Son Of Spunk.* Rare.
* Reissued as *No Future UK?* Matrix: GD 001. In yellow/black deluxe ps. Labels: blank (one side white, the other black). This album is often referred to by the pseudo-title *Spunk Rock.* Fairly Rare.
* Also a copy with blank black labels. In same yellow/back ps. Fairly Rare.
* Also issued in 81 in a green/black ps. Once again, both labels are blank black. Fairly Common.
* Also a copy in a fold-open green/black deluxe ps. Features original deluxe *Spunk* gun labels. Matrix: GD 001/002. Fairly Rare.
* Recently rebooted in the US as *Golden Bullets.* In a white jacket with attached orange/black pic of Johnny. Features plain blue labels with sticker strip (a-side *Golden Bullets*; b-side *The Filth And The Fury*). Matrix: BLA 169. Fairly Common.
There is also a Rolling Stones double bootleg album entitled *Nasty Songs.* The Stones are on the cover, it plays the Stones but . . . disc one's labels are yellow *Spunk* gun labels

Even the Americans got in on the act of 'rebooting' Spunk *! – this one is on TAKRL (The Amazing Kornyfone Record Label).*

Despite the title, this live bootleg was recorded at the El Paradise Club, Brewer St, Soho, London, 4 Apr 76.

(w/black writing); while disc two features the yellow Monique D'ozo yellow labels (again w/black writing). Fairly Rare.
Some years back a small-time bootlegger coupled *Spunk* with another Pistols boot (*Indecent Exposure?*) and put the whole she-bang into a different sleeve. 50 copies were produced. Very Rare.

Miscellaneous Live in The UK Boots

St Albans Bash 28 January 1976
* An Australian bootleg. Live at El Paradise Club, Brewer St, Soho, London, 4 Apr 76. Cat. /matrix no. SEX 3523. Sleeve: glossy deluxe ps. Labels: black with track listing. Sound: a-side very poor, b-side fair. Tracks: 'Stepping Stone', 'No Feelings', 'No Fun', 'Substitute', 'Problems', 'Satellite', 'No Lip', 'NY'/*Carri On Some Product* (Volume 2). The date and title given on the label and jacket are incorrect. Fairly Rare.

Sex Pistols – Live At The Nashville
* UK 86. Live at the Nashville Rooms, Kensington, London, 23 Apr 76. Cat. no. Sex 24. Matrix: SPA. Sleeve: in superb deluxe colour cartoon cover, a direct steal from Warner Bros' US *Bollocks* promo campaign. Labels: white with track listing. Tracks: 'Did You No Wrong', 'No Lip', 'Lazy Sod' ('Seventeen'), 'NY', 'Watcha Gonna Do?', 'Stepping Stone', 'Submission', 'Satellite'/ 'No Feelings', 'Vacant', 'No Fun', 'Substitute', 'Problems', 'Understanding', 'Did You No Wrong'. Sound: very good. Fairly Rare.
The last two tracks on side two are incorrectly

No Fun – it's not a Pistol in the pic, but the drummer of punk band the Worst Ian Hodges crouching over a number 13 hole!

claimed to be live from Maxwell (Vale) Hall, Friars, Aylesbury, 2 Feb 76, when in actual fact they're an encore from the Nashville Rooms, 3 Apr 76 – either way this is the only rendition of 'Understanding' I've ever come across.
* UK 86. There is also a pressing with blank labels (a-side orange/b-side green). Matrix: SEX 24A (original matrix SPA is scraped off). Fairly Rare.

No Fun (The Good Time Music Of The Sex Pistols)
* UK July 77. Live at the Lesser Free Trade Hall, Manchester, 4 June 76. Cat. no. PFP (aka Punk For Pleasure)/No Fun 1. Matrix: NO FUN. Sleeve: b/w deluxe front cover is pic of Preston's vintage punk band the Worst's drummer Ian Hodges crouching over a number thirteen hole on some golf course. Back is a collage of pics and tracks. Labels: green/white with track listing. Sound: good mono. Tracks: 'Outa My Head (Did You No Wrong)', 'Pushin' And Shovin' (No Lip)', 'I'm A Lazy Sod', 'Stepping Stone', '??? (NY)', 'Watcha Gonna Do?'/ 'Substitute', 'Vacant', 'Problems', 'No Fun'. Supposedly only 90 copies issued. The date given on cover (6 June) is incorrect. Reviewed in *Melody Maker* 13 Aug (mention), 20 Aug 77 and *NME* 30 Jul 77. Very Rare.
This was one of a pair of live albums to come from Manchester on the PFP label, the other being the Clash's first bootleg album Take It Or Leave It.
* Subsequent UK issue with original front sleeve photocopied and used as an insert. Fairly Common.
* Euro reboot in a white, rubber-stamped

'Anarchy In The UK Tour' sleeve. With PFP green/white labels. Matrix: No Fun/CRS. Sound: mono. Fairly Rare.
* As the latter, except most copies issued without the stamp on front. Fairly Rare.
* Rebooted in UK, Aug 77, as *The Good Time Music Of The Sex Pistols*. Cat. no. Wise/PFP. Matrix: SP 1. Sleeve: blue/white deluxe ps front is splendid shot of Johnny and Steve on stage. Back is the same as original pressing except it's in blue/white. Labels: blue 'acid speed 3'. Features same back ps as *No Fun*. Supposedly only the first 100 copies were issued in actual ps. Rare.

100 Club Sex Pistols Party (Anarchy In The UK)
* UK 77. Live at the 100 Club, 100 Oxford St, London, 20 Sept 76. Cat. no. SP 3086. Matrix: SP 2. Sleeve: blue/white deluxe ps. Labels: blue 'acid speed 5'. Sound: quite good. Tracks: 'No Feelings', 'Substitute', 'Vacant', 'Problems', 'No Fun', 'Anarchy'/ 'Seventeen', 'NY', 'No Lip', 'Stepping Stone', 'Satellite', 'Submission'. Very Rare.
The cover incorrectly lists 'I Wanna Be Me'.
* Also available in a b/w mimeographed ps on a black cover. Fairly Common.
* Shabbily rebooted in a white jacket with photostat ps in yellow/black. Fairly Common.
* Also booted in Japan. Features a slightly different cat. no. – SP 3068 (not SP 3086) - and matrix: SP 3068, plus black labels. Sound: fair mono. Very Rare.
* There is also a second Japanese pressing with cat. no. (spine and matrix) SP 3086. With blank black labels (except, each side has a red/white 'side 1' and

Like Spunk, Indecent Exposure *saw several reissues and reboots. This is the original edition that hit the London streets in Oct 78.*

'side 2' sticker on them). Very Rare.
* There is also a pressing wrongly entitled *Indecent Exposure (Live At The 100 Club 24 Sep 76)*, which also comes in a white jacket with attached orange lewd ps (man flashing bollocks). Incidentally this sleeve states both the tracks and date incorrectly (the accurate date being 20 Sept 76). Fairly Common.

Indecent Exposure (It's A Dirty Business)
* UK Oct 78. Live at the 76 Club, Burton-On-Trent, 24 Sept 76. Cat. no. Stereo SEX B-005. Matrix: SX PX 1A. Sleeve: fold-open b/w deluxe ps with red logo titles and collage of newspaper clippings. Labels: plain white, with small b/w stickers: 'side 1' and 'side 2'. Sound: very good stereo. Tracks: 'Anarchy', 'I Wanna Be Me', 'I'm A Lazy Sod', 'Pills (NY)', 'No Lip', 'Stepping Stone', 'Submission'/ 'Liar', 'Substitute', 'No Feelings', 'No Fun', 'Vacant', 'Problems'. Some copies came with an additional album-sized b/w lewd ps. Reviewed in *Melody Maker*, 28 Oct 78 and *Record Mirror*, 4 Nov 78. Fairly Rare.
This was the original vinyl release of the classic gig and is easily identifiable by its tiny report on the back recounting how Branson was once busted for merchandising Deep Purple bootlegs!!! . . . like Spunk, IE *has seen loads of reissues.*
* Rebooted in Belgium with different subtitle: *Hot Off The Press/Live At The 100 Club, London Sep. 24, 1976*. Cat. no. SP-6148 (sleeve)/Raven Records Includes 58-3032 (label). Matrix: SP 6148. Sleeve: in white jacket with attached b/w collage insert. Labels: yellow/black stating 'side three' and 'side four' respectively. Fairly Rare.

This is a Euro reboot of the original British Indecent Exposure. *Though the images are different, the design is similar.*

Original Indecent Exposure *cover – amongst the welter of Pistols press clippings, hawk eyes may spot a report on Virgin supremo Richard Branson's bust for selling Deep Purple bootlegs!*

The venue is incorrectly stated on the cover, the appropriate venue being the 76 Club.
* Cat. no. 6148 (label). Matrix: SP 6148. Sleeve: white jacket with attached green/black lewd ps. Labels: b/w, a-side has pic of Johnny, b-side has classic pic of group with Chris Spedding. Once again, the sleeve gives the wrong venue. Fairly Common.
* Different version of the labels in a plain white cover with attached newspaper pic: 'Establish The Name Sex Pistols.' Very unprofessional to say the least. Fairly Common.
* With incorrect subtitle: *Live at the 100 Club, London Sep. 24, 1976*. Sleeve: white jacket with attached b/w pic of Johnny singing (while sitting on floor in the 100 Club). Yet again the bootleggers got their venue wrong. Fairly Common.
* Matrix: SP 6148. Sleeve: in plain white jacket. Labels: yellow with 'side 1' and 'side 2' respectively (mine state 'Sex Pistols Live *Indecent Exposure*' in large red marker on

labels). Fairly Common.
* Cat. no. 5047. In fold-open b/w deluxe ps, the cover incorrectly claiming to be live at the 100 Club. Fairly Common.
* Another Euro reboot with the subtitle *Hot Off The Press*. Issued c.78. Matrix: 5047. In fold-open b/w deluxe sleeve with red logo titles. Different to original release. Labels: plain white. Fairly Rare.
* The latter is also available in a brown wax edition. Otherwise it is identical except it includes an additional lewd ps insert. Fairly Rare.
* Cat. no. Rotten SEXB 005. Sleeve: with insert. Labels: plain white. Fairly Common.

All Crimes Are Paid
* European boot. A mixture of live/studio recordings. Cat. no. Viril. Matrix: VIRIL SBP-301. Sleeve: b/w attached ps. Labels: a-side blank blue; b-side blank red. Sound: poor mono. Tracks: 'Watcha Gonna Do?' (stu-

dio 76, excellent mono), 'Substitute', 'Did You No Wrong' (live, 76 Club, 24 Sept 76), 'Satellite' (studio 76, excellent stereo), 'EMI' (live, Happy House, Student Karen, Stockholm, 28 July 77, excellent mono), 'No Feelings' (76 Club, 24 Sept 76)/'Watcha Gonna Do?' (live, Nashville, 23 Apr 76), 'Belsen Was A Gas' (live, Winterland 14 Jan 78, excellent mono), 'Belsen' (Sid and the Heartbreakers, live, Max's Kansas City, NYC, 30 Sept 78), 'Belsen' (PiL, live, Rainbow Theatre, 26 Sept 78, fair mono), 'NY', 'Understanding' (incorrectly credited as 76 Club, 24 Sept 76). Limited edition of 500 numbered copies. Rare.

The Summer 77 Tour Of Scandinavia
Anarchy In Sweden 77 (Live On Stage)
* Dutch 78. Live at the Discotheque, Beach Disco, Halmstad, Sweden, 15 July 77. Cat./matrix no. GUN 001. Sleeve: white fold-open jacket with 'Sex Pistols' stamped in red ink, sealed by a safety pin. Labels: deluxe yellow. Tracks: 'Anarchy', 'I Wanna Be Me', 'Seventeen', 'NY'/'EMI', '(No) Feelings', 'Vacant', 'Problems', 'GSTQ'. The track listing on the inside flap incorrectly lists 'Holidays' instead of 'NY'. Sound: very good mono. Very Rare.
* As the latter except tracks on inside flap are amended. Very Rare.
The latter pair came in a limited edition of 300 units.
* Repressed with purple ink stamp. The band are credited on the sleeve as 'Sex Pistolz'. This third batch limited to 500 copies. Very Rare.
* Fourth pressing had a plain white jacket (no

Anarchy in Sweden cover, complete with a safety pin piercing the top righthand side.

As with their legal counterparts, the Japanese bootleg manufacturers delivered prime product: Tour of Scandinavia 1977 *was issued in a deluxe sleeve.*

stamp). At least 1,000 copies produced. Rare.
* Booted in Japan as *Tour Of Scandinavia 1977.* Cat. no. SP 3117. Matrix/label: ZAP 7961. Sleeve: deluxe blue/white ps. Labels: deluxe green. Sound: fair mono. Features same tracks as the latter Dutch release, except b-side features an extra four studio tracks (excellent stereo): 'I Wanna Be Me', 'Did You No Wrong', 'No Fun' and 'Satellite'. This album is one of the original boots from the Pistols era. Rare.

Bad Boys
* Switzerland bootleg. Live at the Happy House, Student Karen, Stockholm, Sweden, 28 July 77. Cat. no. Pecca. Matrix: BB 77. Issued in a parody of the classic Beatles' *Sergeant Pepper* sleeve. Labels: blank white. Tracks: 'Anarchy', 'I Wanna Be Me', 'I'm A Lazy Sod', 'NY', 'EMI'/'Submission', 'Problems', 'GSTQ', 'Vacant'. This was limit-

ed to a run of 1,000 units. A fine original item, positively superb sleeve. Rare.
* Rebooted in the UK in 85 as *Scandinavian Tour 77.* Cat. no. 4395518. Matrix: S1009. Sleeve: deluxe b/w ps. Labels: black with the cat. no. This album is the same as *Bad Boys* but with an extra track on side two, 'I Wanna Be Me' (not from this gig). Fairly Rare.

Sweden
* Double album set from Japan. Features both the 15 July and 28 July Swedish gigs. Cat. no. (label)/matrix: UD 6557/6562. Sleeve: blue/white (the classic shot from the 12 Feb 76, Marquee gig) ps. Sound: excellent. Limited edition of 300. Very Rare. Record one: deluxe white labels, a-side with pic of Johnny, live 28 July Sweden. Record two: deluxe white labels, a-side has (different) pic of Johnny, live 15 July Sweden.
Note: The dates/venue on the sleeve are given in reverse order: it lists the 28 July gig incorrectly as 21 July.
* Rebooted in Australia as *Bad Boys In Sweden.* Single album containing both the 15 July and 28 July gigs. Cat. no./matrix: SEX 3521. Sleeve: glossy deluxe ps. Labels: deluxe with tracks. Fairly Rare.
The dates/venue on the labels are given in reverse order, it lists the 28 July date incorrectly as 21 July.

First US Show! (Atlanta Jan 78)
* US Aug 78. Live at the Great South East Music Hall and Emporium, Atlanta, GA, 5 Jan 78. Cat. no. Odd-Two Stereo. Label cat. no. 75001. Matrix: ODD TWO. Sleeve: white jacket with attached black/orange deluxe ps. Labels: green misprint of *Von Grossenshush/Teufel Folk Songs.* Tracks: 'GSTQ', 'I Wanna Be Me', 'Seventeen', 'NY', 'Bodies', 'Submission'/ 'Holidays', 'EMI', 'No

Feelings', 'Problems', 'Vacant', 'Anarchy'. Fairly Rare.
* There is also a pressing in the same sleeve which states 'Trademark of Quality', with b/w pic labels layered over the original green labels: a-side live (Thames cruise) shot, b-side Johnny singing. My labels have track titles biro'ed onto Tippex. The back cover also contains a large gig photo (loose). Fairly Rare.

First US Show! (Atlanta Jan 78)
* Early US edition featuring Von Gross labels, in white sleeve with light blue insert featuring the shot of the four band members out walking in the park. Fairly Rare.
* Recently rebooted in the States as *My Name Is John.* Cat. no. (sleeve): Amnesia recs. LG

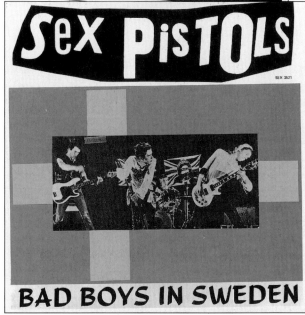

Bad Boys In Sweden was an Australian reboot of the original Japanese Sweden *bootleg.*

SWEDEN **SEX PISTOLS**

This Japanese double album featured a deluxe sleeve and picture labels. The cover pic is of Johnny groping bare-breasted Pistols camp follower Jordan.

001. Labels: b/w pix of Johnny. Matrix: LG 001. In a b/w deluxe jacket: nice shot of da boyz live on front, c/w is track listing. Fairly Rare.
* Rebooted as *Live In Atlanta (Rot 'N' Roll)*. Cat. no. K&S Records 023 – Important ODD TWO. Matrix: ODD TWO. Sleeve: white jacket with attached yellow/black deluxe ps. Labels: plain white. This limited edition was in multi-coloured wax. Fairly Rare.
* *Live In Atlanta (Rot 'N' Roll)*. There is another (standard black wax) press which is similar except that it doesn't contain the small K&S Records cartoon in the bottom right corner. The ps is similar but the colour is pale blue/white. Also note: the plain white labels have 'Side 1' and 'Side 2' on them. Fairly Rare.
* Rebooted as *Shock USA (Depression Over)*. Cat. no. ODD 2230 LP. Matrix no. ODD TWO. Sleeve: b/w deluxe ps. Labels: blank white. Fairly Rare.
* Rebooted in Australia as *Anarchy In The USA (Sex Pistols Fuck Forever)*. Cat./matrix no. SEX 3522. Sleeve: glossy deluxe ps. Labels: black with track listing. Sound: very poor. The date is incorrectly given as 8 Jan. Fairly Rare.
* There is also a double album bootleg from this gig titled *Whiskey Flat*. Cat. no. The Amazing Kornyfone Record Label. Matrix: TAKRL 2409. Sleeve: (front) blue with black logo titles; (back) black/yellow deluxe. Labels: deluxe pic labels, (record one) yellow-black; (record two) blue/black. Included a four-page 'TMQTAKRL' (The Amazing

Kornyfone Record Label/Trade Mark Of Quality) booklet, which gives wrong gig date of 1 Jan 78 and claims 'only 500 pressed'. Also note: the very end of side D (Record two, b-side) has a unique conversation between an unidentified girl and Johnny, although the sound is rather poor. Fairly Rare.
* There is a subsequent issue of *Whiskey Flat* which is very similar except the sleeve is a dark brown and has 'Trade Mark . . .'. It also features a central picture of Johnny in his crucified stance. Rare.
* The Atlanta gig was recently rebooted as

US bootleg *Welcome to the Rodeo wrongly dates the Pistols' Texan gig as 10 Jan 77 – one year before it actually happened.*

Pistols Shock USA. Cat /matrix no. ODD TWO A/B. In a glossy deluxe b/w ps. The labels are plain cream. Fairly Rare.

Welcome To The Rodeo
* US, Aug 78. Live at the Longhorn Ballroom, Dallas, TX, 10 Jan 78. Cat./matrix no. SP 2800. Sleeve: black jacket with attached b/w deluxe ps. B/w pic labels: a-side group pic; b-side pic of Johnny. Tracks: 'GSTQ', 'I Want To Be Me', 'Seventeen', 'NY', 'EMI', 'Bodies'/'No Feelings', 'Problems', 'Vacant', 'Anarchy', 'No Fun'. Sound: very good stereo. The date on the front cover is incorrectly stated as 10 Jan 77. Reviewed in *Melody Maker*, 18 Nov 78. Fairly Rare.
* Rebooted in Germany in same sleeve (10 Jan 77) and cat. no., etc. However this pressing has those Ruthless Rhymes Deluxe

labels. Fairly Rare.
* *Pistols Anarchy In The USA Tour – Sex Pistols In Texas*. Another German reboot. Features a different insert: b/w attached logo ps on a heavy cardboard plain white jacket. Also features the Ruthless Rhymes Deluxe labels. Matrix: SP 2800. Fairly Rare.
* Another pressing exists in a white jacket with attached cream/red deluxe ps. Labels: (Full Tilt rec EF 6339/Serious Endeavour) gold misprint. Date on front cover is correct (78). Fairly Rare.
* Shabbily rebooted with six pics glued on back cover. The date is incorrect (77). Features the Ruthless Rhymes Deluxe labels. Fairly Common.

Gun Control
* US, Jun 78. Live at Winterland Ballroom (last gig), San Francisco, 14 Jan 78. Cat. /matrix no. SP 2900. Sleeve: white jacket with attached green/brown deluxe ps. Labels: red misprint (Full Tilt rec EF 6339/Serious Endeavour). Tracks: 'GSTQ', 'I Wanna Be Me', 'Seventeen', 'NY', 'EMI', 'Belsen Was A Gas', 'Bodies', 'Holidays'/'Liar', 'No Feelings', 'Problems', 'Vacant', 'Anarchy', 'No Fun'. Sound: very good mono. Reviewed in *Melody Maker*, 18 Nov 78. Fairly Rare.
* There is another copy with different attached yellow/black ps. Cat. no. BRF (Bang Record Factory) – BAENG 02 edition 1 SP 2900. Labels: (Dragonfly Records) yellow misprint. Matrix is same as original. Fairly Rare.
* There is yet another variant of the latter w/same labels, etc. However, the different attached ps is now pink/black. Fairly Rare.
* Rebooted in West Germany with those Ruthless Rhymes Deluxe labels. Sleeve: white jacket with front attached b/w deluxe ps (same as latter). Sound: very good mono. Cover cat. no. Bang Record Factory SP 2900 (not BAENG 02). Fairly Rare.
* Also available in pale blue/white attached ps. Fairly Common.
Some editions of the latter had four pics glued to reverse: three b/w and one colour.
* Also available in green/black attached ps. Fairly Common.
* Rebooted on Slipped Discs. Cat. no. SXTT 979. Fairly Common.
* Rebooted in West Germany as *Live At Winterland*. Cat. no. TAKRL 916. Matrix: SP

2900. Sleeve: beautiful b/w deluxe ps with shot of boys on rear. Labels: Ruthless Rhymes Deluxe. The cover claims to be a TAKRL release, but it's not! An extremely hard-to-find item. Very Rare.

* An American reissue with superbly unique labels: a-side is Johnny wearing diving goggles; b-side is a pic of Sid. Cat. no. SP 2900. Without sleeve. Fairly Rare.

* There is an American mispressing, from the Burton-On-Trent gig. Cat. no. TAKRL 916. Sleeve: b/w deluxe ps. Sound: good stereo. As the title says, this album should be live SF, also sides one and two are identical. Very Rare. *There were probably two or three other variants of this mispress: one came in a plain white sleeve and had* Spunk *labels. Very Rare. There is a* Spunk *album with original gun labels, except they're yellow. Matrix: TAKRL 916. Another edition came in the b/w Winterland deluxe ps, another 'same-sided' mispressing. And it's also been rebooted in a white jacket with attached orange ps. The rarest edition of all was pressed on pink wax with identical a- and b-sides. All Very Rare.*

* Rebooted yet again in England as *The Blank Tapes* in Apr 81. Cat. no. (label): Blank records UK 5. Matrix: UK 5. Sleeve: white jacket with small green title sticker. Labels: black with track listing. Fairly Rare. *The guy who brought out this release had the audacity to distribute it via the music press – 'just in from America' – for the entire world to see, including someone from the British*

Phonographic Institute! Needless to say, the album was 'withdrawn' and few now exist.

* Repressed with cat. no. TAKRL 916. Labels/matrix as latter. Sleeve: b/w deluxe ps. Once again this is not a TAKRL release. Fairly Rare.

* Recently rebooted in the US as *The Very Best Of . . .* Cat. no. Blank UK 5. Matrix: UK 5 a/b. Sleeve: wrap-around of Sid and Nancy at Phil Lynott's place; back is three different shots of the group or Sid and Nancy. Fairly Rare.

* Reissued as *Live In America* with cat. labels/matrix no. as *The Blank Tapes*. Sleeve: white jacket with attached b/w ps. Sound: good mono. Fairly Rare.

* Rebooted as *Chelsea Bath (The Very Best Of The Sex Pistols)*. Matrix: UK 5 (A)EG. Sleeve: white jacket with attached wrap-around pink/black deluxe ps. Labels: blank cream. Fairly Rare.

Boot Box Sets

Sex Pistols File (1976 – 1978 A Four Record Set)

* US 81. A four album box-set in a b/w wrap-around ps. The four albums came in standard white paper inners.

Record one: **The A&M Tapes (Spunk)**. Matrix: BLA 169. Labels: plain blue. The actual album has twelve tracks, but claims fifteen.

Record two: **Live At The 100 Club London Sep 24 1976**. Labels: red Unmitigated Audacity Records. Matrix: SP 6148. This platter falsely claims to be live at the 100 Club, when it's the 76 Club, 24 Sept 76.

Record three: **Live In Dallas, Texas, USA Jan 10 1978 (Welcome To The Rodeo)**.

Record four: **Winterland San Francisco Jan 14, 78 (Gun Control)**. Labels: blank white The first pressing consisted of a numbered edition of 250. Main pressing in same box/wrap-around ps. However all the records have deluxe pic labels. Very Rare.

London's Outrage

* UK Jan 91. A three album box-set that included an insert, long sleeved T-shirt, individually numbered concert ticket, a b/w 100 Club poster and a single titled 'The Official Sex Pistols Fan Club - Another Sex Pistols Christmas Record'.

Record one: **Destroy! Live At The 100 Club**. Cat. no. Bel End LULLA 1. Labels: nice pic labels, matrix erased. Deluxe b/w (*100 Club Party*) sleeve.

Record two: **Where Were You In 77?** Similar to the semi-legal, although the labels indicate

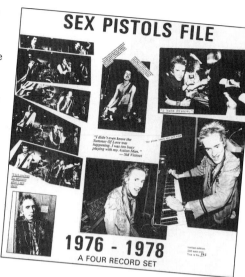

A quad-box album set issued in America in 1981.

it's a re-run edition.

Record three: **Power Of The Pistols.** Again same as its semi-legal counterpart.

The whole thing was issued in a limited edition of 1,000 units. Very Rare. *The single was recorded live at Ivanhoes, Manchester Road, Huddersfield, Xmas Day 77 and features 'GSTQ' and 'No Fun'. Cat. no. Bell End LULLA 1_. Matrix is also erased. In a fold-open pink deluxe jacket. Labels: plain pink.*

Sid Vicious Bootleg Albums

(The Sid Vicious Experience): Jack Boots And Dirty Looks

* UK May 86. Live at the Electric Ballroom, Chalk Farm Rd, London, 15 Aug 78. Cat. no. New Cross rec JACK 001. Matrix: MPO Anthler 37. Sleeve: b/w deluxe ps. Labels: blank white. Tracks: 'C'mon Everybody', 'Stepping Stone', 'No Lip', 'I Wanna Be Your Dog'/'Belsen Was A Gas', 'Chatterbox', 'Tight Pants', 'My Way'. Fairly Rare. *The band and gig were billed as the Vicious White Kids and 'Sid Sods Off' respectively. This original not to be confused with the recent semi-legal pressing in a similar jacket.*

Vicious Burger (Take A Chance On Me)

* Japanese bootleg. Live at Max's Kansas City, NYC, 7 Sept 78. Cat. no. UD 6336. Label cat./matrix no. UD 6535. Sleeve: white jacket with red shiny wrap-around deluxe ps. Labels: white with tracks stated. Tracks: 'Search And Destroy', 'I Wanna Be Your Dog',

Gun Control was another bootleg of the San Francisco Winterland debacle.

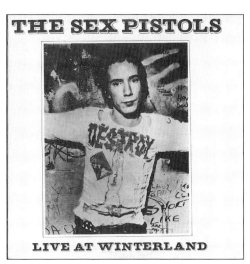

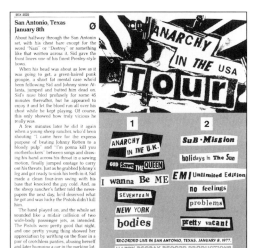

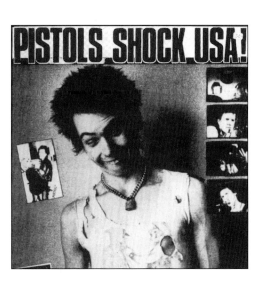

What the bootlegs of the 1978 US tour lacked in sound quality, they made up for with garish covers. Clockwise from top left: My Name Is John – an American reboot of the first show in Atlanta, Georgia; Live At Winterland – the most famous Pistols bootleg after Spunk; Anarchy In The USA (front and back covers, bottom and centre right) – despite wrongly crediting the live recording to the San Antonio, Texas show (in 1977, one year before it occurred), this is an Australian reboot of the Atlanta show; Chelsea Bath – this is actually the San Francisco/Winterland gig; the most recent reboot of the Atlanta show – again under the title Anarchy In The USA (centre left).

The original Japanese Vicious Burger *bootleg was recorded live at Max's Kansas City, NYC, 7 September 1978.*

'No Lip', 'Something Else', 'Belsen'/ 'Stepping Stone', 'Chinese Rocks', 'My Way', 'Take A Chance On Me'. Sound: good stereo. Rare.
* American reboot titled *Live*. Sleeve: black with splendid red wrap-around deluxe ps. Labels: plain white. Matrix: JSR-21 (acronym for 'John Simon Ritchie – aged 21 yrs'). Sleeve neglects 'No Lip', which is on the album, and wrongly titles 'Take A Chance On Me' as '10 Min Ago'. Rare.
* Re-pressed in white jacket with paper insert. Fairly Rare.
* Rebooted with 'creative artistry includes' labels. Fairly Common.
* Swedish pressing titled *(Sid Vicious Group): Who Killed Nancy?*. Cat. no. JSR-21 Innocent. Matrix: JSR 21. Sleeve: white jacket with b/w front news story ps. Labels: blank white. The cover incorrectly claims 'Made in USA'. Fairly Rare.
* Another Swedish pressing titled *Sid Vicious*. Exactly the same, except the sleeve pic is rearranged and additionally states 'excellent stereo' on the bottom left. Also, it doesn't have either the group or album titles.

Fairly Rare.
These are the recordings of the Max's Kansas City gigs.

Boot Singles

Belsen Was A Gas/Anarchy In The USA
* UK Oct 78. Cat. no. Rotten Role SUK 1. This first issue was mispressed with red labels. NOC. Issued without ps. Supposedly only ten exist, either way it's very scarce. Reviewed in *Melody Maker*, 28 Oct 78. Rare.
* UK mass-produced reboot of the original. Basically the same (no ps), except the labels are green. Fairly Rare.
* American reboot of original. Once again it's similar, but the labels are now blue. Fairly Common.
Some of this latter US issue came in a ps.
* **And We Don't Care EP.** West German 80 release of the May 76, Majestic Studio demos recorded by Chris Spedding. Cat. no. Rotten Boys RB 1320. Tracks: 'Problems'/'No Feelings', 'Vacant'. Came in a deluxe ps. Fairly Rare.

Regular SF 'Ippies And Assorted Longhairs EP. UK bootleg of Winterland, 14 Jan 78. Without cat. no. Labels: blank green. Tracks: 'KSAN Report'/'Bodies', 'Holidays', 'Vacant', 'Anarchy In The USA'. The record was pressed in blue wax and came in a fold-open green/black deluxe ps of Johnny looking like a hippy. NOC. Fairly Common.
* There is also a copy in a yellow/back ps. Common.

Pirate Audiography

Tapes of live/studio recordings and interviews. Sound rating (s:) up to 10 (best) and a time lising (in minutes) follow each entry. If a concert is also available on vinyl, then coinciding tracks are not given (consult the appropriate boot album).

The Gigs

* **Nashville Rooms,** 3 Apr 76 – encore – two tracks – only – s:8, t:8 – also vinyl. Common.
* **El Paradise Club,** Brewer St, Soho, London, 4 Apr 76 – twelve tracks, four more than the wax edition: 'Did You No Wrong', 'Seventeen', 'Submission', 'Vacant' – s:6, t:45 – also vinyl. Common.
* **Nashville Rooms,** Kensington, London, 23 Apr 76 – thirteen tracks – the classic night of pandemonium, when both Steve and Johnny join in, leaving them one less venue to play – s:8, t:50 – also vinyl. Common.
* **Lesser Free Trade Hall,** Peter St, Manchester, 4 June 76 – fourteen tracks, four more than the wax edition: 'No Feelings', 'Submission', 'Satellite', 'No Fun' (twice) – s:8, t:60 – also vinyl. Common.
* **100 Club,** 100 Oxford St, London, 6 July 76 – twelve tracks: 'I Wanna Be Me', 'No Lip', 'Seventeen', 'Stepping Stone', 'NY', 'Watcha Gonna Do?', 'Submission', 'Satellite', 'No Fun', 'Substitute', 'Vacant', 'Problems' – s:6, t:45. Rare.
* **Barbarellas,** Birmingham, 14 Aug 76 – twelve tracks: 'Flowers Of Romance', 'I Wanna Be Me', 'Liar', 'Substitute', 'Seventeen', 'NY', 'Stepping Stone', 'No Fun', 'Satellite', 'Vacant', 'Problems', 'Anarchy' (part) – as far as I know, this is the only version of 'Flowers' that exists – s:7, t:45. Rare.
* **100 Club,** London, 31 Aug 76 – fourteen tracks: 'Anarchy', 'I Wanna Be Me', 'Seventeen', 'Did You No Wrong', 'Pushin' And Shovin'', 'Stepping Stone', 'Satellite', 'Submission', 'Liar', 'No Feelings', 'Substitute', 'Vacant', 'Problems', 'No Fun'.

Most dealers incorrectly give this date as: 30 Aug – s:8, t:45. Fairly Common.

* **Chelmsford Maximum Security Prison**, 17 Sept 76 – nine tracks: 'Anarchy', 'I Wanna Be Me', 'Seventeen', 'NY', 'No Lip', 'Stepping Stone', 'Satellite', 'Submission', 'Liar' – s:9, t:50. Subsequently given a semi-legal release in Summer 90 on an American label (remixed). Also vinyl. Common.

* **100 Club (Punk Festival)**, London, 20 Sept 76 – fifteen tracks, three more than the vinyl edition: 'I Wanna Be Me', 'Liar', 'Anarchy' (twice). This was the last time the Pistols played the 100 Club – s:8, t:50. Also vinyl. Common.

* **76 Club**, Burton On Trent, 24 Sept 76 – thirteen tracks – this gig has seen extensive vinyl repackaging courtesy of the semi-legal releases, but it's still a brilliant performance – s:9, t:45. Also vinyl. Common.

* **Bogarts**, Birmingham, 20 Oct 76 – nine tracks: 'Anarchy', 'I Wanna Be Me', 'Seventeen', 'Satellite', 'Substitute', 'Liar', 'No Feelings', 'No Fun', 'Vacant' – s: vocals extremely low, t:35. Rare.

* **Notre Dame Halls**, Leicester Place, London, 15 Nov 76 – thirteen tracks: 'Anarchy', 'I Wanna Be Me', 'Seventeen', 'Vacant', 'No Feelings', 'No Lip', 'Watcha Gonna Do?', 'Did You No Wrong', 'Seventeen', 'Stepping Stone', 'Satellite', 'Problems', 'NY'. Some of this concert went out on TV (see 'Pistols Videography') – s:7, t:40. Fairly Rare.

* **Leeds Polytechnic**, Leeds, 6 Dec 76 – nine tracks: 'Anarchy', 'I Wanna Be Me', 'Seventeen', 'Stepping Stone', 'No Future (GSTQ)', 'Substitute', 'No Feelings', 'Liar', 'No Fun'. Debut gig of the abortive Anarchy In The UK Tour – s:7, t:30. Fairly Rare.

* **Winter Gardens**, Cleethorpes, 20 Dec 76 – nine tracks: 'Anarchy', 'I Wanna Be Me', 'Stepping Stone', 'Satellite', 'GSTQ', 'Substitute', 'Liar', 'No Feelings', 'Vacant' – s:7, t:35. Fairly Rare.

* **Paradiso Club**, Amsterdam, Holland, 5 Jan 77 – eleven tracks: 'Anarchy', 'I Wanna Be Me', 'Seventeen', 'NY', 'Satellite', 'GSTQ', 'Substitute', 'No Feelings', 'Vacant', 'Liar', 'Problems' – s:7, t:40. Matlock's last gig. Fairly Rare.

* **Screen On The Green**, Islington, London, 3 Apr 77 – eleven tracks: 'GSTQ', 'I Wanna Be Me', 'Seventeen', 'NY', 'Satellite', 'EMI', 'Liar', 'Vacant', 'Problems', 'No Feelings', 'Anarchy'. Sid's first public gig (his first took place two weeks prior, at the private Notre Dame Church Halls gig, in Leicester Sq, London, on 21 March 77, filmed by US NBC

TV crew) – s:8, t:35. Fairly Rare.

* **Thames Riverboat Trip**, London, 7 June 77 – six tracks: 'Anarchy', 'GSTQ', 'Holidays', 'Anarchy', 'Vacant', 'Problems'. Once again, the night ends in chaos. Dealers incorrectly give the date as June 15 (or 16) – s:7, t:20. Fairly Rare.

* **Daddys Dancehall**, Copenhagen, Denmark, 13 July 77 – eleven tracks: 'Anarchy', 'I Wanna Be Me', 'Seventeen', 'NY', 'Satellite', 'No Feelings', 'No Fun', 'Holidays', 'Problems', 'Vacant', 'GSTQ' – s:8, t:45. Fairly Rare.

* **Daddys Dancehall**, 14 July 77 – ten tracks: 'Anarchy', 'I Wanna Be Me', 'Seventeen', 'NY', 'EMI', 'No Feelings', 'Vacant', 'Problems', 'GSTQ', 'No Fun' – s:8, t:35. Fairly Rare.

* **Discotheque**, Beach Disco, Halmstad, Sweden, 15 July 77 – nine tracks – s:8, t:35. Also vinyl. Common.

* **El Mocambo Disco**, Helsingborg, Sweden, 16 July 77 – nine tracks: 'Anarchy', 'I Wanna Be Me', 'Seventeen', 'NY', 'EMI', 'Problems', 'No Feelings', 'Vacant', 'GSTQ' – s:9, t:30. Fairly Rare.

* **Pingvinen Restaurant**, Oslo, Norway, 20 July 77 – ten tracks: 'Anarchy', 'I Wanna Be Me', 'Seventeen', 'NY', 'EMI', 'No Fun', 'No Feelings', 'Problems', 'Vacant', 'GSTQ' – s:7, t:40. Fairly Rare.

* **Happy House**, Student Karen, Stockholm, Sweden, 28 July 77 – ten tracks, includes one more track ('No Fun') than its wax counterpart. Along with the 15 July gig, it's seen substantial repackaging via the recent spate of semi-legal albums – s:9, t:35. Also vinyl. Common.

* **Huize Maas**, Groningen, Holland, 10 Dec 77 – fourteen tracks: 'I Wanna Be Me', 'Seventeen', 'NY', 'EMI', 'Bodies', 'Belsen', 'Holidays', 'No Feelings', 'Problems', 'Vacant', 'Anarchy', 'No Fun', 'Liar', 'Submission' – s:8, t:50. Fairly Common.

* **Maf Centrum**, Maasbree, Holland, 11 Dec 77 – fourteen tracks: 'GSTQ', 'I Wanna Be Me', 'Seventeen', 'NY', 'EMI', 'Bodies', 'Belsen', 'Holidays', 'No Feelings', 'Problems', 'Vacant', 'Anarchy', 'No Fun', 'Liar' – s:6, t:60. Fairly Common.

* **Brunel University**, Uxbridge, 16 Dec 77 – sixteen tracks: 'GSTQ', 'I Wanna Be Me', 'Seventeen', 'NY', 'EMI', 'Bodies', 'Belsen', 'Holidays', 'Submission', 'No Feelings', 'Problems', 'Vacant', 'Anarchy', 'No Fun', 'Liar', 'GSTQ' – s:8, t:60. Fairly Common.

* **Mr Georges**, Coventry, 17 Dec 77 – eight tracks: 'Seventeen', 'NY', 'EMI', 'Bodies', 'Belsen', 'Holidays', 'Anarchy', 'Vacant' – s:8,

t:35. Fairly Common.

* **Nikkers Club**, Keighley, Yorks, 19 Dec 77 – thirteen tracks: 'GSTQ', 'I Wanna Be Me', 'Seventeen', 'NY', 'EMI', 'Bodies', 'Belsen', 'Holidays', 'No Feelings', 'Problems', 'Vacant', 'Anarchy', 'No Fun' – s:7, t:60. Fairly Common.

* **Stowaway Club** – may have been recorded at Village Hall, Newport, 23 Dec 77 (different venue) – fifteen tracks: 'GSTQ', 'I Wanna Be Me', 'Seventeen', 'NY', 'EMI', 'Bodies', 'Belsen', 'Holidays', 'No Feelings', 'Problems', 'Vacant', 'Anarchy', 'No Fun', 'Submission', 'Liar'. Subsequently released on one of those semi-legal albums (*Where Were You In 77?*) – s:7, t:60. Common.

* **Links Pavilion**, Cromer, 24 Dec 77 – thirteen tracks: 'GSTQ', 'I Wanna Be Me', 'Seventeen', 'NY', 'EMI', 'Bodies', 'Submission', 'Belsen', 'Holidays', 'No Feelings', 'Problems', 'Vacant', 'Anarchy' – s:7, t:50. Fairly Common.

* **Ivanhoe's Club**, Manchester Road, Huddersfield, 25 Dec 77 – supposedly recorded by John 'Boogie' Tiberi (roadie) although the bootleggers claim only two tracks are currently available: 'GSTQ' and 'No Fun'. These were subsequently reissued on the bootleg 45 that appeared in the *London's Outrage* box-set – s:9, t:10. Fairly Common.

* **Great South-East Music Hall And Emporium**, Atlanta, GA, USA, 5 Jan 78 – twelve tracks: – US debut: 'Well my name's John and this is the Sex Pistols' – s:8, t:45 – also vinyl. Common.

* **Taliesyn Ballroom**, Memphis, TN, USA, 6 Jan 78 – twelve tracks: 'GSTQ', 'I Wanna Be Me', 'Seventeen', 'NY', 'EMI', 'Bodies', 'Belsen', 'Submission', 'Holidays', 'Vacant', 'Anarchy', 'No Fun' – s:7, t:45. Fairly Common.

* **Randy's Rodeo**, San Antonio, TX, USA, 8 Jan 78 – eleven tracks: 'GSTQ', 'I Wanna Be Me', 'Seventeen', 'NY', 'EMI', 'Holidays', 'Submission', 'No Feelings', 'Problems', 'Vacant', 'Anarchy In The USA' – s:9, t:40. Fairly Common.

* **Kingfisher Club**, Baton Rouge, LA, USA, 9 Jan 78 – fourteen tracks: 'GSTQ', 'I Wanna Be Me', 'Seventeen', 'NY', 'EMI', 'Bodies', 'Belsen', 'Submission', 'Holidays', 'No Feelings', 'Problems', 'Vacant', 'Anarchy', 'No Fun', 'Liar' – s:9, t:50. Fairly Common.

* **Longhorn Ballroom**, Dallas, TX, USA, 10 Jan 78 – thirteen tracks, with two extra than boot album: 'Belsen' and 'Holidays'. Also features US FM radio broadcast – s:8, t:60 – also vinyl. Common.

* **Winterland Ballroom,** San Francisco, CA, USA, 14 Jan 78 – fourteen tracks and US KSAN broadcast. Johnny expresses gratitude to Californians via 'Bodies', abusing them throughout – s:9, t:50 – also vinyl. Common. *Memo to pirates: this was professionally recorded, though not as yet released.*

* **Finsbury Park,** London, UK, 23 June 96 – UK radio broadcast – s:10, t:65. Common.

* **Finsbury Park,** London, UK, 23 June 96 – different mix – s:10, t:65. Common.

* **Naval Museum,** Stockholm, Sweden, 26 June 96 – s:8, t:45. Common.

* **Roskilde Festival,** 28 June 96 – s:7, t:50. Common.

* **Le Zenith,** Paris, France, 4 July 96 – s:10, t:55. Common.

* **Curva Stadio,** Rome, Italy, 10 July 96 – s:9, t:60. Common.

* **Arena Spettacoli,** Milano, Italy, 11 July 96 – s:8, t:50. Common.

* **SECC,** Glasgow, Scotland, 16 July 96 – s:10, t:70. Common.

* **Sheperds Bush Empire,** London, 17 July 96 – s:10, t:85. Common.

* **Beach Festival,** Zeebrugge, 20 July 96 – s:6, t:65. Common.

* **Phoenix Festival,** Stratford-On-Avon, UK, 21 July 96 – eight tracks – s:10, t:55. Common.

* **Live at Fairfax,** Washington DC, USA, 6 Aug 96 – s: 9, 75m. Common.

* **Universal Ampitheatre,** CA, USA, 22 Aug 96 – s:6, t:55. Common.

* **Hollywood Palladium,** LA, CA, USA, 23 Aug 96 – s:9, t:75. Common.

* **Bumbershoot Festival,** Seattle, WA, USA, Aug 96 – s:7, t:70. Common.

* **Live At Tokyo,** Japan, 22 Nov 96 – s:10, t:90. Common.

Studio Recordings

* **Chris Spedding Demos – recorded at: Majestic Studios, London, May 76** – three tracks: 'Problems', 'Vacant', 'No Feelings' – The lads' first time in the studio, and, contrary to press claims, Spedding's *not* on the actual recording. Glen reckons Mickie Most paid for this session – s:9, t:15.

* **Spunk/No Future UK** – studio outtakes, mixture of two sets of recordings with Dave Goodman: (1) Sex Pistols' Rehearsal Studios, Denmark St, London, 13/30 July 76; (2) Goosebury Studios, Gerrard St, London, 27 Dec 76. Goodman was rumoured to be playing guitar on these sessions, but that is certainly not the case here – (fifteen tracks in total) – s:10, t:50 – also vinyl. Common. *Dave mixed some of these sessions at Hammersmith's Riverside studios.*

* **1st Anarchy Session – Wessex Studios, London, Oct 76** (with Dave Goodman) – nine tracks: 'Anarchy', 'I Wanna Be Me', 'Substitute', 'Stepping Stone', 'No Fun', 'No Lip', 'Johnny B. Goode', 'Roadrunner', 'Watcha Gonna Do?'. These were the cuts that eventually surfaced on the *Swindle* double album – strictly speaking, this was the *2nd Anarchy Session* as they had previously attempted to record 'Anarchy In The UK' in Lansdowne Studios, Holland Park, London on 10 Oct 76 (also with D. Goodman). Yet still, this was not destined to be the final released (EMI) 7" version – that required another visit to the Wessex Studios on 17 Oct 76, this time with Chris Thomas as producer – s:9, t:50. Common.

* **Mike Thorn Session, EMI Studios,** Manchester Sq. London, Nov 76 – five tracks: 'No Future' (ext'd vers), 'Liar', 'Problems', 'Anarchy', 'No Feelings' (instrumental!) – s:9, t:16. Common.

* **Dave Goodman Session – Goosebury Studios,** 17/20 Jan 77 – six tracks: 'No Future', 'Problems', 'Vacant', 'Liar', 'EMI', 'New York' – from what was to be their fourth and final session with Dave – s:9, t:20. Common.

* **Chris Thomas Session, 3/4 Mar 77** – ten tracks: 'Anarchy', 'Anarchy' (alt. vers), 'Anarchy' (second alt. vers), 'Submission', 'No Feelings', 'No Future', 'No Future' (alt. vers), 'Vacant', 'EMI', 'Liar'. Some dealers incorrectly give date as Apr 77 – s:9, t:40. NB: there are rumoured recordings of a 'small session' at Kingsway Studios, but this session *never* happened. Common.

Interviews/Appearances

* **Radio Luxembourg** – Dec 76, Johnny and Malcolm – s:7, t:25. Common.

* **LBC Radio,** 18 May 77, Malcolm interviewed – s:9, t:12. Common.

* **The Heyday 1977** (see legit tapes) – my boot features a news review of the *Swindle* flick plus a report on Nancy's death, and, amazingly, an interview with Sid after his indictment for her murder – s:7, t:70. Common.

* **Rotten Radio Show: 'The Punk And His Music'** – Capital Radio, 16 July 77 – (Johnny chooses the music, while being interviewed by Tommy Vance) – s:9, t:60. Common.

* **Radio M'bourgh,** Aug 77 – s:9, t:5. Common.

* **Radio Tees** – 1 Sept 77, John, Paul, Steve and Sid – s:9, t:5. Common.

* **Radio Luxembourg** – Sept 77, Johnny and Sid – s:8, t:5. Common.

* **Radio Clyde Interview** – 19 Nov 77, John, Paul and Steve – s:9, t:55. Common.

* **Radio Notts Interview** – Nov 77 – Johnny – s:9, t:20. Common.

* **Radio Metro** – Nov 77, John and Paul – s:8, t:50. Common.

* **Radio Trent** – Nov 77, Johnny – s:9, t:25. Common.

* **BBC Radio 1 *Rock On* Interview** – 12 Nov 77, Johnny and Sid – s:9, t:30. Common.

* **Dutch Radio Session** – Dec 77 – includes four tracks from the earlier Maf Centrum gig at Maasbree: 'Vacant', 'Anarchy', 'No Fun', 'Liar' – s:8, t:15. Common.

* **Dutch Radio Interview** – Dec 77, Paul and Steve – s:8, t:10. Common.

* **Rock On Radio One** – 12 Dec 77, Johnny and Sid interviewed by John Tobler (slagging off McLaren) – s:10 t:30. Common.

* **Radio 3XY Molly Ledrum** – Dec 77, Aussie radio, Paul and Steve – s:9, t:15. Common.

* **Radio K-SAN** – 13 Jan 78, Paul and Steve, aptly described by a *Creem* journalist as a 'no-holds barred' interview – an all time classic – s:8, t:75. Common.

* **Radio K-SAN** – 14 Jan 78, Johnny and Sid (before the gig) – s:8, t:12. Common.

* **Ronnie Biggs, Steve and Paul Interview** – 13 Feb 78 – s:9, t:10. Common.

* **BBC Radio 1 'Newsbeat'** – May 79, Paul and Steve – s:9, t:2. Common.

* **Radio London** – July 79, interview with Paul Cook – s:9, t:35. Common.

* **BBC Radio 1** – 85, Paul and Glen talk about the semi-legals – s:9, t:20. Common.

* **German Radio Broadcast** 85 – Pistols retrospective – s:8, t:30. Common.

* **BBC Radio 1: From Punk To Present** – 14/21 May 85 – s:9, t:65. Common.

* **100 Club Reunion Press Conference,** London, UK, 18 March 96 – s:9, t:18. Common.

* **BBC Radio 1** – May 96. Exclusive band interview – s:10, t:50. Common.

* **BBC Radio 1: Sex Pistols – The Reunion Concert** – 23 June 96, 8pm – live from Finsbury Park, London – s:10, t:180. Common.

* **RTE Radio 1** – 5 March 97 – Irish Radio – legendary Irish rock critic B. P. Fallon offers a personal assessment of the Sex Pistols – s:10, t:43. Common.

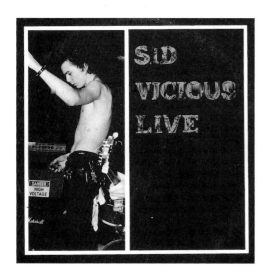

Clockwise from top left: And We Don't Care *(front and back sleeve, top left and right) – this West German bootleg EP features the earliest Pistols studio demos, recorded by Chris Spedding (seen with the band, second from right) at the Majestic Studio in May 1976, plus a US KSAN radio report;* Jack Boots And Dirty Looks *(front and back sleeve, centre and bottom right) – credited to 'the Sid Vicious Experience', this was actually Sid's 'Vicious White Kids' farewell gig in London;* Sid Vicious Live – an American reboot of the Nipponese Vicious Burger; Regular SF 'Ippies And Assorted Longhairs – this EP contains tracks from the Pistols' last US 78 date, at San Francisco Winterland.*

OTHER PiSTOLS COLLECTIBLES

Eight-Track Cartridge

* **Never Mind The Bollocks, Here's The Sex Pistols** – US Warner Bros, M8 3147, Nov 77. In eight-track stereo window box. Long since deleted. Rare.
There also exists a pirate eight-track edition.

Laser Discs

* **The Great Rock'N'Roll Swindle.** Jp Virgin, MP 141/24 VN, 85. Original LD release. With insert. Very Rare
Re-released on a regular basis – see below.
* Jp Virgin, SHRM 2003. From the Legend Rock series. Rare.
* Jp Polygram Video, POLP 1015. NTSC format. Rare.
* Jp Polygram Video, POLP 1611. With unique yellow/black banding which runs horizontally across the top as against the standard vertical position. From the Super Stars Nice Price Collection series. NTSC format. Rare.
There were at least five different Nipponese laser disc issues alone.
* US Warner Reprise Video 9 38319-6, 24 Nov 92. NTSC format, 104 mins, digital sound stereo. Fairly Rare.

* **Winterland Concert.** Jp Videoarts VALJ 3420 CLV, May 95. NTSC format. With banding. In spectacular full-colour deluxe sleeve. The inner has English and Japanese lyrics. Also with small inner ad card. Fourteen tracks from their final performance of the seventies. Rare.

* **Live At Longhorns.** Jp Videoarts VALC 3430 CLV, Dec 95. NTSC format. With banding. In spectacular full-colour deluxe sleeve. With inner containing band history in Japanese. Also has small inner ad card. Eleven tracks from Dallas, Texas, 10 Jan 78. Rare.

* **Filthy Lucre – Live In Japan.** Jp VALJ 1027, Jan 97. NTSC format. Live in Japan, Autumn 96. Rare.

* **(Various Artists) Sid And Nancy – Love Kills.** US Embassy Home Entertainment 13096, 86. NTSC format. Three different discs containing the 111-min. movie. Digitally mastered and mono compatible. Fairly Rare.
* US The Criterion Collection 241, 86. NTSC format. This is the LBX Edition (Letter Box Edition) and features extra cuts, the making of the movie, etc. It comes in a completely different sleeve to the standard LD issue. With black/gold 'Special Edition' sticker on front. Rare.

Digital Compact Cassettes

* **Kiss This.** UK Virgin, 463 167 5, Oct 93. Fairly Common.

Mini Discs

* **Never Mind The Bollocks, Here's The Sex Pistols.** US Warner Bros BSK 3147, 92. Fairly Common.
* **Never Mind The Bollocks, Here's The Sex Pistols.** At Virgin V 2086, 92. Fairly Common.
* **Kiss This.** At Virgin, MDV 2702 (0777 7 86489 3 2), Oct 93. Common.

DAT Tape

* **SPOTS.** Nineteen-second and nine-second radio ads on UK DAT promo tape, 77. Fairly Rare.

Pistols Acetates

The expensive side of record collecting. An acetate is basically the master disc of a particular recording and usually comes in the format of a metal, occasionally lead, disc coated in wax. They are extremely limited releases, usually only a handful are ever produced. The credits are handwritten or typed. Owing to their rarity, values are susceptible to dramatic increase. Watch out for counterfeits.

'Submission' acetate – recorded at EMI's Abbey Road studios, London.

7" Singles

* 'Anarchy In The UK'/'No Fun' – Townhouse – Very Rare.
* 'Anarchy' – EMI Abbey Road – studio sleeve – Very Rare.

10" Singles

* 'Anarchy' – Townhouse – one-sided – Very Rare.
* 'Anarchy'/'No Future' ('GSTQ') –

Poster advertising official Sex Pistols merchandise.

Albums

* *God Save The Queen* – UK acetate for early copy of the *Bollocks* album – Very Rare.
* *Never Mind The Bollocks, Here's The Sex Pistols* – UK acetate – Very Rare.
* *Never Mind The Bollocks* – US Warner Bros two x one-sided acetates – with mispressed labels, both sides claiming same tracks – Very Rare.
* *Never Mind The Bollocks, Here's The Sex Pistols* – US Capitol 72256 – Very Rare.
* *The Great Rock'N'Roll Swindle* – two PYE Studio LPs – Very Rare.
* *Some Product – Carri On Sex Pistols* – UK Utopia – studio sleeve – Very Rare.
* *Live At The Electric Circus* – UK Abbey Road/EMI – beautiful labels – studio sleeve – Very Rare.
* *Live At Birmingham, 14 Aug 76* – acetate sleeve – Very Rare.
* *The Mini Album* – Very Rare.

* 'Anarchy' – Abbey Road – one sided acetate – different to other Abbey Road acetate – supposedly only six made – Very Rare.
* 'Anarchy' – Chaos – one-sided – Very Rare.
* 'Anarchy' plus two – (see 10" for details) – US Capitol/EMI audio disc – Very Rare.
* 'God Save The Queen'/'No Feelings' – A&M black label, lead based – Very Rare.
* 'GSTQ' – PYE acetate – their most valuable platter: the tidy sum of £2,200 was realised at a summer 94 auction at Christie's – Very Rare.
* 'GSTQ' – unreleased version, from an unidentified recording session – one-sided – in special 'Pyral' custom sleeve – no label, and only the outer inch is actually vinyl. Very Rare.
* 'Did You No Wrong' – PRT Studios – one-sided – in special 'Pyral' custom sleeve (3m 09s) – Very Rare.
* 'Pretty Vacant' – EMI Abbey Road – studio sleeve – with handwritten labels – one-sided – Very Rare.
* 'Vacant' – EMI Abbey Road/Chaos – from the Dave Goodman sessions, subsequently released on the Spunk boot – one-sided – Very Rare.
* 'Holidays In The Sun' – one-sided – Very Rare.
* 'Submission' – UK Abbey Road Studios – one-sided – Very Rare.
* 'Submission' – Abbey Road/Chaos – glossy studio sleeve – one-sided, supposedly only six made – Very Rare.
* 'Belsen Was A Gas' (live) – one-sided, with no labels – Very Rare.
* 'Bodies' – US – one-sided – Very Rare.
* 'Who Killed Bambi?' – lacquer – Very Rare.

EMI - handwritten white labels – Very Rare.
* 'Anarchy'/'EMI'/'No Future' – US Capitol/EMI labelled audio disc – 'Anarchy' is the *Great Rock'N'Roll Swindle* (double album) version (see 7") – Very Rare.
* 'Liar' – US Warner Bros. – one-sided – Very Rare.
* 'Problems' – US Warner Bros – one-sided – Very Rare.
* 'Did You No Wrong' – PRT Studios – Very Rare.
* 'Submission' – one-sided – Very Rare.
* 'Vacant' – Townhouse – one-sided – Very Rare.
* 'GSTQ' – one-sided – Very Rare.
* 'GSTQ' – Townhouse – Very Rare.
* 'Bodies' – US – Very Rare.
* 'Seventeen' – US Warner Bros – two x one-track acetate – Very Rare.
* 'Submission'/'Vacant' – US Warner Bros 77 – Very Rare.
* 'EMI' – US – Very Rare.
* 'Silly Thing' – metal plate – Very Rare
* 'My Way' – Townhouse – Very Rare.

12" Singles

* 'No One Is Innocent' – Townhouse – Very Rare.
* 'Bodies' – one-sided, labelled, album version acetate – Very Rare.

14" Singles

* 'Vacant' – UK Chaos – only one exists! Very Rare.

CDs

* 'GSTQ' – TV karaoke version – Virgin Gold recordable CD-ROM acetate, with custom title sleeve and printed disc – Rare.

DVDs

* **The Filth And The Fury**. UK Filmfour/Virgin Sept 2000/ US Warner Home Video Oct 2000. Julien Temple's comprehensive documentary overview of the Pistols, containing much previously unreleased footage. Extras include the theatrical trailer and the directors' commentary. Common.

Sid Vicious Album Acetates

* *Live At The Electric Ballroom* – Abbey Road master acetate – splendid company labels and sleeve – Very Rare.
* *Sid Sings* – see 'The Great Rock'N'Roll Auctions' – Very Rare.

ODDS 'N' ENDS
Calendars

* Blue four-page 100 Club calendar for May 76 – Fairly Rare.
* 78, 79, 80, 81 – Fairly Common.
* 82, 83, 84, 85 – Common.
* 86, 87, 88, 89 – Common.
* 90, 91 (two different), 92, 93, 94, 95, 96, 97 (two different), 98, 99, 00, 01, 02 and 03. Common.

'Pretty Vacant' sheet music.

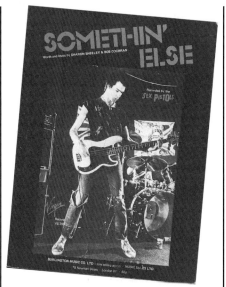

'Somethin' Else' sheet music.

Sheet Music

* 'Anarchy In The UK' – Fairly Rare.
* 'Pretty Vacant' – US Warner Bros, classic shot of da boyz out walking – four pages – Fairly Rare.
* 'No One Is Innocent' – UK promo shot of Pistols/Biggs *et al* – Fairly Common.
* 'Something Else' – superb shot of Sid on cover – Fairly Common.
* 'C'mon Everybody' – shot of Sid, head thrown back, eyes closed, 'really into the music', as his mother says in *The Sid Vicious Family Album*. Fairly Common.

Press Kits/Tour Programmes

* EMI press release/media pack, eight pages printed on yellow/pink paper, Dec 76 – Rare.
* Glitterbest press kit, 28pp – Rare.
There is at least one other Glitterbest press kit out there.
* **The Filth And The Fury!** – original US Warner Bros kit for *Never Mind The Bollocks* in deluxe fold-open collage jacket, including superb cartoon *Sex Pistols* poster and ten large, glossy b/w photos of the group – Very Rare.
* **The Great Rock'N'Roll Swindle** – authentic press pack with 10" album cover, eight-page booklet, some stills and a world premiere ticket – Very Rare.
* Tenth anniversary convention kit (includes photo info, laminate, etc.) – Common.
* **Anarchy In The UK 92** press kit, including video and CD single – Common.
* **The Great Rock'N'Roll Swindle** – US

Warner Bros Reprise press release for the home video, s/t and laser disc issued in the USA on 24 Nov 92, includes three pages and photo – Fairly Common.
* **Sex Pistols 1996 Reunion Press Kit** – deluxe UK press pack in fluorescent pink folder with inserts and photograph, also including *Filthy Lucre Live* promo CD – Fairly Rare.
* **Sex Pistols 1996 Reunion Press Kit,** as the latter except without the CD and the folder is white/pink – Fairly Rare.
* **Mean Fiddler Presents – Sex Pistols – The Filthy Lucre Tour – Finsbury Park, Sunday 23 June 1996** – large 20pp colour tour programme – Fairly Common.
* **Sex Pistols US Summer 96 Tour Press Kit** – one photo and twenty pages of tour dates and magazine reproductions (plus Never Trust A Hippy) all in a folder – Fairly Rare.
* **Sex Pistols Filthy Lucre Press Kit** – includes biog, press release, etc. – Fairly Rare.
* **The Great Rock'N'Roll Swindle** – Japanese programme, Rare.
* **The Filth And The Fury** – UK eight-page promo from the movie's London premiere, contains quotes, pictures, background information, credits, wrapped in Japanese-style obi. strip, with Union Jack pattern – Farily common.
* **Pistols At The Palace** – UK programme for 27 July 2002 reunion/Jubilee gig, with colour and b/w photos throughout – Fairly common.

Tickets, Backstage Passes And Handbills

* **Anarchy In The UK Tour** (includes the

Clash and the Damned), original Plymouth 76 ticket – Fairly Common.
* **Anarchy In The UK Tour** laminated backstage pass – Common.
* Ticket for cancelled 20 Dec 77 concert at Hamilton, Birkenhead – Very Rare.
* Ticket for 23 Dec 77 concert at Huddersfield – Rare.
* Ticket for Xmas Day concert at Huddersfield (last UK gig) – Very Rare.
* **Leona Theatre – Pennsylvania 30 Dec 77** unused backstage pass since gig was cancelled – Fairly Rare.
* Atlanta (first US appearance) backstage pass – Fairly Rare.
* **Winterland Ballroom, San Francisco 14 Jan 78** (final Pistols appearance) backstage pass – Fairly Rare.
* **Satin Pass for Winterland** – Common.
* **The Great Rock'N'Roll Swindle –** blue/white Aussie insert/handbill to promote movie – Common.
* **Never Mind The Sex Pistols . . . Here Comes The Filthy Lucre Tour** – Australian promo handbill for 22 Oct 96 gig – Common.
* **Filthy Lucre Tour** Japanese promo handbill for ticket and tour date info – Common.

Presentation Discs

* **Something Else** presentation disc – Very Rare.
* **Never Mind The Bollocks** UK Virgin gold disc – Very Rare.
* **Never Mind The Bollocks** US Warner Bros/RIAA gold disc signed by surviving band members Johnny Rotten, Paul Cook and Steve Jones – Very Rare.
* **Never Mind The Bollocks** – US WB/RIAA platinum presentation to Johnny Rotten for 1M US unit sales. Very Rare.
* **The Great Rock'N'Roll Swindle** UK Virgin gold disc – Very Rare.

Unusual Posters

* **The Great Rock'N'Roll Swindle** film poster (large/framed) – Very Rare.
* **The Great Rock'N'Roll Swindle** fold-open cardboard poster (Virgin) – Fairly Rare.
* **Sex Pistols Fuck Forever** original silk-screened poster, used for exhibition by Jamie Reid – Fairly Common.
* **Dickens/Oliver Twist** poster, given out at only one live concert on Xmas day 77 (for these and other superb rare poster illustrations, consult Jamie Reid's book *Up They Rise*) – Very Rare.
* Six original posters from the film, 2' by 6',

Warner Bros backstage pass for the American Tour.

all in bright fluorescent colour: *The Great Rock'N'Roll Swindle*, 'They Swindled Their Way To The Top', 'The Only Notes That Matter Are The Ones That Come In Wads', 'Believe In The Ruins', 'Cash From Chaos' and 'Never Trust A Hippy' – Very Rare.

* Cartoon strip in colour, poster sized, mounted on card, framed and glazed, autographed by all – Very Rare.

* **Charcoal Drawing of Johnny Rotten** by Bradford John Salamon, 24" x 20" – Very Rare.

* Sid Vicious promo poster for the tracks 'Born To Lose', 'Something Else', 'My Way' and 'I Killed The Cat' – Very Rare.

Strippings/Roll-Outs

* **God Save The Queen** original promo strip (long cream/black) – Rare.

* **Pretty Vacant** promo strip (long red/b/w) – Rare.

* **We Stock Sex Pistols While Stocks Exist** promo strip (yellow/orange 10" x 20") – Rare.

* **Great Rock'N'Roll Swindle** advertising strips (five different colour versions) – Very Rare.

Right: original Who Killed Bambi *badge used to promote the* Swindle *flick. Far right: original promotional badge for 'God Save The Queen'.*

Selected Postcards, Badges And Stickers

* **Sex Pistols** sew-on (long yellow/navy blue) – Common.

* **God Save The Queen** original promotional sticker – Common.

* Two b/w Xmas (78) cards of Johnny and Sid – Common.

* **Guns 'N' Roses/Sex Pistols** badge – Common.

* **God Save The Queen** badges (uncut sheet of six originals) – Rare.

* **Anarchy In The UK** original postcard from the heyday – Fairly Common.

* **Holidays In The Sun** original postcard from Oct 77 – Common.

* **Sex Pistols Fuck Forever** orange postcard in mailing envelope with 'Demand The Impossible' message inside – Common.

* **Anarchy In The UK** large promo sticker from 92 – Common.

* **Damaged Goods 93** postcards (full colour reissues) – among them 'Anarchy', 'GSTQ', 'Vacant' and *Bollocks* – Common.

* **Filthy Lucre** promo sticker (A5 yellow/pink) for tour and album – Common.

* **Filthy Lucre Live** decals (yellow and grey) – Common.

* **Filthy Lucre Live** stickers (two sets) – Common.

Miscellaneous

* Sex Pistols logo A3 heavy duty transparent plastic pink/yellow carry case – Rare.

* **God Save The Queen** film script which subsequently became the *Swindle* movie, written before J. Rotten left and including him in the plot – Very Rare.

* **Who Killed Bambi?** film script (very thorough revision of the above, my copy was presented to Paul), 290pp, A4 – Very Rare.

* **Punk** bubblegum set of cards – Fairly Rare.

* **God Save The Queen** special punk pack, including T-shirt, poster, badge and mug, 50 copies given away by *Record Mirror* in 18 June 77 issue to promote the single – Very Rare.

* **God Save The Queen** T-shirt, ripped and torn – Very Rare.

* Signed concert contract for Market Hall, Scotch Street, Carlisle, Friday Dec 17 76 – Very Rare.

* **I Wanna Be Me** autographed sleeve, framed and glazed, mounted with b/w print – Very Rare.

* Polyfoam colour stand-up head display of Johnny – Common.

* Johnny's T-shirt from the Trondheim gig, Norway, 21 July 77, complete with letter of authentication, ripped to pieces! Very Rare.

* JOHNNY'S RIPPED 'ANARCHY IN THE UK' SHIRT, WORN ON 'ANARCHY' VIDEO – VERY RARE.

* Steve's ripped shirt, as worn on 'GSTQ' – Very Rare.
* **God Save The Queen** T-shirt designed by Jamie Reid – Very Rare.
* **The Sex Pistols/A&M Original Buckingham Palace Contract – 10 March 77** (mounted and framed) has recently been advertised in *Record Collector*, and its sellers appear confident of getting two

Of The Year' magazine cover story signed by Jamie Reid – Very Rare.
* **God Save The Queen** collage of Jubilee souvenirs and 7" ps, signed by Jamie Reid – Very Rare.

This prop was placed on the gates of the school that Steve visits in The Great Rock'N'Roll Swindle *movie.*

grand for it. Very Rare.
* **No Feelings**: original handwritten lyrics by Johnny on Glitterbest paper – Very Rare.
* **Submission**: original handwritten lyrics by Johnny on Glitterbest paper – Very Rare.
* **Anarchy In The UK**: Vivienne Westwood/'Sex'-designed linen shirt for Johnny – Very Rare.
* Handwritten note from Johnny to a fan (1979) – Very Rare.
* Vivienne Westwood-designed T-shirt for Steve, depicting two gay cowboys, naked from the waist down. Very Rare.
* Piece of white paper, 4" x 7", signed by all four members of Sid-era group – Very Rare.
* **1988** proof cover for Caroline Coon's book – Fairly Rare.
* Colour mag photo proof signed by Johnny – Very Rare.
* **Never Mind The Bollocks** original US promo flag showing cover of LP – Very Rare.
* **Never Mind The Bollocks** large full-colour Warner Bros promo cloth repro-ducing both sides of the US album sleeve, beautiful item – Very Rare.
* **Never Mind The Bollocks** full-colour WB promo T-shirt – Very Rare.
* **Sex Pistols – The Filth And The Fury!** gigantic b/w silk cloth of famous 'wall' shot, including two inserts, superb item – Very Rare.
* **Anarchy** concert handout, A4, colour – Fairly Rare.
* **Who Killed Bambi?** camera-ready artwork signed by artist Jamie Reid – Very Rare.
* Tinted Warhol job on 'Young Businessmen

* **Great Rock'N'Roll Swindle** badge-slogan colour proofs signed by Jamie Reid – Very Rare.
* **Never Mind The Bollocks** original colour proof (both sides), designed by Jamie Reid – Very Rare.
* **God Save The Sex Pistols** original colour proof (both sides), design by Jamie Reid – Very Rare.
This was to be the original title of the Pistols' first album, but it was changed at Steve Jones' insistence to his favourite exclamation: 'Bollocks'.
* **Great Rock'N'Roll Swindle** die-cut four-colour cardboard cinema-foyer promo featuring (l-r) Biggs, Rotten, McLaren, Vicious, Jones and Cook – Very Rare.
* **Some Product – Fatty Jones** – heavy flat cardboard artwork for the album – Very Rare.
* **Some Product – Chelsea Hotel** – heavy flat cardboard artwork for the album – Very Rare.
* List of songs used at an early rehearsal, handwritten by Glen Matlock – Very Rare.
* **Letter from Johnny Rotten** dated 31/7/79 – Very Rare.
* **Great Rock'N'Roll Swindle** s/t shop display, 60"x 26" – Very Rare.
* **Great Rock'N'Roll Swindle** fluorescent display (different to above), 14" x 28" – Rare.
* **Sid And Nancy Competition Pack** from Aussie music paper *Juke* (no. 652, 24 Oct 87), including video, poster and s/t album, only five given away – Rare.
* Framed picture mirror – Common.
* **God Save The Queen** proof sleeve for Aussie single – Rare.

* **Kiss This** album promo 6' x 6' facsimile, printed on PVC and mounted on polystyrene, from Tower Records' Piccadilly window display, given away in *Melody Maker* competition – Fairly Rare.
* **Kiss This** 3D freestanding promo fold-out display board, 24" x 24" – Fairly Common.
* **Kiss This** horizontal b/w cardboard promo strip for album – Common.
* **Anarchy In The UK** counter box for shop display, including 'Anarchy' in both single formats (cassingle and CD single) sitting snugly in special pouch at front, splendid item – Fairly Rare.
* **Pretty Vacant** 92 promo counter box – Common.
* **A Box Of Punks** from photographer Ian Dickson, containing seven original hand-printed photos in signed, ready-to-frame mounts (Johnny, the Clash, Damned, Ramones, Jam, Siouxsie Sioux and Shane McGowan) – Very Rare.
* Double-sided wall cloth, Spanish, c. 96, features painting of Johnny incorporating classic 'Destroy' T-shirt design (with exposed penis). Fairly Rare.
* **Filthy Lucre** album cover artwork, 18" x 24" – Common.

A4 Original Flyers/Handbills
* **El Paradise Club – Brewer St. W1**, 4 Apr 76, b/w – Fairly Rare.
* **Nashville Rooms, Kensington, London**, 29 Apr 76, b/w – Fairly Rare.
* **100 Club, Tuesdays In May (11th, 18th and 25th)**, b/w – Fairly Rare.
* **Screen On The Green, Islington**, Monday

17 May 76 (rarest of the set, in that this gig was subsequently cancelled), red/white – Fairly Rare.

* **100 Club, 100 Oxford St, London**, 25 May 76 – Fairly Rare.

* **100 Club, Oxford St, London**, 6 July 76 – Fairly Rare.

* **Screen On The Green, Islington**, 29 Aug 76, b/w – Fairly Rare.

* **100 Club, Oxford St**, Tuesday 31 Aug 76 – Fairly Rare.

* **Pistols in Prison – Chelmsford Maximum Security Prison**, 17 Sept 76, double-sided, b/w – Fairly Rare.

* **London's Outrage – Sex Pistols On Stage!! At Last!** Notre Dame Halls, Leicester Place, Leicester Square, London, 15 Nov 76 – Fairly Rare.

* **Leeds Poly, Monday 6 December**, black print/orange background, mega-rarity since the entire concert was thwarted by officialdom – Very Rare.

* **Anarchy In The UK** EMI colour flyer for debut single – Fairly Rare.

Some dealers have sold these for as much £75 – £150 each! Don't worry about counterfeits as the originals are easy enough to identify.

A3 Original B/W Flyers/Handbills

* **Pistols in Prison – Chelmsford Maximum Security Prison**, 17 Sept 76 – Very Rare.
* **Punk Festival, 100 Club**, 100 Oxford St, London, 20 Sept 76 – Very Rare.
* **Cricket Ground, Northampton**, 9 Oct 76 – Very Rare.
* **Technical College, Dundee**, 12 Oct 76 – Very Rare.
* **Mr Digby's, Birkenhead**, 14 Oct 76 – Very Rare.
* **Queensway Hall, Dunstable**, 21 Oct 76 – Very Rare.

As with their A4 counterparts, expect to pay anything from £100 to £250 a piece. Once again, originals are easily identifiable.

Sid Vicious Odds 'n' Ends

* Framed picture mirror – Common.
* **Sid Vicious Dead** cigarette lighter – Rare.
* *Punk* **Magazine 1979 Calendar**, January pic is of Sid – Fairly Rare.
* **Charcoal Drawing of Sid Vicious** by Bradford John Salamon, size: 24"x 20" – Very Rare.
* **Birthday Bash 1991**, signed silk screen by underground punk artist Frank Kozik, limited

edition – Rare.

Sid And Nancy (Film) Odds 'n' Ends

* US cardboard display for video, 9"/13" – Common.
* Promotional film pack – Common.
* **Love Kills** album cover artwork, 24" x 24" – Common.
* **Sid And Nancy** film programme (French), Nov 86 – Fairly Rare.
* **Sid And Nancy** colour movie flyer (Japanese, 97) – Common.

Pistols Publications

There's certainly no shortage of material on the Sex Pistols. Considering the band came and went in a flash, it's not unusual for all who 'were there' to pen their memoirs of those 26 great months.

Title (and subtitle, if applicable) author(s), publisher, country of origin, date of publication, approximate size (generally A5 or A4), number of pages, and, where relevant, scandal or trivia, are all listed chronologically. All editions are paperback unless otherwise stated, and I've deliberately refrained from providing the ISBN's as some of these books have seen multiple printings.

Anarchy In The UK. The original large tabloid-format fanzine from Glitterbest. Designed by Jamie Reid for the decimated 'Anarchy' tour. With a front cover featuring Sue 'Catwoman' Lucas, this zine has rocketed in value over the past ten years. Very Rare.

Sex Pistols, Fred and Judy Vermorel, Universal, UK Jan 78, A5, 224pp. The authors have revised and re-published their masterpiece on two occasions. *This is* the *Sex Pistols book*. This edition was also published in Greece in a completely different cover. At a mere 80pp, the biographical text is reduced, but the lyrics are given in both English and Greek! Fairly Rare.

Sex Pistols Scrapbook, Ray Stevenson (independently published), UK March 78, A4, 56pp/ 180 photographs. 2000 printed, forerunner of the highly successful *File*. A genuine collector's item. Indispensable. Fairly Rare.
Glitterbest – aka the four band members and McLaren – sued Stevenson upon publication, but all 2,000 units were sold-out in four days! Ray's brother, Nils, was a member of the 'Bromley Contingent' and subsequently pro-

gressed to the position of first Sex Pistols' roadie (replaced by Boogie). Nils also managed Siouxsie and the Banshees.

Les Sex Pistols, Fred and Judy Vermorel, Speed 17, Fr 78, A5, 240pp. Superb French edition of the Vermorels' masterpiece, in completely different jacket with spectacular back cover picture of Johnny and Sid – also features an extra sixteen pages and some different inner photographs. Fairly Rare.

Sex Pistols File, Ray Stevenson, Omnibus Press, UK 78, A4 , 64pp. Omni realised the potential of Stevenson's *Scrapbook* (see above), and purchased the publishing rights. Stevenson was only too glad to trade, since Glitterbest were sending out legal vibes over his initial private publication. Watch for the unique red title. Fairly Common.

Never Mind The Bollocks, That Was The Sex Pistols (songbook), Warner Bros Music Ltd, UK 78, A4, 56pp. Every other page features a full-page photo from the collage poster given away free with *Bollocks*. This original edition is Fairly Rare.

Never Mind The Bollocks, That Was The Sex Pistols (songbook). Reissued in the UK in 88, format is identical to 78 edition although the publisher is now International Music Publications Limited. Common.

The back cover of the 56-page songbook Never Mind The Bollocks, That Was The Sex Pistols.

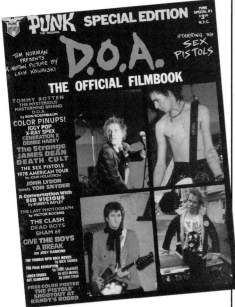

D.O.A. – The Official Film Book – *this 64-page glossy promo mag was published in April 1981 to coincide with the American movie of the same name.*

Here's The Sex Pistols – Never Mind The Bollocks (songbook), BMG Publishing, US, 96, A4, 72pp. Note the difference in the title (in fact the spine spells *Bollocks* as *Bullocks*!). The cover is pink instead of yellow, as per the US album cover. Other changes include different shots of the band in the opening pages and the book is slightly longer than its UK counterparts.

Sex Pistols File (updated), Ray Stevenson, Omnibus Press, UK Nov 78, A4, 72pp. Third revamped edition, revised in the shadow of Nancy's death and Sid's arrest. Watch out for the unique green cover. Fairly Common.

The Great Rock'N'Roll Swindle (songbook), Warner Bros Music Ltd, UK 80, A4, 48pp. Common.

The Sex Pistols, ghost written, High Books Ltd, Italy, Apr 81, A4, 96pp. Italian only. Superb publication with stunning shots and classic full-colour cover. Rare

D.O.A. The Official Film Book – Punk Special Edition, authors include John Holmstrom, Punk Publications, US, no.1, Apr 81, A4, 64pp. Glossy promo mag-cum-book for film of the same name, with superb colour shots of the US tour and other vintage punk rock acts. Holmstrom was behind the legendary NY

Punk magazine. Fairly Rare.

The Great Rock'N'Roll Swindle, Michael Moorcock, Virgin, UK May 81, A5, 128pp. Hawkwind sidekick, recording artist, science fiction novelist, poet and lyricist Moorcock wrote this unique novel in two weeks. It originated in a larger-than-tabloid twelve-page newspaper format for the princely sum of 75p, accompanied with a promotional gimmick: 'Collector's Item – The Cheapest Novel Of 1980.' Fairly Common.

Sex Pistols File (edited and updated), Ray Stevenson, Omnibus Press, UK 81, A4, 72pp. Stevenson enjoys a fourth major overhaul of his classic file of vintage cuttings. This latest edition recounts Sid's death, the *Swindle* flick and the initial court proceedings of Lydon Vs McLaren. Common.

Sex Pistols (The Inside Story), Star Books, Fred and Judy Vermorel, UK Nov 81, A5, 288pp. Update of the Universal book – not essential. Common.

Rebel Rock, Dennis Morris, Epoch Press, UK Oct 85, limited edition: 12" square, wide format, 86pp. 'A photographic record of the Sex Pistols' last tour of Europe and England.' Some comical shots and equally funny descriptive captions. Fairly Common.

Rebel Rock, Dennis Morris, Omnibus Press/Epoch Productions, UK 86, A4, 80pp. Once again, Omni climb on the bandwagon of a proven publication. Common.

Sex Pistols (The Inside Story), Fred and Judy Vermorel, Omnibus Press, UK May 87, A5, 240pp. Second update of the Universal book. This edition was also translated and printed for the Greek market in 96, once again in a shorter edition (144pp) with lyrics to all the songs in both English and Greek. Common.

Sex Pistols (The Inside Story), Reissued in UK in 89, format is identical to 87 edition. Common.

Sex Pistols Diary (Day By Day), Lee Wood, Omnibus Press, UK Aug 88, A4, 96pp. A day-by-day, blow-by-blow account of their career, from the very beginning to the Winterland debacle. Also available in an alternative colour cover. Common.

Sex Pistols Diary (Day By Day), subsequently translated and re-issued in Japan, in an A5

format in Sept 90. Fairly Rare.

Sex Pistols Cut Up!, Ray Stevenson and Dennis Morris, Shinko Music Publishing Co. Ltd, Jp, 89, A4 – 96pp. Japanese only publication – the *File* and *Rebel Rock* merged in a cut-down version with the captions translated into Japanese; b/w throughout in a nice glossy yellow cover. Inessential.

The Sex Pistols 'Chaos' (Bob Gruen's Works), Bob Gruen, Hideki Nishikawa, Japan, 10 May 89, A4, 128pp. Photo book with more pages than its British counterpart, basically b/w with sixteen full-colour pages in the centre, within a superb cover of a bloody Sid Vicious.

Chaos – The Sex Pistols, Bob Gruen, Omnibus Press, UK Feb 90, A4, 128pp. Some nice new shots from the infamous American tour, where Gruen snapped his best shots. Still only a UK clone of the latter – Common.

Sex Pistols Punk, William Mandel, Edizioni Blues Brothers, It, 90. Fairly Rare.

Twelve Days On The Road, Noel E. Monk and Jimmy Guterman, William Morrow and Co. Inc, US Summer 90, 230pp, A5, galley proofs of Monk's US book in pink/black softbound cover, with blank numbered pages instead of photos. Features official info insert and review copy order form. Superb item. Fairly Rare.

Twelve Days On The Road: The Sex Pistols And America, Noel E. Monk and Jimmy Guterman, William Morrow and Co, US, 26 Sept 90, A5, 240pp, h/b. Subsequently reissued in s/b format in 92 by Quill (an imprint of William Morrow and Co). Common.

12 Days On The Road: The Sex Pistols USA Tour, Noel E. Monk and Jimmy Guterman, Sidgwick And Jackson UK Aug 92. Common.

I Was A Teenage Sex Pistol, Glen Matlock with Pete Silverton, Omnibus Press, UK Aug 90, A5, 194pp, h/b. The first member to put his memoirs on paper. Reissued in s/b in Aug 91. Also published in America in 91 by Faber and Faber, 181pp. Finally revamped and reissued in the UK by Virgin in June 96, with a new cover. Common.

NO! (Sid Vicious: Il Nichilismo, L'Eroina, La Morte, Il Punk), William Mandel, Edizioni

Blues Brothers, It 91, 130pp, A6, It. Fairly Common.

Never Mind The B*ll*cks: A Photographic Record Of The Sex Pistols, Dennis Morris, Omnibus Press, UK Aug 91, A4. *Rebel Rock* revamped and reissued with sixteen extra full-colour pages. Omnibus go down the Virgin road of barrel scraping. Common.

England's Dreaming: Sex Pistols And Punk Rock, Jon Savage, Faber and Faber, UK 21 Oct 91, A5, 610pp, h/b. Ultimate biography of the Pistols and the era they ushered in, second only to the Vermorels. Jon was the man behind the 76 punk zine *London's Outrage*. Issued in s/b in the UK in May 92. Common.

England's Dreaming: Anarchy, Sex Pistols, Punk Rock And Beyond, Jon Savage, St.Martin's Press, US Jan 92, h/b, 602pp. Basically as its UK counterpart, although running to eight less pages, completely different jacket and revamped title for the American mass market. Reissued in s/b in the US in Jan 93. Common.

Agents Of Anarchy, Tony Scrivener, Kingsfleet Publishing, UK, Aug 92, A4, 112pp. Pistols diary coupled with *The Complete Discography*. Tony was the man behind the posthumous Pistols fanzine *Hot Off The Press*. Common.

Sex Pistols Retrospective (A Visual History . . . 7"/12"Rare Album Releases), Agent Provocateur, Retro Publishing, UK, 15 June 96. Initial copies had a free poster. Common.

Never Mind The Bollocks, Here's The Sex Pistols, Clinton Heylin, Schirmer Books, US, June 96. From the *Classic Rock Albums* series, concentrating on the origin and production of *Bollocks*. Common.

Destroy: Sex Pistols 1977, Dennis Morris, UK, Oct 98, Creation, p/b, 200pp. A revamped enlarged version of *Rebel Rock*.

Satelite: Sex Pistols (Memorabilia; Locations; Photography; Fashion), Paul Burgess and Alan Parker, Abstract Sounds Publishing, Sept 99, h/b, 180pp, p/b 160pp. Original limited edition h/b featured CD of images from the book: Fairly Rare. P/b edition: Common.

The Filth And The Fury – The Official

Companion To The Fine Line Features Documenary Film, Margo Mooney (designer), St. Martins Griffin, US, March 2000, p/b, 136pp. Stills from the film captioned with dialogue. Withdrawn shortly after publication. Fairly Rare.

Pistols Videography

All titles available in VHS unless otherwise stated (the suffix 'B' in the cat. no. indicates BETA availability). Pirates are acknowledged even if the same titles exist legitimately, since in most cases the pirate was the initial release. There was one gig which was played for the sole reason of recording: Notre Dame Church Halls, Leicester Square, London, 21 March 77, which was recorded by US NBC TV and featured Sid Vicious' debut with the Pistols.

Videos

Sex Pistols No. 1 (When The Air Turned Blue)
* A McLaren/Glitterbest production including the super-rare video for 'God Save The Queen', the TV appearances from late 76 – Bill Grundy, *Nationwide*, *So It Goes* – and some footage from the Anarchy Tour. Released in Apr 77. Shot on 16mm with a length of 22 mins. Rare.

Sex Pistols No. 2 (Never Mind The Sex Pistols, Here's The Problems)
* More vintage footage, including Screen on the Green, Thames riverboat cruise and some interviews, etc. Running time: 30 mins. Rare.

Sex Pistols No. 3
* Another compilation, features Sid and Nancy screwing on a *Never Mind The Bollocks* poster. Time: twenty mins. Rare.

Live In Sweden
* Live from Student Karen, Stockholm, 27 July 77. Available only on pirate copy. T: 60. Fairly Common.

Live In Dallas
* Live 10 Jan 78. Again only available on pirate. T:35. Fairly Common.

The Great Rock'N'Roll Swindle
* UK Virgin VIRV 0101A. Initial working title, *Who Killed Bambi?*, was scrapped. Hilarious movie, hit British cinemas in Summer 80. *Variety* magazine affectionately dubbed it 'the *Citizen Kane* of rock'n'roll pictures'. Director: Julien Temple. This edition was specially

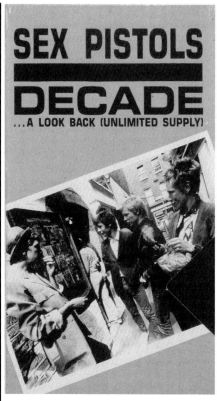

The second of two semi-legal video cassettes released in the US only, featuring relatively more recent footage.

released through mail-order ahead of high-street releases early December 82 and has subsequently been reissued at least three times in the UK alone. Early editions featured a green stamp on the front – 'official pirate video' – and cat. no. 0101A. T: 104. Fairly Common.
* UK main initial release: Virgin/Palace Video VTM/VBM 12, Dec 82. Common.
* UK reissue no. 1: 88, Virgin Vision VVB 010. Common.
* UK reissue no. 2: 88, Virgin Vision VVB 0101 A/B. Common.
* UK reissue no. 3: 92, Virgin Vision. This third issue came in a completely different jacket. Common.
* Italian Virgin Video, 90.
* USA (not officially released at time of UK video release, hence the Japanese edition was pirated for the American home market). Same sleeve and format as Nipponese copy. Fairly Rare.
* USA edition legitimately released on home video by Warner Reprise Video Cassettes with cat. no. 3-38319 on 24 Nov 92. Common.
* Australian edition released on Virgin Video VIR 104 in 82. Fairly Rare.

* Japanese edition VOS 4824, released with subtitles. Came in a superb jacket. Rare.
* Japanese reissue, POVP 1015 – from the mid-eighties.

D.O.A. – A Right Of Passage

* US Lightning 024V, 81. Lech Kowalski was the brains behind this punk rockumentary. Features extensive footage of US tour and a rare interview with Sid and Nancy. Premiered at the Waverly Theatre on 10 Apr 81. T: 90. Fairly Rare.
* Jp columbia HC 364, 81. This Nipponese edition came in a different colour jacket and ran for 99 minutes (nine minutes longer that its US counterpart). In NTSC VHS MONO HI-FI format. Very Rare.
* Pirated in the UK, Common.
* Finally given an official British release by Vision Video in Oct 92.

And We Don't Care

* US pirate video in glossy colour sleeve. Features NBC news report, Prime Time, a brilliant studio version of 'Anarchy' (not on the

The first of the semi-legal US videos, released April 88. Features the infamous Today show with Bill Grundy.

Buried Alive video) and the live gig from Dallas. T: 35. Fairly Common.

Sid And Nancy – Love Kills

* UK feature film July 86/video released Jan 87. The original release was in a pink jacket. T: 90.
All the Sex Pistols tracks in this movie were re-recorded by Glen Matlock, Dave McIntosh and James Stevenson. Lead roles in Alex Cox's film are taken by Gary Oldman (Sid) and Chloe Webb (Nancy). Some trivia: Courtney Love of Hole auditioned for the Spungen role, but came a close second to Webb!
* UK promo-only, issued in a nice 'Display Copy Only' jacket.
* UK budget release from Channel 5 (cat. no. CFV 04022, Jan 89). Issued in a completely different sleeve to the previous releases.
* US Embassy 1309. In a different jacket to any of the UK editions.
* US budget reissue in Mar 88.
* Au Cel (VHS and BETA). Issued for video library release (rental purposes) on 13 Oct 87.

Sex Pistols: Live At Winterland Jan 14 78

* US Target (VHS only) Jan 88. One of those semi-legal issues. Came in a full-colour jacket with tracks scattered across cover. T: 55. Fairly Rare.
* There is also a widely available UK pirate copy of the Winterland concert. Common.

Sex Pistols – Bollocks To Everyone

* US NTSC VHS. Another one of those semi-legal issues. Rare concert footage. T: 90.
I've deliberately neglected any semi-legal videos that appeared on the US market in the last few years. Basically they're either Sweden, Dallas or Winterland repackaged in glossy wrap-around jackets.

Sex Pistols – Banned

* NZ de France Productions Ltd. Compiled and packaged down-under in Auckland, this green/black covered tape features six different segments and loads of tracks. That's a staggering total of four non-stop hours. T: 240. Rare.

Buried Alive – A Documentary

* US Iceworld Outlaw 11.V Apr 88. Includes some of the early UK TV appearances (Today with Bill Grundy, etc.), two different versions of 'Anarchy', 'No Fun' (live) and 'GSTQ'. Issued in a full-colour jacket with sticker. T: 22. Fairly Rare.

Decade – A Look Back (Unlimited Supply)

* US Iceworld Outlaw 22.V 88. Features some of the Rotten interviews from That Was Then This Is Now, some stuff from a punk documentary titled Where Are They In – ?, humorous British 'punk' ads, and finishes up with footage from the Swindle flick. Issued in a nice green jacket with a pic of the band in Paris from Sept 76. T: 32. Fairly Rare.
The latter pair of videos were given independent releases in America by Dave Goodman under the name Iceworld in 1988.

Rebel Rock

* UK promo video (VHS only). Released to promote the book of the same name. T: six. Rare.

The Filth And The Fury

* UK Thunderbird Vision TV 1, Nov 89. Live in Sweden and America. Also includes two tracks from an early UK gig. Almost immediately withdrawn. T: 60. Rare.
* US NTSC version is Common.

Sex Pistols – Anarchy In The UK

* Irish compilation from 94. Features interview with Sid after Nancy's death; original promos for early singles; a live set from the USA; documentary footage and various interviews with the band. T: 70. Common.

Kiss This

* UK Virgin. Original brief advertising promo for the new LP/CD/cassette. T: 30 secs. Rare.
* UK Virgin 92. Official five-track promo video in authentic b/w cover. This edition was quickly deleted and hence quickly booted. T: twenty. Fairly Rare.
* UK pirate 93. Practically identical to the latter. Fairly Common.

Anarchy In The UK

* UK Virgin 92. Original promo for the reissued single. Officially labelled but without jacket. T: three. Common.

Pretty Vacant

* UK Virgin 92. Original in-store promo for the second reissued single. Officially labelled but without jacket again. T: three. Common.

Van Halen/Sex Pistols

* US Warner Bros promo to promote the 92 issue of Swindle flick/CD/LD in the States. Issued on 23 March 93 with official label and jacket. Cuts: 'Right Now' (live)/'Pretty Vacant', 'Anarchy'. T: twelve. Fairly Common.

Filthy Lucre

* UK EPK promo Aug 96. Features tracks and interviews from the reunion. EPK = Electronic Press Kit Video. T: 25. Common.

The Filthy Lucre Tour – Live In Japan
* Jp VAVJ 9017, limited edition. In two video boxes: one with the video, the other has a special T-shirt. T: 70. Rare.

Trailer And Promo Compilation
* June 96, Trailer for the forthcoming Filthy Lucre tour. Includes brief band history and interview clips followed by 'GSTQ', 'Anarchy', 'Vacant', 'C'Mon Everybody' (excerpt), 'My Way' – *a la* most official promo releases, the video is labelled but without a jacket. T: 31. Fairly Rare.

London Press Conference
* US NTSC, 96. Promo video. T: eighteen. Fairly Rare.

Kill The Hippies
* US SIC 1. In nice ps. Unlike the other US videos this is an excellent compilation, featuring a selection of live numbers intercut with excellent band/Warners staff/audience interviews and footage. It includes the infamous Sid and Nancy interview where they are totally stoned. All the songs have English subtitles! T:60. Fairly Rare.

Live At Longhorns
* UK Castle Communications/Pearson New Entertainment Aug 96. Official release in nice jacket. T: 60. Common.

Winterland
* UK Castle Communications/Pearson New Entertainment Aug 96. Official release in nice jacket with b/w 'The Original Sex Pistols Last Live Performance' sticker on front. T: 50. Common.

Live In The USA
* German PAL VHS only issue. Features American concerts and interviews, etc. T: 55. Fairly Common.

Live At Finsbury Park
* Finsbury Park, London, 23 June 96. T: 65. Common.

Live At Roskilde Festival
* Roskilde Festival, 28 June 96. Also includes some Swedish TV reports. T: 50. Common.

Live In Paris

* Le Zenith, Paris, France, 4 July 96. T: 55. Common.

Live In Rome
* Curva Stadio, Rome, Italy, 10 July 96. T: 60. Common.

Live In Milano
* Arena Spettacoli, Milano, Italy, 11 July 96. T: 50. Common.

Live In Shepherds Bush
* Shepherds Bush Empire, London, 17 July 96. T: 85. Common.

Live In Zeebrugge
* Beach Festival, Zeebrugge, 20 July 96. T: 65. Common.

Live At Phoenix Festival
* Phoenix Festival, Stratford-On-Avon, UK, 21 July 96 – eight tracks. T: 55. Common.

Live At Fairfax
* Live at Fairfax, Washington DC, USA, 6 Aug 96. T: 75. Common.

Live In Tokyo
* Live At Tokyo, Japan, 22 Nov 96. T: 90. Common.
This one was professionally filmed.

The Filth And The Fury
UK Filmfour/Virgin Sept 2000/US Warner Home Video Oct 2000. VHS. Julien Temple's comprehensive documentary overview of the Pistols, containing much previously unreleased footage. Common.

The Great Rock 'N' Roll Auctions
I am indebted to Pippa from Christie's, Steven Maycock from Sotheby's, Nicholas J.Orringe from Phillips and Mark Paytress from *Record Collector*. They kindly furnished me with the listings, back catalogues from the sales and some invaluable photographic material. Also see 'Odds 'N' Ends' section for equally valuable items sold at private auctions over the past 21 years.

The mega-bucks business of rock'n'roll auctions was initiated by Sotheby's on 22 December 1981. The other two grand houses, Christie's and Phillips, followed suit on 4 July 1985 and 28 January 1987 respectively, followed in their turn by Bonhams and Fleetwoodowen, to name but two. The total

price of Pistols material sold by the main auction houses is now well into six figures. (Allowing for inflation and the crazy rate at which rock'n'roll ephemera is spiralling upward in price, in terms of its real value the figure is probably nearer £1 million.) If you're curious as to the contents of Sotheby's first rock'n'roll sale, the original catalogue itself now changes hands for upwards of £200.

Christie's
London, 4 July 85
* 7" 'Anarchy In The UK' – Abbey Road acetate.
* 134 colour transparencies, plus a folder of ephemera relating to their career with EMI.

London, 19 Dec 85
* 7" 'God Save The Queen' – A&M.
It's interesting to note that, at the time, the price of £250 was regarded as phenomenal! (Charity auction.)

London, 28 Aug 87
* 'Anarchy' – Abbey Road acetate.
* 10" 'Anarchy' – acetate.
* 10" 'GSTQ' – acetate.
* 10" 'Pretty Vacant' – acetate.
* 10" 'My Way' – Townhouse acetate.

The auction also included extensive artwork from Pistols designer/situationist/artist Jamie Reid:
* 'Anarchy' – unreleased material.
* 'Holidays In The Sun' – unreleased material.
* 'GSTQ' – unreleased cover proof.
* Three signed items.
* Two framed 'Bodies'.
* Stickers and posters (framed).
* *Great Rock'N'Roll Swindle* artwork.
* Four posters with signatures.
* *Goodbye To Virgin* – unreleased material.
* 'Something Else' – silk screen attributed to Reid.

London, 25 Aug 88
* 'Anarchy In The UK' concert poster signed by Jamie Reid – 'Cash From Chaos' streamer and comic strip poster.
* 'GSTQ' promo artwork, signed by Jamie Reid.
* Two Jamie Reid promo posters: *Never Mind The Bollocks, Here's The Sex Pistols* and 'Anarchy'.
* Framed *Bollocks* sleeve, signed and inscribed by Sid Vicious.
* Film scripts for *The Swindle* and *Who Killed Bambi?*.
* Two reel-to-reel quarter-inch *Bollocks* studio

tapes.
* Two typescript agreements and publicity handouts
* John Lydon's *Still Life Study Of A Rag Doll*.

The auction also included extensive Sid Vicious memorabilia. Clothing was made available by Sid's mother, Ann Beverley, for the charity Children In Need.
* *Sid Sings* album – acetate, test pressing and proof sleeve
* Black t-shirt along with four others.
* Waistcoat, Levis and jacket.
* Rubber shirt and wet-look t-shirt.
* Belts, spurs, studs, chains, etc.
* Two-piece suit and shirt.
* Leather jacket with badges.
* Set of four Kiss dolls.
* Cream tuxedo worn for 'My Way'.

London, 27 Apr 89
* Printed inner sleeve, decorated with photomechanical portraits of John, Paul, Steve and Sid (US *Bollocks* inner) – signed and inscribed 'Love from Sid Vicious'.
* 'Anarchy' promo poster and streamer from *The Swindle*.
* *Swindle* and 'Something Else' promo posters.
* Colour transparencies and press releases from 76.
* Promo handbill, signed and designed by Jamie Reid.
* Two studio reel-to-reel tapes recorded 16 and 25 September 1977, annotated by Johnny.
* Original proof for *Bollocks* sleeve.
* (PiL): *Metal Box* – signed.
* (Various Artists) Sex Pistols and Jimi Hendrix test pressings.

London, Aug 89
* Sid Vicious' signature (framed).
* Inner sleeve signed by Sid (framed).
* Steve Jones' mackintosh, (authenticated).
* Proof for 'GSTQ' sleeve by Jamie Reid (authenticated).
* 'Holidays' poster signed by Jamie Reid, plus other promo items.
* 7": 'Anarchy' – signed on the label by John, Paul and Steve.
* *Bollocks* sleeve, fully signed.

London, Apr 90
* Glen Matlock's acoustic guitar.
* Autographed *Bollocks*.
* Malcolm McLaren's jukebox.
* Pistols autographs (including Sid).

* Sid Vicious celluloid film strip.
* Pair of Sid's trousers.
* Two Pistols promo handbills.
* Pistols handbill and promo material.
* 'GSTQ' handbill.
* Two Spanish Pistols promo posters.

London, Dec 90
* *Bollocks* – signed by group (Sid line-up).
* Two American concert tickets from 8 Jan 78, mounted with photos.
* Reel-to-reel demo tape including 'No Future' 'Liar' and 'Problems' – from 76.
* Signed 'Anarchy' and 'Vacant' singles (Sid line-up).
* Publicity photo signed by band (including Sid).
* Malcolm's felt hat.
* Collection of Pistols records, posters and memorabilia.
* Collection of punk clothing, including Pistols T-shirts.
* Signed *Bollocks* poster (autographs include Sid's and Malcolm's).
* Sid Vicious and Sue Catwoman punk dolls.
* Unpublished Pistols photo from EMI House, with collection of punk mags and posters.

London, Apr 91
* Handbill signed by Jamie Reid, plus four badges.
* Three promo posters, all signed by Jamie Reid.
* *Bollocks* poster signed by Jamie Reid.
* Italian *Swindle* poster showing Sting!
* Two handbills for 100 Club shows.
* Two tickets for Texas show, plus photos.
* Banned *Swindle* pic sleeve mounted with group photo.
* Three handbills for early concerts, signed by Jamie Reid.
* 1977 Uxbridge show handbill, signed by Jamie Reid.
* Photo of Sid signed by Pistols.

London, Aug 92
* Sid Vicious' signed passport, from 77.
* Eight promotional paper flags for 'GSTQ'.
* Signed publicity photo.
* Letter from Johnny to zine editor, Jan 78.

London, Aug 93
* 65 photographs of the Pistols – some previously unpublished.

London, 26 May 94
* 'God Save The Queen (No Future)' UK PYE acetate – £2,200.
* 80pp-xerox of film script and press releases.

* Chewing gum wrapper and handbill, signed by Johnny.
* Letter to a fan from Johnny.
*As above, with two additional notes.
* *Bollocks* album signed by group.

London, Summer 94
* Three signed Pistols' letters.

London, 25 May 95
* Anarchy Tour poster, 1976, plus Clash poster.
* 'Anarchy'/'EMI'/'No Future' 10" acetate, unreleased versions.
* Photo of Pistols parodying Beatles' *Please Please Me* LP cover and fanzines, etc.
* Autographed T-shirt, Dec 77.

London, 6 June 96
* Four punk concert and promo posters – incuding 'Anarchy'.
* Six punk concert and promo posters – including *Bollocks*.
* Anarchy In The UK, 10 Dec 76, Charlton Theatre, Preston.
* White cotton sleeveless *Bollocks* promo T-shirt.
The following six celluloid strips are from the *Swindle* flick: –
* The Pistols on board the Good Ship Venus.
* Sid Vicious looking threatening, wearing chain.
* Johnny Rotten in a doorway.
* Sid in a bedroom scene.
* Sid Vicious barging through door – 'Something Else' ps.
* Mean-looking Sid Vicious – multiple image.

London, 9 May 97
* Scrap of paper used as a shopping list and inscribed, 'For the Geezer Over There – Fuck Off.' Very Rare.
* Half-inch reel-to-reel tape featuring early mixes of 'No Future' and 'No Feelings' – PYE Recording Studios. Very Rare.
* Four promotional banner posters for *The Swindle*, and a 'GSTQ' promo poster. Very Rare.
* 'Vacant' lyrics autographed by Glen Matlock . Very Rare.
* Autographed *Alternative Press* magazine cover from 95. Rare.
* Sid autograph reading 'To Allan from SV', mounted alonside a recent autographed photograph of the original line-up. Very Rare.

London, 4 Sept 97
* Withdrawn A&M 'GSTQ', in company sleeve.

Very Rare.

* White Remo Weather King drumhead, signed in blue-felt pen by the band on their 96 American Filthy Lucre tour. Rare.
* Crestwood Stratocaster-style electric guitar, signed by the band on their 96 American Filthy Lucre tour. Very Rare.

London, 10 Dec 99
* Original Seditionaries 'Cowboy' t-shirt signed by Vivienne Westwood, Johnny Rotten, Paul Cook, and Malcolm McLaren (1994).
* Seven promo posters – including 'Swindle' single (American Express design, British quad poster), 'C'mon Everybody', 'Vicious Burger', 'Friggin' In The Riggin'', and 'Never Mind The Sex Pistols, Here's The Problems'.
* Two withdrawn trial print-outs for the sleeve of 'God Save The Queen', plus a mug sticker of the same design, used by the Pistols/Glitterbest staff.
* Two promo posters for Bollocks plus corresponding banner: 'Never Mind The Bollocks, We Stock Sex Pistols'.

Phillips

London, 28 Jan 87
* Two Pistols promos.
London, 26 Aug 87
* 7"s: 'Submission' VDJ 24 (promo) and 'Vacant' VS 184 (stock).

London, 6 Apr 88
* Bollocks album press kit – including hand-printed t-shirt and a printed folder in plastic zipper case
* Album sleeve proofs for Bollocks, each signed by Jamie Reid.
* Signed promo copy of Bollocks.
* Promo poster for Bollocks – pink/yellow, framed and glazed.
* B/w 'GSTQ' proof ps.
* Miscellaneous memorabilia, including two t-shirts, three 7"ers and press folder.
* 'Cheap Holiday' cartoon, postcard size, framed and glazed – signed by Jamie Reid.
* 'Never Mind The Bans' tour poster, Dec 77 – signed by Reid.

London, 24 Aug 88
* Miscellaneous memorabilia, including stickers and booklets.
* Miscellaneous memorabilia, including Fuck Forever t-shirt.
* 'Holidays' promo poster.
* 'Something Else' promo poster.
* Six streamers to promote Swindle album.
* Swindle (film) promo poster.

* 10" 'GSTQ' one-sided acetate.
* Paul's drum kit (used throughout the Pistols era).

London, 26 Apr 89
* Six Jamie Reid promo streamers.
* B/w bromide proof for a 'Vacant' poster promoting a half-hour film made in Apr 77, signed by Jamie Reid.

London, 23 Aug 89
* 'Anarchy' promo poster, Union Jack flag, EMI 2566.
* 'Vicious Burger' bromide proof artwork used for the single 'C'mon Everybody' – framed and glazed, signed by artist.
* Swindle film poster, unreleased.

London, 24 Apr 90
* Miscellaneous items, including two Evening News posters showing the headline 'Sid Vicious Faces Murder Court' – also Pistols scrapbook, etc.
* Two pieces of paste-up artwork for 'Vacant' single.
* Printed material relating to Bollocks album.
* Collection of ephemera comprising promo handbills, fanzines and a newspaper.
* Telegram from Malcolm to the Evening Standard dated 28 February 77, concerning Sid Vicious joining the group, two pages.

London, 22 Aug 90
* 145pp-script for the cancelled Who Killed Bambi? movie.
* Proof artwork for 100 Club poster.
* Bollocks poster by Jamie Reid.
* Fuck Forever poster.
* Silk 'Anarchy' flag and 'GSTQ' t-shirt.
London, 24 Apr 91
* Bollocks sleeve without track listing, signed on the front by band.

London, Aug 92
* Pistols posters, scrapbook and news sheet.

Sotheby's

New York, 29 June 85
* Miscellaneous punk rock/new wave memorabilia including fanzines, photographs and posters – some 99 items in all, much relating to the Pistols.

London, 5 Aug 87
* Eighteen posters, one patch and 72 badges.

London, 7 Apr 88
This auction featured extensive Jamie Reid

artwork:
* God Save Dick Turpin screenprint poster, framed and glazed.
* Some Product – Carri On Sex Pistols screenprint poster.
* 100 Club concert poster for 20 Sept 76 – also a handbill for the 31 Aug 76 gig at the same venue.
* 'No Future' sticker (mounted) and bromide.
* Nine original stickers (1972-74): 'Save Petrol, Burn Cars', etc.
* Six original Pistol streamers from 78 to promote the Swindle album.
* Lithographic album proofs for Bollocks and God Save The Sex Pistols.

London, Aug 89
* Bollocks gold disc.
* Three Jamie Reid posters.
* 'Herbarium' sign from the Swindle film.
* John Lydon design for PiL record sleeve (signed).
* God Save The Sex Pistols cover proof.
London, 21 Aug 90
* Photographic Pistols portrait, 76.
London, 27 Aug 92
* Vivienne Westwood dress designed for Bow Wow Wow's Annabella Lwin.
* Handwritten lyrics for 'Problems', by J. Rotten, Esq., 1977.
* Bollocks gold disc presented to Johnny in 77.

London, 27 July 93
* Celluloid strip from the Swindle flick, 79.
* Sid Vicious' t-shirt.
* Two 'GSTQ' promo t-shirts.
* Original Bollocks proof sleeve.
* 100-watt P.A. used by Pistols.
* Letter from Malcolm McLaren agreeing payment for Pistols at 100 Club Punk Rock Festival, Oxford St, London, Sept 76.

London, Summer 94
* Poster for Screen on the Green gig, 76.
* 'Anarchy' posters.
* Poster collection – also includes the Jam, Clash, etc.
* Sid's tuxedo from 'My Way' film clip.
* B/w Sid poster
* 'GSTQ' Pye acetate and unused A&M labels for withdrawn 45.
* 'GSTQ' A&M.
* Signed 'Vacant' 45, plus unpublished photo
* McLaren and Westwood 'Cowboys' t-shirt.
* Steve's cheesecloth 'Cowboys' t-shirt.
* McLaren and Westwood bondage trousers
* Johnny's handwritten 'New York' lyrics.
* US Bollocks poster

Adam And The Ants, Fred and Judy Vermorel, Omnibus Press, Apr 81. Common.

And God Created Punk, Erica Echenberg and Mark P, Virgin, 96, 144pp. Common

And I Don't Want To Live This Life, Deborah Spungen, Corgi, UK Feb 84, A5, 336pp. The 'blame it all on Sid Vicious book' – which seems a little ironic, in that all who knew Nancy largely accredit the disintegration of the band to her. Nonetheless a bestseller. Issued in at least three different jackets. More recently updated (including a new chapter) and published by Fawcett Crest in 94. Common.

The Bible, Mark Perry, Dempsey, 78, 84pp. Includes free copy of the author's classic fanzine *Sniffin' Glue* no. 12. Fairly Rare.

Ronald Biggs – Odd Man Out, Ronald Biggs, Bloomsbury, 94, 282pp, h/b. Common.

The Bollocks, Japanese scrapbook of the life and demise of Sid and Nancy, A4, 52pp. Press cuttings and some super-rare photographs. Fairly Rare.

The Book Of Rock Quotes, various artists, Omnibus Press, 120pp, Nov 77. Includes Johnny and Sid. Fairly Common.

The Boy Looked At Johnny – The Obituary Of Rock'N'Roll, Julie Burchill and Tony Parsons, Pluto Press, UK Nov 78, A5, 96pp. Indispensable work from two now-famous writers who lived through the punk era. Reprinted in Britain in different jacket. The US edition published by Faber & Faber in 87 has 108pp, another different jacket and a new introduction by Lenny Kaye and some nice new pics of various UK/US punk rock-new wave groups inside. All Common.

Richard Branson – The Inside Story, Mike Brown, Michael Joseph Publications, 88, 280pp, h/b. Common.

Classic Rock Stars, Peter Herring, Magna Books, 226pp, h/b. Common.

Cool Cats (25 Years Of Rock'N'Roll Style), Tony Stewart, Eel Pie, 81. Common.

Crimes Of The 20th Century (A Chronology), various authors, Crescent Books, 91, 320pp, h/b. Common.

Destroy (The Definitive Histoy Of Punk), Alvin Gibbs, 15 Apr 96, Britannia Press Publishing, 288pp. Common.

El Sid, David Dalton, St. Martin's Press, US 97, h/b, A5, 222pp. Common.

Impresario: Malcolm McLaren And The British New Wave, The New Museum of Contemporary Art/MIT Press, Paul Taylor, US 89, A4, 80pp. Inaccurately known to fans and collectors as 'the other biography', it's actually a catalogue-cum-book based on 'a retrospective exhibition of the work of Malcolm McLaren' that the New Museum of Contemporary Art hosted in New York from 16 Sept – 20 Nov 88. Fairly Rare.

In The Fascist Bathroom: Writings On Punk, 1977-1992, Greil Marcus, Viking, July 93. Common.

In The Gutter, Val Hennessy, Quartet Diversions, Autumn 78, A4/A5 sized, 96pp. With almost as many b/w full-sized photographs. Fairly Rare.

Irish Rock (Where It's Come From – Where It's At – Where It's Going), Tony Clayton-Lea and Richie Taylor, Gill and MacMillan, 92, A4, 128pp. Story of emerald rock, includes Lydon, etc. Common.

Joe Strummer With The 101'ers And The Clash, Julian Leonard Yewdall and Nick Jones, Image Direct, Dec 92. Common.

Johnny Rotten In His Own Words, Dave Thomas, Omnibus Press, UK Aug 88, A4, 96pp. More barrel-scraping. Common.

Lipstick Traces (A Secret History Of The Twentieth Century), Greil Marcus, Secker and Warburg, 89, 492pp. Reprinted by Penguin in Aug 93. Common.

The New Music Record and Tape Guide, Omnibus Press, Ira Robins, 87, 176pp. Common.

New Wave Explosion (How Punk Became The New Wave Became the 80s), Myles Palmer, Proteus Press, 81, 128pp. Common.

New Wave On Record – England And Europe 1975-78 – A Discographical History, Greg Shaw, Bomp Books, US Dec 78, larger than A4. Only 1,000 issued. Features Pistols on cover. Fairly Rare.

1988: The New Wave Punk Rock Explosion, Caroline Coon, Orbach and Cambers, Oct 77, 128pp. Subsequently re-issued by at least three different publishers: Hawthorne, Wyndham and Omnibus Press. Most are Common.

Note Di Pop Inglese (2^a edizione), Roberto Cacciotto and Giancarlo Radice, Gammalibri, It, A5, 220pp. Various artists/pop-fan book with the 'wall shot' of Pistols on front of jacket. Fairly Rare.

100 Nights At The Roxy, Michael Dempsey, Big O, Aug 78. Fairly Rare.

The Penguin Book Of Rock'N'Roll Writing, Clinton Heylin, Viking/Penguin, Nov 92, 700pp. Common.

Photo Past '66-'86 (Access Nearly All Areas), Ray Stevenson, Symbiosis, Apr 89, 72pp. Common.

PiL: Rise/Fall, Clinton Heylin, Omnibus Press, UK July 89, A4, 96pp. Biography and chronology of Lydon's lot. Common.

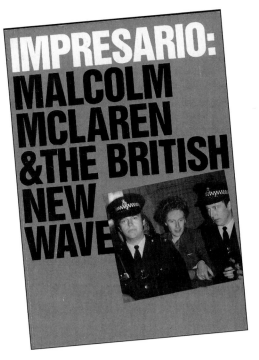

Pointed Portraits, Chalkie Davies, Eel Pie, 81. Common.

Portrait Of A Decade (The 1970's), Elizabeth Campling, Batsford, 89. Common.

Punk! Terry Jones and Isabella Anscombe, Big O Publications, Jan 78. Fairly Common.

Punk (Seventeen Rock), Stéphane Pietri and Alexis Quinlin, Régine de Forges, 77. Original French punk book from the heyday, includes lotsa photos of the Pistols *et al.* My copy is signed by Stéphane Pietri to Malcolm! Fairly Rare.

Punk Rock, Richard Allen, New English Library, Jan 78. Fairly Common.

Punk Rock, John Tobler, Phoebus, Dec 77. 'A complete guide to British and American new wave music.' Fairly Common. There is also a nice Dutch edition published by Nederlandse Uitgave and a Greek edition. All Fairly Rare.

Punk Rock'N'Roll/New Wave, Heather Harris, Almo Music, July 78. Various artists songbook, with biogs, etc. Fairly Rare.

Punk (An A-Z), Barry Lazell, Hamlyn, UK, 95, 160pp, large h/b format. Issued in two different colour covers. Common.

Punk '77 – An Inside Look At The San Francisco Rock'N'Roll Scene, 1977, James Stark, Stark Grafix, 92, 104pp. Common.

Punk: Punk Rock/Punk Style/Punk Stance/Punk People/Punk Stars/That Head the New Wave In England And America, Isabelle Anscombe and Dike Blair, Aug 78. There were two different editions, one for the UK, the other for the US market (Urizen

Books Inc). Both could be bought as *The Punk Pack* on special offer at time of publication. Fairly Rare.

The Punk, Gideon Sams, Polytantric Press, Oct 77, 62pp. Sams was fourteen when he penned this novel!

The Punk: (The First Punk Novel 'Romeo and Juliet'), Gideon Sams, Corgi.

Punk The Original: (A Collection Of Material From The First, Best And Greatest Punk 'Zine Of All Time!) John Holmstrom, Trans-High Corporation, US, July 96, 128pp. Common.

Rock'N'Roll Babylon, Gary Herman, Plexus, 82, 194pp. Subsequently reissued in a different cover. Common.

Rock'N'Roll Comic #14, Revolutionary Comics, US, Aug. Band's history traced in comic-strip style.

Rotten: No Irish, No Blacks, No Dogs (The Autobiography), John Lydon, with Keith and Kent Zimmerman, Hodder and Stoughton, UK, 31 Mar 94, A5, 342pp, h/b. Well worth the wait, features some previously unreleased photos – including a shot of Johnny and Paul at their very first gig at St. Martin's College of Art, 6 Nov 75. Subsequently reissued in s/b, Dec 94, and 'bestseller' s/b Feb 95. The German edition, published by Hannibal in 95, came in a completely different jacket to all the others. All Common.

Rotten: No Irish, No Blacks, No Dogs (The Authorized Autobiography – Johnny Rotten Of The Sex Pistols), John Lydon, with Keith and Kent Zimmerman, St.Martin's Press, US Apr 94, A5, 330pp, h/b. As the British edition except the customary change in subtitle, also a reduced number of pages and the overall layout is slightly re-hashed. Avoid unless you're a completist! Reprinted in the US in s/b in Apr 95 by Picador. Common.

Rotten: No Irish, No Blacks, No Dogs (The Authorized Autobiography – Johnny Rotten Of The Sex Pistols). Pre-press copy in large s/b format issued in late 93, without photos but with 372pp. Perfect bound and announcing eventual publication details. Rare.

Sex And Drugs And Rock'N'Roll, Bobcat Press, 96pp. Common.

Sex Pistols – Buy This Book, Rock Fantasy Comics no. 7/Sex Pistols no. 1, US, Apr 90. This entire issue based on Pistols.

Shockwave, Virginia Boston, Plexus, UK, 78 A4, 128pp. The US Penguin/Viking edition was issued in a completely different cover with a title change to *Punk Rock*. Both Fairly Rare.

Sid And Nancy, Alex Cox and Abbe Wool, Faber & Faber, UK July 86, A5, 144pp. The script, positively superfluous. Common.

Sid And Nancy (novel), Gerald Cole, Methuen, UK July 86, A5, 186pp. Hilarious. Common.

Sid Vicious – Rock'N'Roll Star, Malcolm Butt, Plexus, UK, Apr 97, A5, 144pp. Common.

Sid Vicious – They Died Too Young, Tom Stockdale, Parragon/Magpie Books 95, 78pp, pocket-sized h/b. There is also an Australian edition by the Book Company. Common.

Sid's Way (The Life And Death Of Sid Vicious: The Official Biography), Keith Bateson and Alan Parker, Omnibus Press, UK, Sept 91, A4, 96pp. 'Born in nineteen fifty-seven, fun and young a punk in heaven' – but then again, he did do it his way. Common. There is also an A5 Japanese edition, with banding, a completely different detachable dust cover and different photographs, and the order of the authors' names reversed. It sold 18,000 copies in its first 48 hours on the shelves in Tokyo. Fairly Rare.

The Sid Vicious Family Album, Ann Beverley, Virgin, UK, Sept 80, A4, 32pp. Photographic memoirs from 'Ma Vicious'. Fairly Common.

Smash Hits Yearbook 1984, includes four-page cartoon/pictorial 'Sex Pistols Story' by Arthur Ranson. Common.

Starmakers and Svengalis, Johnny Rogan, Macdonald and Queen Anne Press, 88, 290pp, h/b. Common.

Subculture: The Meaning Of Style, Dick Hebdige, Methuen New Accents, Nov 79. Common.

Johnny Thunders: In Cold Blood, Nina Guidio, Jungle/Omnibus Press, 87, 128pp. Common.

Twenty Years Of Rolling Stone, edited by Jann Wenner, Ebury Press, 87. A US edition is available from Friendly Press. Both Common.

The Uncyclopaedia Of Rock (The Way It Really Was), Jeremy Pascall, Angus Deayton and Geoffrey Perkins, Ebury Press, 87 128pp. Common.

Up They Rise: The Incomplete Works Of Jamie Reid, Jamie Reid and Jon Savage, Faber & Faber, UK, June 87, A4, 144pp. Features all the addictive visuals Reid created for the explosive, disaffected young Sex Pistols. As its title suggests: past, Pistols and prospective. Common.

Virgin (A History Of Virgin Records), Terry Southern, A Publishing Co. Ltd, UK, 95, 256pp. Common.

The Wicked Ways Of Malcolm McLaren, Craig Bromberg, Harper and Row/Perennial

Library, US, Dec 89, A5, 330pp. Talcy Malcy's story right from the very beginning, 1947, through to his manipulation of the Dolls, Pistols, Ants, Boy George, Bow Wow Wow and on into his own highly successful solo career. Published in the UK by Omnibus Press in Sept 91 in a completely different jacket. Both Common.

The World's Greatest Rock'N'Roll Scandals, David Cavanagh, Octopus Books, Apr 89, 160pp. Common.

Xcapees (A San Francisco Punk Photo Documentary), Raye Santos, Richard McCaffrey, f Stop Fitzgerald and Howie Klein, Xcapee Press, Jan 80, 72pp. Scarce Californian book, features SF gig. Fairly Rare.

Key To General Terminology

Key To Countries

Ar	Argentina
At	Austria
Au	Australia
Au/NZ	Australasia
Be	Belorussia
Bg	Belgium
Bz	Brazil
Ca	Canada
Dn	Denmark
EC	European Community
Fr	France
Ge	Germany
Gr	Greece
HK	Hong Kong
In	India
Io	Indonesia
Is	Israel
It	Italy
Jp	Japan
Lx	Luxembourg
Ma	Malaysia
Mx	Mexico
Nl	Netherlands
NZ	New Zealand
Pd	Poland
Ph	Philippines
Pl	Portugal
ROC	Rep. Of China
Ru	Russia (USSR)
SA	South Africa
SK	South Korea
Sp	Spain
Sv	Scandinavia (Sweden or Norway only)
Sw	Sweden
Sz	Switzerland
Th	Thailand
Tu	Turkey
UK	United Kingdom
US	United States
Uy	Uruguay
WG	West Germany

Key To Discography

* A&R = Artist and Repertoire.
* as = art sleeve.
* bio = biography.
* cs = custom sleeve. Normally issued by the record company with their own logo on the sleeve instead of a ps, or when ps's have been exhausted.
* c/w = comes (complete with).
* del = deluxe.
* DJ = disk jockey edition.
* EP = Extended Player.
* ext'd vers = extended version (usually a 12" single).
* g/f = gatefold jacket.
* JB = juke box copy.
* LP = Long Player.
* NOC = No Original Centre. This is where the centre piece is approximately one inch in diameter as opposed to the usually much smaller hole (this mainly relates to jukebox or European 45s).
* obi. = Japanese term for the wraparound paper-strip which is standard with all Japanese albums. This is also commonly known as banding, belt or a title-strip.
* ost (also s/t) = original soundtrack.
* ps = pic sleeve.
* st = stereo.
* s/t = soundtrack.
* w/ = with.
* wltp = white label test pressing.